the **heart** *of* **teaching** *series*

Ginger Tucker's

First Year Teacher

Notebook

Revised Edition

"In a completely rational society, the best of us would aspire to be teachers and the rest of us would have to settle for something less, because passing civilization along from one generation to the next ought to be the highest honor and highest responsibility anyone could have." -- Lee Iacocca

---

Ginger Tucker

GKT Consulting, Inc.
806-353-7291
ginger@gingertucker.com
www.gingertucker.com

Ginger Tucker's

First Year Teacher

Notebook

Revised Edition

© 2013 by Ginger Tucker
Printed in the United States of America
ISBN 978-0-9860039-0-5

Published by:
GKT Publishing
GKT Consulting, Inc.
Amarillo, Texas
806-353-7291
www.gingertucker.com

Printed by Cenveo Printing in Amarillo, Texas

3/4/13

Contents

As you work through each chapter, notice the *Heart of Teaching* symbols.

❧ The larger symbols highlight each chapter's concept statement and topics.

❧ The smaller symbols point to an activity to complete or to a discussion.

This book is dedicated to all who choose to
make a difference as teachers.

I want to thank my colleague and friend,
Justin Richardson, for his dedication to
learning and the learner.

I want to especially thank a master teacher
and my friend, Carolyn Miller, for her careful
and kind editing and proofreading.

Introduction

The purpose of the *First Year Teacher Notebook* is to provide new teachers and others with the foundational resources and support to enjoy a successful teaching career. It is designed for use in new teacher training before and during the first year of teaching. I believe, however, that the information is useful for any teacher any time. Effective teachers are always learning and growing.

Dear First Year Teacher,

Thank you. Thank you for choosing the most important, most challenging, and most rewarding profession in the world. You are about to embark on the adventure of a lifetime! It is my heart's desire that you will benefit from the content and support you receive from being part of a First Year Teacher learning community and from these materials.

Being a teacher comes with good news and bad news. The bad news is that it is hard! And it doesn't get easier. But the good news is that even though it doesn't get easier, you get better! As you experience all the aspects of being a teacher during this first year, you learn more and more how to do so effectively.

It is my hope and prayer for you that you have a system of support at your campus and in your district and that you welcome and benefit from that support.

My first year of teaching was a nightmare! I didn't have any idea of what I was doing! I had wanted to be a teacher my entire life. I made my brothers and sister play school until they cried; and then I practiced discipline strategies on them! When I graduated from college and landed a teaching job in my hometown, I was ecstatic. I couldn't wait. I was planning to be the best teacher in America and every student's favorite.

Even before the first day started, I began to struggle. I kept calling the school, asking when I could get a book, when I could see my room, and when I could talk to my fellow teachers. After repeated requests, the assistant principal finally allowed me to come to the school where I finally received a teacher's edition for the history classes I was to teach. I asked about a curriculum guide (We had learned about that at the university). There were none; those were apparently going to come out later. I also learned at that time that I would be teaching geography also. Geography! I had only one class of geography on my transcript - elementary geography. And...there were no textbooks. I would have to gather my own material. Well, I began to gather and call and search. I found some old textbooks and a retired teacher's old files. The maps were outdated and the material was inadequate.

I have to tell you, however, that I didn't know it was supposed to be different. Because I had never done this before, I didn't know how it was supposed to be. The message I got was, "Every man for himself!" I was prepared with lessons for the first few weeks and a general outline for the entire year. I felt really good about it. I was prepared to lecture by giving notes, having the students do a worksheet, and giving a test. Every week for 36 weeks...that was my plan! And I was one chapter ahead.

What I learned from the very first day was that, while I knew a little about history and a very little about geography, I knew absolutely nothing about teaching. And I didn't know I didn't know how to teach! I re-grouped every night, every weekend. I was doing all I knew how to do. I was teaching the way I was taught in school and the way I was taught to teach at the university in my history classes. It was 1980 and I was prepared for 1960. Because it wasn't working, I began to try to use games and other activities. But instead of increasing learning, it produced chaos and discipline problems. I had no classroom control! The only rules were those I made up as I went along. Well, needless to say, it was not a good year. If I could have done anything else, I would have quit teaching. Actually, I probably should have been fired!

My <u>experience</u> is not so different from that of other teachers. The difference, however, was that there was no <u>support</u> for me in any way. I didn't receive any support or guidance from the administration, the office, the department, the rest of the faculty, or anyone. Because I was new, I didn't know I needed help to be successful; I just thought there was something wrong with me. Everyone else seemed to be getting it. The people at my school were not bad people; in fact, many became life-long friends. There simply was not any system of support and training for a new teacher.

I got better every year I taught, not because campus-wide support increased, but because I began working on my master's degree and was fortunate enough to be exposed to some good teaching and a little training on lesson planning. I never received any training on classroom management, on what to teach, how to teach it, nor how to assess learning. It wasn't until I was out of the classroom that I had the privilege to attend excellent training on curriculum and instruction. Isn't that a shame! All of that wonderful knowledge and experience was out there, but not for me nor for my students.

When I left the classroom to work at a regional education service center, in addition to the great training I received, I was exposed to a new statewide initiative to support mentors and first year teachers. I immediately volunteered to be a part of that effort. Because of my experiences, I have been passionate about this project since that day.

I began providing training and support twenty-one years ago for teachers. These First Year Teacher materials are the product of my experiences with those wonderful teachers—listening to their hopes and concerns, sharing their frustrations and passions, and watching their growth and successes. I am grateful to have learned so many lessons from those who want to teach and who desperately desire to be effective. I am completely convinced that it is our moral obligation to provide a system of support, training, and encouragement to each of you, the new teachers—our future.

Best Wishes and God Bless,
Ginger

Don't be in any rush to become a teacher, my friends. Teaching is highly responsible work. Teachers are held to the strictest standards.
James, *The Message*

To teach is to learn twice.
Joseph Joubert

Ginger Tucker's *Heart of Teaching*
and
First Year Teacher Academy

Philosophy
Our work as teachers is the most important work there is.
The future of our society depends on a moral, educated population.
Teachers stand in the greatest position for effecting a positive impact on children.
Every teacher can be effective, given the training, support, and time.
Everyone deserves the opportunity to learn in an environment of respect and integrity.
Becoming an effective teacher is a life-long learning process.

Mission
The mission of *The Heart of Teaching* is to support, challenge, and inspire teachers to become competent, confident, and compassionate so that they make a positive difference for their students.

Purpose
Our purpose is to build on the experiences from a new teacher's pre-service training, to apply that learning to the classroom, and to provide new knowledge and skills. As a result of this study,

The First Year Teacher will
➢ Be convinced of the impact he or she has on the lives of students.
➢ Be prepared to start the first days of school with confidence.
➢ Have a well-organized and managed classroom, conducive to learning.
➢ Lead a classroom characterized by respect, compassion, and high expectations for student learning and behavior.
➢ Create a learning environment that meets the needs of all students.
➢ Plan, prepare, teach, and assess lessons in a way that leads to mastery.
➢ Develop a partnership with parents for the benefit of students.
➢ Exhibit professionalism and integrity in and out of the classroom.
➢ Be supported and encouraged through a relationship with trained mentors and colleagues.
➢ Enjoy a healthy and happy first year.

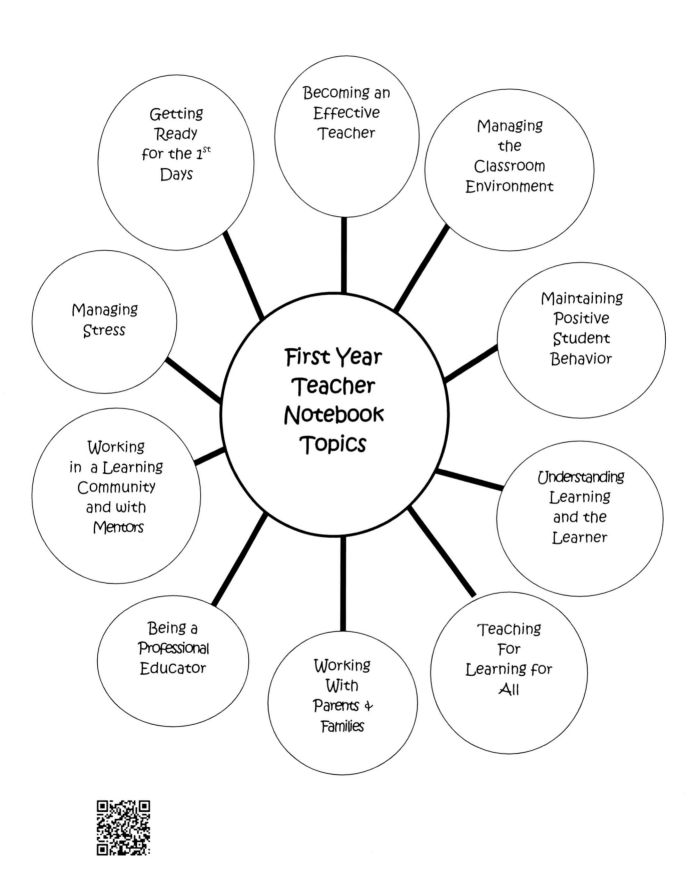

First Year Teacher Notebook Topics

- Becoming an Effective Teacher
- Getting Ready for the 1st Days
- Managing the Classroom Environment
- Managing Stress
- Maintaining Positive Student Behavior
- Working in a Learning Community and with Mentors
- Understanding Learning and the Learner
- Being a Professional Educator
- Working With Parents & Families
- Teaching For Learning for All

Chapter 1
Becoming an Effective Teacher

Fifty years from now it will not matter what kind of car you drove, what kind of house you lived in, how much you had in your bank account, or what your clothes looked like. But the world may be a little better place because you were important in the life of a child.

Author Unknown

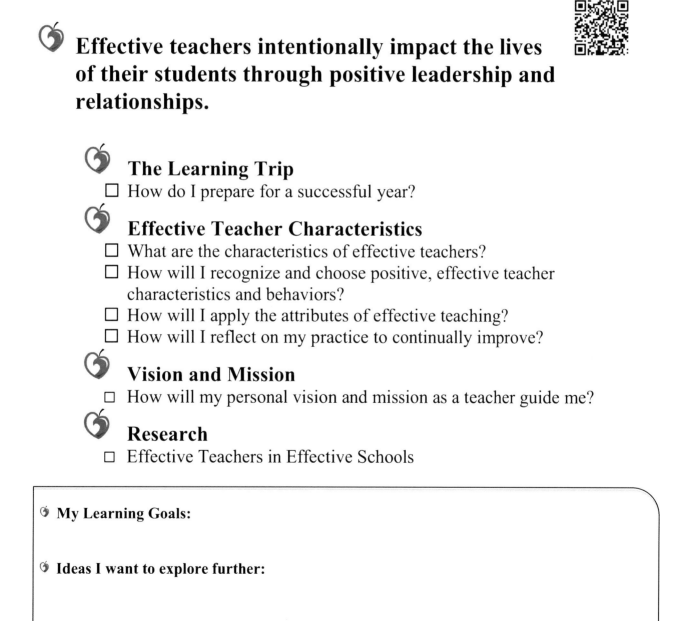

Effective teachers intentionally impact the lives of their students through positive leadership and relationships.

The Learning Trip
☐ How do I prepare for a successful year?

Effective Teacher Characteristics
☐ What are the characteristics of effective teachers?
☐ How will I recognize and choose positive, effective teacher characteristics and behaviors?
☐ How will I apply the attributes of effective teaching?
☐ How will I reflect on my practice to continually improve?

Vision and Mission
☐ How will my personal vision and mission as a teacher guide me?

Research
☐ Effective Teachers in Effective Schools

❂ **My Learning Goals:**

❂ **Ideas I want to explore further:**

The Learning Trip

Let's take a trip! On the learning trip bus. *You* are the driver for this learning trip. It is August and <u>you are ready</u>. You know <u>where</u> you are going and you have <u>your passengers</u>. Turn and look at them…ready to go, all on board. Your job is to move these passengers from where they are to where they need to be. You have never made this trip before, so the road will be new to you. You have actually never driven a bus before, so that will be new also. But you are excited and ready! You take off on this trip with passengers on board. You are moving along at a rapid pace when all of a sudden, you hit a huge bump in the road. You didn't see it coming. You are shaken and you turn to see how your passengers are. You realize that some of them popped right out the window when you hit the bump. You feel terrible about it. You want to stop and get them back on, but you have to get to your destination on time, so you move forward again, hoping someone will maybe pick them up on their way. Back on track and moving forward, you gain a little confidence and speed up. Again, out of nowhere, another bump, this one worse than the one before. You look in the mirror in time to see more of your charges flying out the windows! You are feeling really bad now. But you must continue the journey; you must get to the destination. You continue, speeding up, hitting bumps, and losing passengers. You cannot stop; you must get the bus to your destination. Finally you reach the destination. Hallelujah! You are exhausted, but you made it. You turn, look and what do you see? Oh, no! You are the only one who is still on the bus!

⚘ Some thoughts for discussion:
- ☑ If you worked for a real bus company, what would your supervisor say?
- ☑ Did you notice how your objective changed from getting the passengers to the destination to getting the bus to the destination?
- ☑ If this metaphor represents the learning trip you will lead your students on from August to June, what do the bumps and popped-out passengers mean to you?
- ☑ What do you need to know and do to prepare for a successful trip?

The Bus Trip Lessons

The task—to move people from where they are to where they need to be.

Corollary: **Your task**—to lead learners from where they are to where they need to be.

Results—If the driver's the only one on the bus when it arrives…it's a failed trip.

Corollary: If the teacher is the only one smarter at the end of the year, it is a failed journey.

⚘ **Your thoughts:**

---

4 Phases of a Successful Learning Trip

Think about the things it takes for a professional bus trip to be successful.

☑ **Planning and preparation**
☑ **Knowledge and skills**
☑ **Ability to perform, monitor, and adjust**
☑ **Professional duties**

What's the difference in driving a bus professionally and being a teacher? The teacher has to plan for the trip; get the passengers ready; get the bus ready; organize the bus, manage the people on the bus; keep the bus records; have meetings about the bus, the trip, and the passengers; evaluate the trip; and communicate with all other bus drivers. Not all of the principles apply; many do. There are several **aspects** of making the first year and every year successful. This *First Year Teacher Notebook* will help you in each aspect of your new teacher journey.

1. *The Route*
Planning and Preparation (Is the trip well planned?)
☑ Knowledge of content, students, resources
☑ Selecting learning goals and outcomes
☑ Designing lessons and assessments

2. *The Bus*
Positive Environment (Is the bus ready?)
☑ Organization of space, materials, and time
☑ Management plan for procedures and behavior
☑ Attitude of high expectations
☑ Climate of respect and rapport

3. *The Passengers*
Purposeful Instruction (Is everyone on the bus?)
☑ Clear goals and objectives expressed
☑ All students engaged
☑ Brain-compatible lessons
☑ Learning for all

4. *The Driver*
Professionalism (How can the next trip be better?)
☑ Reflecting on and revising practice
☑ Effective communication with families
☑ Professionalism in manner and actions
☑ Professional growth and collegiality

🍎 Your thoughts:
Describe your confidence and preparation level in the 4 aspects. Where do you feel most and least confident?

Effective Teacher Characteristics
The bottom line is that there is just no way to create good schools without good teachers.
—*What Matters Most: Teaching for America's Future*, NCTAF

Effective educators share certain behaviors and attitudes.

Think back over your entire career as a learner. Think of all the many teachers and learning experiences you had from early childhood through college: in school, scouts, church, sports, family, or other situations. Some of those experiences were probably great; others were not.

- Think of the experiences that were either good or bad because of the teacher. If you separate those experiences into positives and negatives, some tendencies will begin to surface. As you focus on the negative experiences, what characteristics did the teacher possess and exhibit? What made it such a bad experience? What did that person do or not do? List those characteristics on the chart below under "Ineffective."
- Now think of the positive experiences. Think of the best teacher(s) you ever had. What characteristics did that teacher possess and exhibit? What did that person do or not do that caused you to remember the experience even today? List those characteristics below under "Effective."

Ineffective	Effective
-boring	- energetic
-screaming	-out of the box fun
- inconsiderate	-field trips
- no break from the norm	- happy
-single out in front of everyone	- relationship builder
- monotone	-felt comfortable / safe
-rude	- confidant
- unfair	-always looked forward to her class
-sarcastic	-prepared & knew how to get point across
-creepy	-high expectations

- Go over the lists and think about whether the characteristic is mainly about the person or the subject or grade level taught. Mark a *P* by each item that is about the *person*; mark an *S* by each item that is primarily about the *subject*/content taught.
- Do you see a pattern? How would you summarize the chart?

Effectiveness

Over the years as I've asked new teachers those questions about the best and worst teachers, I am amazed at the responses. First of all, I am amazed that every group has a list of terrible teacher characteristics. Secondly, I am amazed because many of the same characteristics seem to appear on list after list. The lists almost always include these qualities: boring, mean, sarcastic, hateful, dirty, sleazy, incompetent, played favorites, yelled, cried, lazy, didn't care, tried to be a buddy, dumb, and so on. How does this happen? What would cause someone to be like this?

Another amazing thing is the best teacher characteristics list. The same qualities appear over and over: competent, caring, consistent, fair, treated us with respect, tough, challenging, sense of humor, loved to teach, etc. The lists are always overwhelmingly about the person, not the subject. As a matter of fact, students who had liked subjects before were often turned off them for life because of the teacher. And the opposite is also true—students who didn't like a subject began to love it because of a teacher. **The power of a teacher can never be underestimated!**

A few years ago there was a young man in my First Year Teachers' Academy who took great offense to my statement that teachers were role models for their students. He said, "I don't want to be a role model. That's not my job. I just want to teach history and coach." I told him I had some bad news for him, "Every teacher is a role model; that's not a choice! When you stand up in front of kids, you're a role model. The choice is whether to be a positive one or a negative one. There's no neutral ground." They are watching. They are watching us and learning how to be adults. Scary, isn't it?

Our goal as teachers is to be effective. How do we do that? How do we stay off the "worst" list? One way we do that is to look at our own experiences and learn from them. We need to look at what effective teachers do and do those things. We need to look at what ineffective teachers do and avoid those things. We can organize effective teacher characteristics, whether they are people skills or cognitive knowledge and skills, into the following qualities that Harry Wong[1] says define effective teachers:

1. They have *High Expectations*
2. They are *Effective Classroom Managers*
3. They *Teach for Mastery for All Students*

These qualities are hierarchical. That is, you cannot teach for mastery unless the classroom is well managed. And you cannot have a well-managed classroom without having high expectations for students and yourself. Almost everything a teacher does fits within one of these three qualities.

---

[1] Wong, Harry and Rosemary. (1998). *How To Be An Effective Teacher The First Days Of School*. Mountain View, California. Harry Wong Publications, Inc.

High Expectations

An effective teacher is convinced of the potential that lies within each of his students and for himself as a professional educator. Effective teacher qualities[2] include

- Being **committed** to making a difference for each student
- Being **convinced** of the possibilities for each student
- Being a person of **character** and **integrity**
- **Caring** about what happens to each student
- Being **compassionate** toward students
- Being **considerate** of others' situations
- Having a sense of **humor**
- Showing **respect** to everyone, even those who don't reciprocate
- Being **passionate** about the profession
- Having a **vision** for teaching and learning

One of my former teachers and friends, Bess Brillhart Sommers, tells of learning a lesson about expectations during her first year to teach math many years ago. She had a student she simply loved; his name was Charles. He was wonderful—great math student, handsome, popular, kind, and dependable. At the first meet-the-teacher night, a woman approached Bess and introduced herself, "Hello, I'm Charles' mother." Bess was surprised. This woman was nothing like what she thought Charles' mother would be. This woman was quiet, unassuming, and appeared a little sad. Bess began, "Oh, I love him! He is one of my favorite students. He is such a joy to have in class…and what a good student…all the other kids love to work with him. You must be so proud!" The woman was stunned, almost speechless, and asked, "My Charles?" "Yes, he's wonderful! And it is so good to meet you."

The next morning in the teachers' workroom, she mentioned this encounter to a fellow teacher who also had wonderful Charles and who said, "You didn't meet Charles' mother last night. She teaches at the junior high and told me she couldn't be here. I don't know who you met, but it wasn't his mother." Confused, Bess went to her room and checked her grade book. Sure enough, there it was—she had another student named Charles in that same class. He was a quiet boy who hardly participated and barely passed. "Oh, no," she thought. When the class with the two Charleses began to come in, she worried whether she ought to say something to the other Charles to straighten it out. He entered the room with bright eyes and a smile—the first she'd ever seen. "My mom said she met you," he said with a shy grin. Now, you know what that mother did as soon as she returned home from meeting the teachers—she reported to Charles and the entire family about how much this teacher liked him and how smart she thought he was.

The miracle of this story is that he became what she mistakenly told his mother he was. She misspoke him into success. Charles became a good math student and eventually a teacher. He rose to what <u>he</u> thought her expectation of him was. <u>That</u> is influence!

---

[2] Tucker, Ginger LaGrone. *The Heart of a Teacher: Sailing the High Cs*. Fifteen characteristics of effective educators.

Effective Classroom Management

Learning simply cannot happen if the classroom is not well managed. Some teachers mistakenly think that active learning means chaos. Yes, learning means activity, movement, and noise at times; but it is always in a safe and structured environment. I have visited some classes where I was the only one paying attention to the teacher who was teaching away without one student being engaged. Well-managed classrooms are organized, managed, safe, and orderly. The teacher is in control of the activities. When I think of the best teachers I know, they have good classroom management and very few discipline issues. Classroom management is a preventive to many discipline problems.[3]

Effective teacher qualities include

- Organizing and managing **space, time,** and **materials**
- Managing student **behavior**
- Being a good **communicator**
- Creating a classroom **culture** for learning

Teaches for Mastery for All Students

Effective teachers teach for mastery; they don't just cover the material. They utilize the latest research on learning and effectively implement strategies to involve all learners. They are learning-focused and teach with learner performance in mind. Effective teachers plan, prepare, and present lessons that are aligned with the curriculum, integrated with other subjects, and have relevance to the learner. Students who are engaged in learning in meaningful ways don't usually have time to cause problems. Students who have mastered knowledge and skills can show you what they know by explaining, describing, applying, demonstrating, teaching, etc. Effective teacher qualities[4] include

- Being **competent** in the process of teaching
- Being **knowledgeable** about the subjects taught
- Utilizing a variety of teaching **methods** to engage all learners
- **Planning, preparing,** and **facilitating** effective **lessons**
- **Assessing** student learning and **adjusting** instruction.

⌾ **Your thoughts**: How will these characteristics define you this year?

---

[3] Chapters 3 and 4 deal with classroom management and behavior management thoroughly.
[4] Chapters 5 and 6 explore teaching and learning.

My Favorite Teachers

I had some great teacher role models: wonderful men and women whom I considered heroes and heroines. One of my favorites was Mrs. Ocoee Holt, teacher extraordinaire. I loved Mrs. Holt and I loved fourth grade because of Mrs. Holt. She was, in my mind, the perfect combination of kindness, toughness, and fun. I still remember lessons she taught. I remember our homonym club; I am partial to homonyms to this day! More than anything I remember the way she treated us. I remember the way she treated kids who were poor and kids who were rich and kids like me. I vividly remember telling her I wanted to write books. She said, "Well, do it!" And I did. I wrote and illustrated my first book that day, called <u>The Adventures of Petunia, The Skunk.</u> Mrs. Holt proudly displayed it in our room for all to see. She made me think it was fabulous.

I had been telling a group of teachers how important it would be if they would call or write teachers who had made a positive impact on their lives. I realized as I described the teacher I wanted to be, I always described Mrs. Holt and that I had never told her that. Finally, I went to visit Mrs. Holt in her nursing home to tell her how much she meant to me and that I wanted to be a teacher just like her.

She had lived in a retirement village for years, not because she needed assistance, but because she enjoyed the friends and activities. Her daughter had informed me that if I was going to visit her, I needed to do it soon, because her mom was beginning to "slip a little."

As I knocked on the door of her little suite, fear gripped my heart that she wouldn't remember me or that she would not be the same person. She opened the door and greeted me with a smile in her silk dress, pumps, and pearls. It was almost dinnertime and she was dressed and waiting. I said, "Mrs. Holt, it's Ginger. Do you remember me?"

"Why, Ginger! How good to see you! Come in here." She always said my name real long and up on the end. My heart flooded with warm memories.

She showed me her apartment, telling me about her schedule, and invited me to stay for dinner. I told her I could only stay a while, so she invited me to sit and visit a minute. When we sat down I said, "Mrs. Holt, you know I became a teacher and taught high school and now I get to work with teachers in professional development."

"My, my, my, yes, I have kept up with several of you children. I had forgotten that you were a teacher. I'm so proud for you."

I leaned toward her and said, "Well, Mrs. Holt, I've been meaning to come by for a long time to visit you. I just wanted to tell you how much you meant to me as a teacher. When I think of all I wanted to be as a teacher, it was you. You are one of the reasons I wanted to teach. I really love you, and I want to thank you for the difference you made in my life as a child."

She was moved and thanked me, "Why, Honey, thank you! You know I always tried to treat all children like they were mine."

I was so relieved that she seemed well and understood and that I hadn't waited too long to let her know. She told a story about a little boy and a lesson she'd taught him about honesty. We laughed and then she looked at me and said, "Now, honey, what do you do?" And I told her again. "Oh! Isn't that nice. Now where do you live?" And I told her again. Then she told the story of the boy again. I listened and laughed with her again. Then she looked at me and said, "Now, Honey, what do you do?"

We had the same conversation until time for her to go to dinner. Sadness engulfed me as I sat there and realized two things. My teacher-hero was leaving her frail little body, bit by bit. And the selfish regret that I had waited too long to tell her the difference she'd made in my life. She wouldn't remember that I had been there. Why hadn't I told her when it could have made a difference for her? Why had I put it off?

I escorted her down to dinner, her arm locked on mine, flashing back to days of wanting to be right behind her first in line to the cafeteria or playground or anywhere else she led.

She has since passed away. Her funeral was a tribute to her impact on the community and as a teacher on the lives of hundreds of children. Although she didn't remember my visit, my comfort comes from knowing that as she joined the Master Teacher, she knew how much she meant to a little girl who wanted to write books and be a teacher. Thank you, Mrs. Holt, for modeling for me what being a teacher is.

Some teachers help us decide what we want to be and help to make us who we are. Such was the case with another favorite teacher, Jane Stephens, my high school history teacher. I had not had great experiences in history classes up to that point-mostly lectures and chapter questions. Mrs. Stephens loved history and it was catching! She had traveled extensively and shared her adventures with us, bringing history to life. It has been a long time, but I still remember some of our class discussions. It was real and it was important—there was a war going on in Vietnam—history mattered. She also had a great sense of humor, great rapport, and great classroom management. I can't recall her ever having to discipline anyone. She was fair and friendly, but was the adult in charge. In looking back, I realize that I never even considered teaching anything other than history after having her as my model teacher. Thank you, Mrs. Stephens.

Your thoughts:

How would you describe your favorite elementary, middle, and high school teachers?

To whom do you need to send a note?

Imagine that you are at the end of your career as a teacher after having taught for many years. You are being honored with a retirement dinner. Your former students are coming back to honor you and will speak about the difference you made in their lives as a teacher. If your career could be what you most desire, what would you hear them say about you?

🍎 In the space below, write several statements you want to hear that would represent what you had hoped to accomplish as a teacher. Write them as if the other person were speaking about you.

🍎 Based on what you want to have said about you at the end of a successful career, list the things you want to do and are committed to do as a teacher.

Vision and Mission

Where there is no vision, the people are unrestrained. Proverbs 29:18

In *Seven Habits of Highly Effective People*[5], Steven Covey says that effective people begin with the end in mind. They know **where** they are going, **why** they are going, and have a **plan** to work toward their desired results. When you focused on what you would like to have accomplished and to have said about you at the end of your career, you were establishing the building blocks of your **vision** and **mission** as a teacher.

Definitions

Vision – statement of the desired result of my efforts, the ideal I am working toward. As a teacher it is what my career looks like in completion and along the way. It represents a place from which I can look back and see the impact I've had. It describes the ideal.

My vision is the constant in the distance toward which I strive.

Mission – statement of what a person commits to do. As a teacher my mission articulates my purpose, promise, and plan. Everything I do as an educator is connected to my mission.

A personal and professional mission drives effective teachers.

The foundation for vision and mission is the **reason** you do what you do. How would you answer the questions?
- ☑ Why do I teach?
- ☑ What difference does it make?
- ☑ What do I believe about teaching and learning, teachers and children?

Answering those questions reflects one's philosophy about teaching based on beliefs and values.

Philosophy – statement of core beliefs about teaching, learning, and students. As a teacher, these are the values that I live by that cause me to be able to do this work.

---

[5] Covey, Stephen R. *The 7 Habits of Highly Effective People*. (2004)

My Vision, Mission, and Philosophy

Using page 18:

    ◕   Write your vision based on what you want to have said about you at the end of your career.

        My vision is…..(what does it look like?)

    ◕   Write your mission statement based on what you promise and commit to do as an educator.

        My Mission is to….

    ◕   Write your philosophy statements based on what you believe.

        I believe….

What does the research say?
Effective Teachers in Effective Schools

Over 30 years ago, Dr. Lezotte[6] and his colleagues Ron Edmonds, Wilbur Brookover, and other Effective Schools researchers identified the common characteristics of successful schools—schools where all children learn. The research of these dedicated individuals refuted the notion that schools had no impact on learning and, in doing so, identified the following *Correlates of Effective Schools*:

Clear School Mission - In the effective school, there is a clearly articulated school mission through which the staff shares an understanding of and commitment to instructional goals, priorities, assessment procedures and accountability. Staff accepts responsibility for students' learning of the school's essential curricular goals.

High Expectations for Success - In the effective school, there is a climate of expectation in which the staff believe and demonstrate that all students can attain mastery of the essential content and school skills, and the staff also believe that they have the capability to help all students achieve that mastery.

Instructional Leadership - In the effective school, the principal acts as an instructional leader and effectively and persistently communicates that mission to the staff, parents, and students. The principal understands and applies the characteristics of instructional effectiveness in the management of the instructional program.

Frequent Monitoring of Student Progress - In the effective school, student academic progress is measured frequently. A variety of assessment procedures is used. The results of the assessments are used to improve individual student performance and also to improve the instructional program.

Opportunity to Learn and Student Time on Task - In the effective school, teachers allocate a significant amount of classroom time to instruction in the essential content and skills. For a high percentage of this time students are engaged in whole class or large group, teacher-directed, planned learning activities.

Safe and Orderly Environment - In the effective school, there is an orderly, purposeful, businesslike atmosphere which is free from the threat of physical harm. The school climate is not oppressive and is conducive to teaching and learning.

Home - School Relations - In the effective school, parents understand and support the school's basic mission and are given the opportunity to play an important role in helping the school to achieve that mission.

Robert Marzano, who is one of the most significant educational researchers today, in his *What Works in Schools Framework*, offers the following **Factors That Influence Achievement:**

School Factors	1. Guaranteed and Viable Curriculum 2. Challenging Goals and Effective Feedback 3. Parent and Community Involvement 4. Safe and Orderly Environment 5. Collegiality and Professionalism
Teacher Factors	6. Instructional Strategies 7. Classroom Management 8. Classroom Curriculum Design
Student Factors	9. Home Environment 10. Learning Intelligence/ Background Knowledge 11. Motivation

Every chapter in this *First Year Teacher Notebook* will guide you as you analyze each of these factors influencing achievement and will help you apply effective strategies as you grow professionally.

Professional teachers are students of teaching and consumers of research.
Richard DuFour, in *Professional Learning Communities at Work*

---

[6] Larry Lezotte. *What Effective Schools Do: Re-Envisioning the Correlates.* (2010) Visit www.effective schools.com.

What does the research say?

The Highly Qualified Beginning Teacher

Source: National Commission on Teaching and America's Future

NCTAF, working with its state partners and building on research and standards developed by the Interstate New Teacher Assessment and Support Consortium (INTASC), the National Board for Professional Teaching Standards (NBPTS), and others, identified a set of criteria to define a highly qualified teacher. These criteria are based on the teaching profession's consensus about what a highly qualified teacher, *including beginning teachers*, should know and be able to do to help students learn.

Highly qualified beginning teachers should be able to meet state licensing standards that require candidates to

☑ Possess a deep understanding of the subjects they teach

☑ Evidence a firm understanding of how students learn

☑ Demonstrate the teaching skills necessary to help all students achieve high standards

☑ Create a positive learning environment

☑ Use a variety of assessment strategies to diagnose and respond to individual learning needs

☑ Demonstrate and integrate modern technology into the school curriculum to support student learning

☑ Collaborate with colleagues, parents and community members, and other educators to improve student learning

☑ Reflect on their practice to improve future teaching and student achievement

☑ Pursue professional growth in both content and pedagogy

☑ Instill a passion for learning in their students.

⟁ Read through the list again and <u>underline</u> the skill or quality once and the descriptor for how, how much, or to what degree twice, if it tells. For example, in the first criteria, underline *subjects taught* once and *deep understanding* twice.

⟁ **Your thoughts:** Would this list be helpful in creating your vision and mission? Would it help you set goals?

---

*There is more on using this list in Chapter 8.

Triangle-Circle-Square Reflection

△	List three important "points" from this chapter.
◯	Based on this chapter, what is something that is "rolling" around in your mind?
☐	What "squares" with your beliefs from this chapter?

Extend: How could you use this reflection format with your students?

Chapter 2
Getting Ready for the First Days

"What you do on the first days of school will determine your success or failure for the rest of the school year. You will either win or lose your class on the first days of school."

--Dr. Harry Wong

Effective teachers are prepared to start the first days of school with confidence.

The First Days' Essentials
- ☐ What 3 categories must be ready for the first day?
- ☐ What do students need to know on the first day?

The First Days' Lessons
- ☐ How should lessons be designed?

The First Days' Checklists
- ☐ What things should I know, ask, or have prepared?

Comprehensive Plan for the First Days
- ☐ What should the plans be for the first days?

❧ **My Learning Goals:**

❧ **Ideas I want to explore further:**

The First Days' Essentials

Where do I start?

You can't do everything on the first day. Some things can wait a couple of days. But there will never be another first day; there will never be a better opportunity to get off to a great start. Impressions are formed immediately and are hard to overcome if we don't start with a good one!

Three categories of things have to be ready for the first day of the Learning Trip...

Think back to our bus metaphor. You, the *driver*, have some things to do before the students, your *passengers*, show up and take their seats on the learning trip. Three things must be ready in order for the Learning Trip to get off to a successful start:

1. The **driver** must be ready. There can't be a bus trip without a driver.
2. The **route** must be decided. Without a clear direction, the destination cannot be reached.
3. The **bus** has to be ready for the passengers. If the passengers can't get on and stay on, what is the point of the trip?

Let's explore those three aspects further. Remember, you might not be able to have *everything* ready, but some things are essential. These are listed in what I believe is their <u>order</u> of importance. Teachers often reverse the order—spend all their time making the room perfect, a little time on a plan, and no time to ready themselves.

1. The teacher – You!
   ☑ You must be rested, nourished, relaxed, and ready. If you start out exhausted, you may never catch up. Get 7 to 8 hours of sleep. Your brain will thank you.
   ☑ Eat breakfast and drink lots of water during the day. It will keep you from being so exhausted and dehydrated.
   ☑ Dress for success—adult and professional. (See chapter 8 for more on professionalism.)

2. The plans –
   ☑ Have a <u>lesson plan</u> for the first week outlined and the first day detailed.
   ☑ Write it out; don't leave it to memory or try to "wing it."
   ☑ Have a <u>management plan</u> ready to share with goals, rules, and procedures. (See Chapter 3 for goals, rules, consequences and procedures)
   ☑ Time spent teaching procedures in the beginning will result in time saved during the rest of the year.

3. The room –
   ☑ Everything doesn't have to be perfect, but at least have what you need for the first days ready. (More on room arrangement in Chapter 3)
   ☑ Check with others on your campus for ideas.
   ☑ Remember the words—safe, effective, and efficient. You can decorate later. Always ask yourself if the room is designed for student learning or for adult comfort and taste.

The most important factor affecting individual student success in schools is the classroom teacher.
(Marzano, Pickering, and Pollack, 2001)

What students need to know on 1ˢᵗ day to feel safe and to be successful:

This chapter and the following chapters will help as you plan your successful trip. Harry Wong suggests seven things students need to know on the first day. Effective teachers plan for the start of each year with those questions in mind. I've added some suggestions to his list of seven.

- ☑ **Am I in the right room?**
    - ☑ Don't let students wander around looking for you. Remember how many classes middle and high school students have to deal with.
    - ☑ Have your name and subject on the door.
    - ☑ Be at the door to greet them and/or their parents.
    - ☑ Hi, I'm Mrs. Tucker and this is World Geography. Welcome!

- ☑ **Where am I supposed to sit?**
    - ▪ Have assigned seat for the first day, even if you don't know names yet. You can assign by giving each student a number as he enters that matches a desk number.
    - ▪ Assigned seating saves time and trouble and takes care of those who are left out of "the group."

- ☑ **What are the rules in this classroom?**
    - ▪ Let them know early on what your expectations are.
    - ▪ See Chapter 3 for information on developing rules.

- ☑ **What will I be doing this year?**
    - ▪ Give them the big picture of the class.
    - ▪ Tell them about the content and the processes.
    - ▪ Let them see your enthusiasm for the subject and for teaching.

- ☑ **How will I be graded?**
    - ▪ Let them know how they can be successful.
    - ▪ Let them see immediately that you are fair and consistent.
    - ▪ Show them everyone has the opportunity to succeed.

- ☑ **Who is this teacher as a person?**
    - ▪ Tell them about your goals for them
    - ▪ Without giving personal details, introduce yourself to them.
    - ▪ They will get a picture of you by what you say, how you act, and how you look. It will be a lasting impression.
    - ▪ Even if you're only three years older than they are, let them see that you are the adult in charge.

- ☑ **Will the teacher treat me as a human being?**
    - ▪ Let them see from the beginning that you are a person of integrity.
    - ▪ Show them and assure them that it will be safe to learn in your room.
    - ▪ Let them know you have high expectations for everyone.

Do you notice that these questions deal with physical needs, social needs, cognitive needs, and emotional needs?

The next time you attend a staff development session or meeting, see if you don't have many of those same seven concerns.

How will you answer each of those questions? Use this space to brainstorm the things you want to do to meet students' needs.

First Days' Lessons –Tips For Success

Lesson planning and guided instruction date back to the 1700s. Various philosophers and scholars offered steps and criteria for instruction. In the 1970s and 1980s, Madeline Hunter asserted that improving learning required improving teachers—schools needed master teachers. Her book, *Mastery Teaching*[7], became the foundation for lesson planning and curriculum design for schools across the nation. Today there are many variations and "takeoffs" of Hunter's lesson design. The Lesson Cycle basics include the following components:

The Lesson Cycle based on Madeline Hunter's Mastery Teaching

Instruction
Explain, define, model, question

Focus
To create interest in learning; to connect to prior or future learning

Monitor and adjust

Guided Practice
Monitored application of learning

Closure
To connect all learning to the stated objectives

Independent Practice
To see if learning has happened

Every lesson plan should have a clear goal—stated objective with learner performance objectives (what the learners are able **to know** and **do) and should have these components:**

☑ Focus (anticipatory set) - to generate interest in learning; tie to prior learning
☑ Instruction – explanation, definitions, modeling, questioning, processing activities
☑ Guided practice – monitored application of learning; re-teaching the concepts not mastered
☑ Independent practice – to see if learning has taken place
☑ Closure – connect all learning to the objective; reflect on learning

A Lesson Cycle may be completed in one class session or over many days.

As a teacher in the 1980s and 1990s, Madeline Hunter's work was a true gift. I learned to organize my instruction and I began to be a better teacher. The drawback for today's classes is that Hunter's model focuses on improving the teacher while today's schools **focus on the learner**—*high levels of learning for all*. **For effective use today, Hunter's model can be altered to make it more learner-centered, or schools can adopt other frameworks for planning units and lessons.**

(In Chapter 6 we will look at another format for planning lessons, the **5E Model** for lesson design.)

---

[7] Hunter, M. (1982). ***Mastery Teaching.*** El Segundo, CA. TIP Publications.

Teaching Schema for Master Learners (from Jane Pollock)

Jane Pollock offers the *Teaching Schema for Master Learners* (TSML)[8] with the following six steps "to prepare students for learning, help them connect new information to prior learning, and to cement those ideas or skills." I have added descriptions and some simple examples to the schema to connect to the components of a guaranteed and viable curriculum.

Sample Lesson:

Unit Title: The geographic grid   **Lesson Title:** Absolute and relative location
Grade Level: High School World Geography

1. Goals/Learning Targets (GO): The teacher identifies the **key concepts** and the **essential understandings** for the lesson.
Example: The student understands the concept of location. The student is expected to apply knowledge about the geographic grid and absolute location and to use map skills to locate places using coordinates.

2. Access Prior Knowledge (APK): The teacher plans an activity, a question, or a demonstration to spur or fire activity in the student's neural network. The goal is to provide stimulus that relates to the lesson, not just to get the students excited.
Example: As students enter the classroom, they notice the diagram of a football field on the board without gridlines. In pairs ask the students to talk about how the game would be different without the lines. Using a KWL chart, ask students to brainstorm what they know about the grid system and would like to learn.

3. Acquire New Information (NI): The teacher deliberately plans for declarative (facts and information) and procedural (skills and processes) knowledge, using instructional strategies that are effective.
Example: Students use the two-column note-taking method to write definitions, descriptions, and label the grid components.

4. Apply Knowledge (APP): The students practice the new knowledge or skills to create sense and meaning.
Example: Students practice finding locations, using the classroom as a grid with each desk having coordinates. Then students transition to their map worksheets to mark several locations, using coordinates with a partner first and then alone.

5. Generalize/Summarize (GEN): Closure is the time after learning when the learner reflects on or summarizes what he knows and/or can do in relation to the learning targets. Pollack calls this step "putting a tab on the folder."
Example: After reviewing their 2-column notes in the left column and depictions of the concepts in the right column, students write summary statements and share their summaries with a partner. Students add the final column to the KWL chart.

6. Homework, if necessary (HW): Students complete relevant reading, notes, or other tasks to extend learning. Homework is never assigned as punishment or an unnecessary task.
Example: Assign students to look for other grid systems and their purposes at home and in the community.

Continuous Feedback during and after the lesson: Feedback should be directly related to the essential understandings so that students can improve.

🍎 **Practice:** Use the format above to sketch out a lesson you will soon teach or have recently taught.

---

[8] Pollock, Jane S. (2007). *Improving Student Learning One Teacher at a Time*. ASCD.

Teaching Schema for Master Learners (based on Jane Pollock's work)

Unit Title:
Lesson Title:
Grade Level:

Goals/Learning Targets (GO):

Access Prior Knowledge (APK):

Acquire New Information (NI):

Apply Knowledge (APP):

Generalize/Summarize (GEN):

Homework, if necessary (HW):

Continuous Feedback:

First Days' Checklist

Questions to ask: Notes:

- ☐ Do you have keys to your classroom and other rooms you may need access to?
- ☐ Do you have the necessary furniture for your room?
- ☐ What are the procedures for obtaining classroom books and for checking them out to students?
- ☐ What expendable supplies are available, and what are the procedures for obtaining them?
- ☐ What technology equipment is available, and what are the procedures for obtaining it?
- ☐ What is the required paperwork for the first days of school, everyday attendance, and lunch procedures?
- ☐ What is the procedure for the arrival of students on the first day of school and for the following days?
- ☐ How do students leave at the end of the day?
- ☐ What are the school's policies about rules and consequences, suspension, keeping students after school or during lunch for makeup or for detention?
- ☐ Are there special events or assemblies you need to be aware of during the first weeks? What are your responsibilities for sponsoring or attending events?
- ☐ What time do your students go to lunch, PE, music, recess, and library?
- ☐ Do you have a class roster?
- ☐ What are the attendance procedures?

- ☐ What is the procedure for late and early arrivals?
- ☐ Are there hall and office passes?
- ☐ Do you have a copy of the bell schedule?
- ☐ Do you have a copy of the school calendar?
- ☐ Do you have a map of the school campus?
- ☐ Do you have a copy of the faculty roster?
- ☐ Do you have students with special needs? If so, when can you expect modification sheets?
- ☐ Do you have students with handicapping conditions which will require a special room arrangement?
- ☐ Do you have students who will be leaving your classroom for help or other reasons?
- ☐ Are aides available and, if so, what are the procedures for working with aides?
- ☐ In what circumstances do parents need to be notified?
- ☐ What time are you required to be at school and when may you leave?
- ☐ What is the procedure for duplicating materials?
- ☐ How do you get assistance from the office for emergencies, illness, or discipline problems?
- ☐ Who is your mentor teacher?
- ☐ When is the principal available and when should he/she be consulted?
- ☐ What is the procedure for referring students to the nurse?
- ☐ What is the procedure for referring students to the counselor?
- ☐ What janitorial services are available for your room?
- ☐ Are you familiar with the building? Restrooms? Library? Lunchroom? Workroom?
- ☐ Where can you hold parent conferences?

- ☐ What is the procedure for securing a substitute?
- ☐ Is there a required curriculum?
- ☐ How do you access your lesson plans and grade book?
- ☐ Are you required to turn in lesson plans? Electronic or paper? When?
- ☐ When are faculty meetings?
- ☐ Are you a member of any team or committee?
- ☐ Do you have school insurance information?
- ☐ Do you have teacher organization information and forms?
- ☐ Do you have a place to store the supplies students will bring (elementary)?
- ☐ What is the expectation for dress during beginning of school professional activities?
- ☐ What teams or committees will you serve on?
- ☐ Are you part of a professional learning community?
- ☐ What are your "duty" assignments?
- ☐ Who is your "go to" person for questions/help?

Add your questions:

☐

☐

☐

☐

☐

The <u>First Day</u> Checklist

- ☐ Do you have a written lesson plan for the first day?
- ☐ Do you have a team building activity for the first day?
- ☐ Do you have a checklist of the required paperwork to distribute and collect?
- ☐ Do you have a prepared handout and/or bulletin board for rules, consequences, procedures, and course requirements?
- ☐ Do you have a seating arrangement planned?
- ☐ Do you have sponge activities (worthwhile time fillers) ready in case you have extra time?
- ☐ Do you have a letter/email ready to go home to parents introducing yourself and explaining your class expectations?
- ☐ Do you have folders or files for each student?
- ☐ Do you have a procedure for collecting student work and information?
- ☐

- ☐

- ☐

Sample First Day Plan – Secondary Example

Depending on your schedule for the first days, you may do these things over several days.

Objectives: Students will understand the rules, schedules and procedures
Students will become familiar with the teacher's system and expectations

- ☐ Before the bell or before class starts
  - ○ Smile and greet them at the door – friendly and professional
  - ○ Welcome them – "Hi, I'm Mr….., Welcome to Biology"
  - ○ Explain how to find a seat
  - ○ Explain what to do—get them to work on one of the following:
    - ▪ Problem
    - ▪ Read
    - ▪ Puzzle
    - ▪ Journal
    - ▪ Pretest
    - ▪ Student information sheet
- ☐ Begin class as soon as bell rings
  - ○ Introduce yourself
  - ○ Introduce the class or course –"What you will learn"
  - ○ Explain your goals for them
  - ○ Take roll
  - ○ Do other clerical requirements for the first day
- ☐ Explain procedures (only the ones needed now; teach others as needed)
  - ○ Entering and leaving room
  - ○ Tardy policy
  - ○ Class participation
  - ○ Quiet signal
  - ○ Using resources and supplies
  - ○ Getting your attention
  - ○ Phone buddy for makeup work or assignments
- ☐ Instructional matters
  - ○ Explain course requirements
  - ○ Explain grading policy
  - ○ Required supplies and materials
  - ○ Check out textbooks or equipment (you may want to wait until classes are leveled)
- ☐ Teach the class rules or expectations
  - ○ Have them posted
  - ○ Be positive
  - ○ Explain consequence system
- ☐ Explain materials pick up and delivery system
  - ○ In-basket
  - ○ Makeup work folder or system
  - ○ Student files of completed work
- ☐ Conduct a class-building (get acquainted) activity

Sample First Day Plan - Elementary Example

Depending on your schedule for the first days, you may do these things over several days.

Objectives: Students will become familiar with the rules, schedules and procedures

Students will begin to adjust to school

☐ Before the bell or before class starts
- o   Smile and greet them at the door – friendly and professional
- o   Welcome them – "Hi, I'm Mrs….., Welcome to 3rd grade"
- o   Explain how to find a seat
- o   Explain what to do—get them to work on one of the following:
  - ▪ Problem
  - ▪ Read
  - ▪ Puzzle
  - ▪ Journal
  - ▪ Pretest
  - ▪ Student information sheet

☐ Begin class as soon as bell rings
- o   Introduce yourself
- o   Introduce the class –"What you will learn"
- o   Explain your goals for them
- o   Have them complete a name tent or color a page
- o   Do other clerical requirements for the first day while they are working
- o   Learn everyone's name with an activity

☐ Explain procedures (only the ones needed now; teach others as needed)
- o   Quiet signal
- o   Restroom
- o   Getting your attention
- o   Hallway
- o   Others, appropriate to age

☐ Teach the class rules or expectations
- o   Have them posted
- o   Be positive
- o   Explain consequence system
- o   Model with students how it looks in role play

☐ Appropriate instructional activities to allow students to get used to system and to assess what they can do.

☐ Conduct a class-building (get acquainted) activity

 # First Day Plan

Before—
Learning targets:

Materials needed:

During—
Procedures:

    Introduce yourself –

    Introduce the class or course -

    Explanation -

After—
Clerical tasks:

Reflections on today:

After your first week of school, use this to reflect on your week and plan for the future.

Looking Reflection

Looking at the details	What happened this week that I want to remember? Think of the good & bad.
Looking at myself	What was I prepared for? What was unexpected? What did I do very well? Where would I like to improve?
Looking ahead	How does what happened change my future planning?

Chapter 3
Managing the Classroom Environment

I've come to the frightening conclusion that I am the decisive element in the classroom. It's my personal approach that creates the climate. It's my daily mood that makes the weather. As a teacher, I possess a tremendous power to make a person's life miserable or joyous. I can be a tool of torture or an instrument of inspiration. I can humiliate or humor, hurt or heal. In all situations, it is my response that decides whether a crisis will be escalated or de-escalated and a person humanized or de-humanized.

--Hiam Ginott

Effective teachers have a well-organized and well-managed classroom that is characterized by high expectations and is conducive to learning.

Effective Classroom Management
☐ What is good classroom management?
☐ Do I understand the difference between classroom management and discipline?

4 Aspects of Classroom Management
☐ What is my organizational plan for supplies and materials?
☐ How will I develop an effective system for time management?
☐ What is my plan for functional classroom arrangement and usage?
☐ What do I need to know to be able to set goals for student behavior?

Planning for Classroom Management
☐ What do I need to know to be able to plan and prepare procedures to teach?
☐ How will I design classroom rules and consequences?
☐ Will I be able to create an environment that will prevent most discipline problems?

◌ **My Learning Goals:**

◌ **Ideas I want to explore further:**

Effective Classroom Management
What is Classroom Management?

It's not, "Start hard, end up easy";
It's, "Start consistent, stay consistent."
With management and discipline it's easier to "lighten up" than to "tighten up."

Definition:
Effective classroom management consists of teacher behaviors that produce high levels of student involvement in classroom activities, minimal amounts of student behavior that interfere with the teacher's or other students' work, and efficient use of instructional time.[9]

☞ Unpack the above definition by highlighting the key words and phrases. Underline the three results of effective classroom.

Effective teachers lead and manage; ineffective teachers are always having to discipline. (Harry Wong)

Characteristics of Effective Classroom Managers:
✓ With-it-ness—having a pulse on what is happening, not naïve
✓ Smoothness—transitioning between activities
✓ Momentum—keeping everyone on the "bus"
✓ Group alerting—using a quiet signal, finished signal, etc.
✓ Individual attention accountability—expectation of involvement, random calls

--from J. Kounin

Characteristics of Better Classroom Managers:
✓ Planned rules and procedures carefully
✓ Systematically taught these to students
✓ Monitored student work and behavior closely
✓ Organized instruction to maximize student task engagement and success
✓ Communicated directions and expectations clearly

--from C.M. Evertson

Effective classroom management is *preventive* and *proactive*;
disciplinary actions are *reactive* and *time-consuming*.

---

[9] Evertson, Carolyn, Emmer, E.T., & Worsham, M.E. (2003). *Classroom Management for Elementary Teachers*, 6th Edition. Boston: Allyn and Bacon. and Emmer, E. T., Evertson, Carolyn and others. (2003). *Classroom Management for Secondary Teachers, 6th Edition.* Boston: Allyn and Bacon.

Four Aspects of Classroom Management
Snapshot View

✓ Organizing and managing time
- ⑥ Schedule time to <u>plan</u>.
- ⑥ Have a system. Use a <u>planner</u> or day timer.
- ⑥ Set goals and <u>prioritize</u>.
- ⑥ Capture time that would otherwise be wasted.

✓ Organizing and managing materials
- ⑥ With mail and memos use the "touch it once" concept.
- ⑥ Develop a system for filing.
- ⑥ Create an office in your classroom.
- ⑥ Have a central system—a tub or notebook for the essentials.

✓ Organizing and managing space
- ⑥ The arrangement must be <u>safe</u>.
- ⑥ The arrangement must be <u>effective</u> for the purpose of the lesson.
- ⑥ The arrangement must be <u>efficient,</u> requiring the least effort and confusion.
- ⑥ 3 Keys to classroom arrangement

✓ Organizing and managing student behavior
- ⑥ Establish the goals you have for your students.
- ⑥ Teach procedures – how to get things done.
- ⑥ Teach rules – expected norms of behavior.
- ⑥ Establish and teach consequences.

Time Management

The bad news is that you cannot get everything done! So what can you do?

Time Management: Key Words-Plan, Prioritize, Planner

⇨ The effective teacher is an effective planner. There is more to do than time to do it, so focusing on priorities is essential.

⇨ Stephen Covey[10] proposes one way to organize and prioritize demands on your time: to divide all your activities into four categories, depending on their <u>urgency</u> and <u>importance</u>.

I. Urgent / Important	II. Not urgent/ Important
☑ Crisis ☑ Last-minute meetings ☑ Rushing to meet deadlines ☑ Problems	☑ Preparation ☑ Planning ☑ Skill Improvement ☑ Getting job done ☑ Relationships ☑ Needed Relaxation
III. Not Important/ Urgent	**IV. Not Urgent/ Not Important**
☑ Interruptions ☑ Unimportant calls ☑ Some meetings ☑ Some paperwork	☑ Junk mail ☑ Busywork ☑ Idle chit chat ☑ Time-wasters

✎ Make a list of everything you need to do and then place the items from your list in the appropriate quadrant.

I	II.
III.	IV.

---

[10] *Seven Habits of Highly Effective People*, New York: Simon and Schuster, 1989

 The Heart of Teaching Series, 2013 Edition   42   © GKT Consulting, Inc. 2013

🍎 Daily Planner

Date: _____

Things to do before school:

☐ _____
☐ _____
☐ _____
☐ _____

Things to do at school:

☐ _____
☐ _____
☐ _____
☐ _____
☐ _____
☐ _____
☐ _____
☐ _____
☐ _____

Things to do after school:

☐ _____
☐ _____
☐ _____
☐ _____

✓ = Complete   ● = in progress   ➜= forward to tomorrow

Notes:

Time-Saving Tips

☑ Make a to-do list every day. Check items off when completed.

☑ Keep these lists for future reference and documentation.

☑ Teach students to hand in papers, right side up, with their names at the top.

☑ Have a basket for each subject or class so papers are sorted for you.

☑ For older students, assign each a partner. When a student is absent, his partner can gather notes, handouts, and assignments for the absent student.

☑ Give students the number, which corresponds to the number in your grade book. Have them write their name and number on all papers. You or a student can quickly put the papers in order for grading and recording. You can also see easily whose papers are missing.

☑ Use an answer column along the right margin of the paper for easy grading.

☑ Make a stencil to cut out or hole punch to grade multiple-choice tests.

☑ For short warm-up activities or bell work, cut worksheets into mini-strips.

☑ Place assignments and instructions on the board in the same place every time. Teach students to look there to get started.

☑ Write frequently used instructions on a chart and laminate it. When needed hang the chart on the chalkboard.

☑ Keep a traveling office for the times you are away from your room and have time to work. A cleaning supply tub or flip-top box works well. Keep pens, paper clips, scissors, tape, etc., in the box. Leave room for a file or set of papers to grade. When you are waiting at the copier or on hold on the phone, you will have what you need.

☑ Keep everything you need to plan with in a system file or notebook.

☑ Use one calendar for everything; don't have several.

☑ Identify your supplies with those little personalized mailing labels, or make your own.

☑ Designate one day a week as filing day for student papers, teaching files, and office files.

☑ Make two blank copies of student worksheets and tests, one for the file for future reference and one to make an answer key.

☑ Have a personal care kit for you in your desk with pain medicine, Band-Aids, needle and thread, etc.

☑ Create form letters and notes on the computer that you can fill in quickly.

☑ Store materials near where they are used.

☑ When you are going to do a project, gather all needed materials ahead of time and put them in a basket or box with a handle so you can move them or transport them easily.

☑ When you put up a new learning center or bulletin board, take a picture of it and make a list of everything needed. Tape those inside the box or folder where it will be stored, so that next year you won't have to try to remember what to use.

☑ Create a checklist of frequently needed supplies and make copies so all you have to do is mark the items you need as you run out.

☑ Keep a list of names of people who borrow books or supplies from you so you can locate those easily. It would even be better if you had library pockets in all your books and other items you might lend.

☑ Have your students create things such as bulletin board letters to save you time.

☑ If you can't print an electronic copy, put each student's name on little sticky notes and place them on your seating chart grid. Make copies and use them to quickly check roll, keep up with consequences, etc., when you need to change seating, rearrange sticky notes and make new copies, instead a spending time writing names over.

☑ Turn an entire wall or bulletin board into a monthly calendar, using tape or ribbon for the grid lines. Color-code daily assignments, tests, birthdays, events, etc., on index cards and tape or staple them in the date space. You can also staple a manila folder in each space and place worksheets for students who are absent. Teach students to look for what they missed or need to do in advance.

☑ Have a Rolodex or index file box handy with sponge activities. These can be puzzles, stories, activities, worksheets, etc., for when students finish early. Every time you think of one, place it in the file for future use.

☑ Check student homework to see if it is done as they come into the room. Mark blank or incomplete work with a highlighter. Have students grade their own work in class and hand it in. You can quickly see how much to deduct for work not done.

☑ Keep a roll of stick-on file labels handy to write notes about discipline and other items. At the end of the day, peel labels and place in students' folders.

☑ Take a pen with you to the mailbox and, if possible, fill out forms right away and return to the person's box.

☑ Make copies of the names in your grade book (without the grades). Use these as check lists any time you need to—field trips, permission slips, etc. Place one in the student in-basket for work and have them mark off their name as they turn in papers. Staple or clip the list to the papers. If a volunteer grades for you, she can record the grades on the list without seeing your grade book.

☑ Use double-knit fabric to cover bulletin boards and then add a colorful paper border. As the border fades or wears, it can easily be replaced. It will never fade or show staple marks. The one I made in 1984 is still being used today and is still bright purple!

☑ Keep a sub-tub with plans, instructions, worksheets, and activities that could be used at any time in the event you are ill or have to be absent and don't have time to plan for it. Update the tub from time to time.

☑ Best advice: watch what others do and borrow those ideas that work!

☑ **Add ideas from others:**

Materials Management

Mail and Memos

The **"touch it once"** concept for time and material management.
When you get mail from your box, sort it immediately.

1. **Trash** – throw it away; don't take trash to your room. When you are in doubt, ask your mentor or another teacher if it is something to keep or toss.

2. **Keepers**—take to your room and put the mail in your "In Box" if you can't sort it immediately.

- ☑ Every day, when you schedule the time, sort it into these categories (and others if needed).
    - ☑ **Hold** (or Send) – for materials to be sent to others. Put a sticky note with the recipient's name on it.
    - ☑ **Do Today** – urgent things to attend to.
    - ☑ **Do Later** – things that can wait until the end of week. – But don't forget! Put them on your list.
    - ☑ **File** – items to be filed - Deal with these items when you have time to put them where they go. (see file system below)
    - ☑ **Read** – articles, etc.
- ☑ Immediately enter those dates and reminders in your calendar. If you do this and check your planner every day, you won't be embarrassed by missing a meeting, a deadline, or a conference.
    - ☑ These tips apply as well to electronic mail.
    - ☑ Find out what your campus policy is about receiving, handling, and sending email, texts, and social media.

Central System

If you could only take one thing with you, what would you take and still be able to carry on? Organize a notebook or tub with those items in it. You might include

- ☑ Calendar/journal/planner
- ☑ Checklists
- ☑ Lesson plans
- ☑ Schedules
- ☑ Seating charts
- ☑ Sub information

Your Filing System

You will need to set up a filing system with several types of files. These are the ones that worked for me. You will have to decide what your needs require.

Filing cabinets

- You will need at least these three types of files.

1. **Curriculum files**-*lessons and resources*
    I organized mine by the units I taught and color-coded the following folders:
    - Blue tab for the detailed lesson plan, notes, and resource list
    - Yellow tab for student worksheets, assignments, projects, etc.
    - Green tab for bulletin board pictures and "stuff" for unit
    - Red tab for tests and other assessments—regular, modified, and re-take

2. **Professional files** –
    You will want to create a folder for each category as you need them. Some examples are insurance, committees, certificates, your absence forms, evaluations, etc.

3. **Student files** – *portfolios and student work samples*
    I kept a file for every student and recycled the folders every year. For a parent conference or ARD, you can grab that folder and go.

Storage areas

Boxes for units, seasonal items
Bookshelves
Bulletin board stuff

Ask about empty copier paper boxes. They make great storage boxes. Large detergent boxes with the sturdy handles are good too, but be sure to clean them out first.

Your Office

Create an office in your classroom, if you can. The office is for you to do your professional work, not for student access. It is where you will do your planning, preparing, and storing of confidential student information. Keep the things nearby that you will need to use. These are a few of the files you will want near your work area.

Desk files

- ☑ Forms and writing supplies
- ☑ Dictionary, resource books
- ☑ School calendar
- ☑ Confidential student information in a drawer you can lock.

Mail files

- ☑ Hold or Send
- ☑ Do Today
- ☑ Do Later
- ☑ File
- ☑ Read

Handy files

- ☑ Sponge activities—activities for when you have time left.
- ☑ Daily/Monthly files--have a set of five folders, one for each day of the school week and a set of 31 folders, one for each day of the month. Keep these in a standing file near your desk. File things according to the date needed in the monthly files. Each week move the content to the weekly files. You'll never forget anything.
- ☑ Tickler files-a folder for each month where you can quickly file ideas from magazines, etc., for future lessons.

Student Work files

- ☑ In basket
- ☑ Out basket

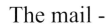 # Your Plan for Materials Management

The mail -

Filing system-

Central system -

Your office -

Space Management

Three keys to safe, effective, efficient classroom arrangement:

⚷ Visibility –
- Can you see every student?
- Can every student see you?
- Can every student see the instructional materials?

⚷ Accessibility
- Can you get to every student?
- Can you get to your resources?

⚷ Distractibility
- Is anything a distraction from the learning?
- Is there too much visual stimulation in the room?

☑ I usually recommend that for the first week or so new secondary teachers start students out facing the teacher in rows until they are confident about their management skills. You can later move into clusters or teams.

☑ Sometimes there are things you have no control over, such as lab tables or chairs bolted to the floor. Look at what you have and how you can work around the problems with your space.

☑ Sometimes teachers don't have one classroom, but move from class to class. It is so difficult to teach without a home base! Here are some tips:
  - Talk with the teachers whose rooms you'll be sharing and ask where you can have some space—shelves, drawers, desk, etc.
  - Get some type of rolling teacher center, like a media cart, and keep everything you need to teach with on it. Ask the librarian for suggestions.

Sample Classroom Setup
Analyze this arrangement for safety, effectiveness, and efficiency

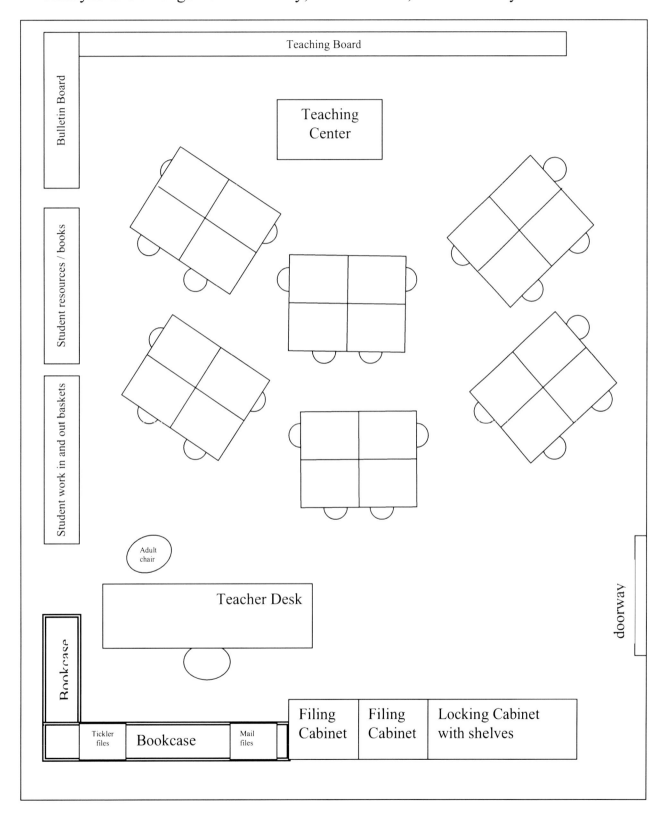

🍎 Use this page to design your classroom:

Behavior Management Plan
Remember: *It's easier to lighten up than tighten up!*

The **purpose** of a behavior management plan is to prevent discipline problems and to create a safe learning environment.

The **goal** is to have a plan that will minimize classroom disturbances and maximize learning.

Your beliefs about student behavior and your attitude will impact everything you do in the classroom, especially how you manage behavior. Think about what your beliefs and values are as they relate to behavior and discipline.

Which of the following match your beliefs?
- ☑ Behavior is a choice.
- ☑ In order to be successful in life, students can and must learn to make appropriate choices and be held accountable for the choices they do make.
- ☑ We cannot make students behave.
- ☑ We must create a system whereby students can choose to cooperate and behave successfully.
- ☑ When students know what to do, when to do, how to do, why to do, and where to do, we must hold them accountable for their choices.
- ☑ Many first-year teacher discipline problems are teacher caused.

A good behavior management plan has four major components:
- ☑ **Goals**—the broad behavioral characteristics you desire for your students to have—Goals serve as the foundation for the others.
- ☑ **Procedures**—how to do things
- ☑ **Rules**—expected norms of behavior
- ☑ **Consequences**—reinforcements for behavior

Remember: Rules and procedures are developed in order to achieve and support your goals!

Student Management Plan

Goals for my students—to establish goals, ask yourself what you want your students' behavior to be like in order for them to be successful. Create your goals by synthesizing that list. Here are the ones I had for my students.

⇨ **Be Respectful**
⇨ **Be Responsible**
⇨ **Be Ready**

Procedures-how to do things

- Procedures have to be taught, like lessons.
- Six *Ps* may help you remember how to teach a procedure:

Prepare to teach it
Purpose – tell why & how
Picture it for them-model it
Practice-rehearse it
Positive feedback or reteach
Plan to reteach when necessary
Examples of procedures to teach:

Entering and leaving a room
End of period dismissal
Responding to questions
How to ask for help
Passing in papers
Getting materials
Going to the library
Lining up
Going to the cafeteria
How to put the heading on papers
Walking in the hall
Going to the restroom
Getting a drink
Checking out equipment
Responding to an adult
If you are suddenly ill
Tornado and fire drills
When visitors enter the room
When you finish early
Keeping your materials
When you are absent
How to sit in chair

Rules – how to behave

- Rules have to be explained and modeled
- Rules have consequences
- Here are some simple guidelines for developing rules—

Rules should be
☑ Stated positively—describe what they are to do
   Enter the room quietly
☑ Stated behaviorally— describe action required
   Follow directions
☑ Few in number—no more than 3-6
☑ Consistent with school rules
   Follow all school rules
☑ Consistent with your goals and beliefs
   Speak politely to everyone
☑ Always applicable

See following page for sample rules

Consequences—are actions that follow a behavior and serve to do one of three things:

☑ Reinforce or maintain it – **Positive**
   Example-praise, reward
☑ Stop or eliminate it – **Negative**
   Example-loss of privilege
☑ Teach a new behavior – **Corrective**
   Example: student contract / growth plan for calling out in class

Sample Rules & Consequences

Class Rules

Speak politely

Listen quietly

Keep hand and feet to yourself
Follow directions

Follow all school rules

(for lower elementary)

Class Expectations

- Speak politely to everyone
- Listen quietly when others are speaking
- Keep hand and feet to yourself
- Cheerfully follow directions
- Bring necessary materials to class
- Turn in quality work on time
- Follow all school rules

(for upper elementary / lower middle school)

These are the expectations I had for my high school class. I used our school mascot to create the rules.

Soaring Eagles
Class Covenant

- Speak politely to Everyone
- Use Appropriate language
- Give your attention when others are speaking
- Be in your seat with all materials ready to Learn when the bell rings
- Turn in Excellent work on time
- Follow all School rules

(for middle and high school)

Consequences
1. Warning
2. Detention
3. Note / Call home
4. Office Detention

(for middle and high school)

Consequences
1. Warning
2. Move color to yellow (time out)
3. Move color to red – (Note home)
4. Office visit
5. Great Day-Move color to blue!

Student Management Plan

Goals for my classroom

Procedures

Rules

Consequences

☝ **Questions:**
- ☐ What procedures, rules, and consequences are campus/district-wide?
- ☐ What is the procedure for asking the office for help when I need assistance?

The Perfect Blend of Classroom Management and Love

Let me tell you about a classroom I visited that oozed the characteristics of caring, consideration, and compassion. I visit classrooms often to observe teachers and students. This day was different for me, though; I was visiting a teacher who invited me to come just for fun, while I was waiting to observe others. The teacher is Miss Marianne McGinnis, music teacher extraordinaire. I think she is a perfect mix of "teacherness": great classroom management and organization – not too easy, not too tough; she loves her subject; she loves her students.

I entered the class just as the fourth-graders were preparing to leave. It was the kind of classroom that made you feel good. Not fancy, just warm and inviting. You can tell that learning happens in this room. Moments after the older children left, the kindergarteners were lined up at the door in perfect order, waiting for a signal. As she said, "banana split!" twenty little ones scurried for their assigned spots on the floor where music notes had been painted, forming a grid. In less than three seconds, every child was in his spot sitting at attention, smiling back at this cheerful teacher.

From the end of the line, the special education teacher brought in a child with cerebral palsy in a wheelchair. This beautiful child was rolled in his chair over to his music note spot. As the other children were doing their procedural warm-ups and roll check, I was fascinated as this special teacher unstrapped the child from his chair and stood him up, facing out, his feet on her feet. She wrapped her arm around him running the fingers of her hand through his belt loops to hold him next to her. With the other hand she cradled his head.

Miss McGinnis said, "Apples" or oranges (I can't remember which fruit meant standing and ready to sing) and all eyes were on her. The music started and my tears didn't stop until the class was over. It was just one of those beautiful scenes when one is so overcome with the love and joy and pleasure of watching the miracle of children. These little musicians sang and danced to one tune after another. The special education teacher sang and danced with her little charge on her feet as he laughed until I was afraid he would pass out. All through the dance, this teacher patted, smiled and loved on that child. After a few songs, his teacher placed him back in his wheelchair to leave him in the music teacher's care. She reached down, spoke to him and lovingly patted his face and kissed his cheek before leaving him.

Miss McGinnis started a second series of songs. Spontaneously, throughout the series of songs, one child after another left his spot and went to the special child. Some patted his cheek, a couple kissed his cheek or hands, one bear-hugged him and the chair. As each returned to his spot, Miss McGinnis gave a private wink or smile. At one point, Miss McGinnis said, "Grapes!" which meant to "bunch up" around her. One of the boys went behind his classmate in the wheelchair and, popping a wheelie, pushed him up to join the rest of the bunch. There he joined his classmates in playing instruments with the help of Miss McGinnis.

This little one was showered with tender affection from the moment he entered the room until he was wheeled out by an unlicensed five-year-old driver. He was never treated with sympathy or even caution; he was treated with respect and love as a little boy who just happened to need a different kind of transportation.

No one told these children to do this; it wasn't an assignment. Where did they get the idea to treat this child with such love and affection? They saw it. It was modeled. And it wasn't just because there was a visitor. I could tell; I could feel it. It was real.

(Story from *The Heart of a Teacher: Sailing the High Cs,* by Ginger Tucker)

Quick Review....

◉ List the characteristics of effective classroom managers you want to remember:

- ☑
- ☑
- ☑
- ☑
- ☑
- ☑
- ☑
- ☑

Four Aspects of Classroom Management

◉ Complete the graphic organizer with everything you can remember about the 4 things that must be managed in your classroom. Use colors, symbols, and depictions as well as words.

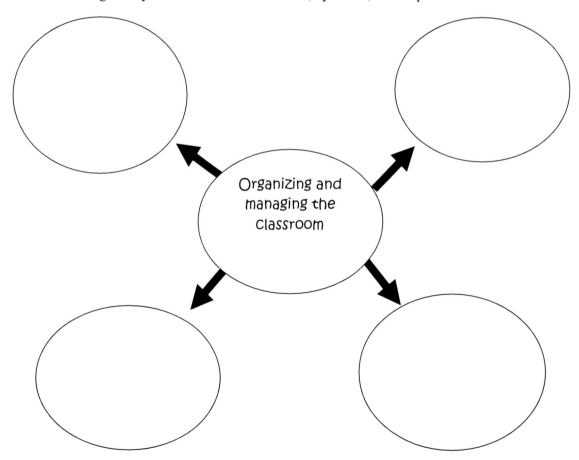

Chapter 4
Maintaining Positive Student Behavior

*When kids don't live up to your expectations,
don't treat it as a crime, but as a problem to be solved.*

--Scott Willis

 Effective teachers establish a classroom that is characterized by respect, compassion, and high expectations for behavior and achievement.

Effective Behavior Management
- What is behavior management?
- What is a standard operating procedure for maintaining positive behavior and avoiding conflict?

Understanding Misbehavior
- Why do students misbehave?
- Why should I be able to analyze causes of misbehavior?

Discipline Management Plan
- How will I intervene at the lowest level to effectively solve a problem?
- How will I be fair, consistent, and respectful in applying consequences?
- How will I work as a partner with others to manage student behavior?

My Learning Goals

Ideas I want to explore further

🍎 Think of student behaviors you are experiencing that you would classify as misbehavior or discipline problems. Use the chart below to brainstorm and then analyze those behaviors, thinking of why it is misbehavior.

🍎 Just do the first two columns now. You will complete the last two after studying the rest of this chapter.

What is the Behavior?	Which *Goal & Classroom Rule* does behavior violate?	Possible cause?	Possible solution?

Effective Behavior Management

So, what do you do if they choose not to cooperate with your wonderful rules?

That's when we have to implement an effective discipline management plan. The <u>behavior management plan</u> is designed to PREVENT problems. The <u>discipline plan</u> is our tool when a problem has occurred—when we have to hold a student accountable for the choices he has made. **Remember: our goals for our students are still the same, even when they misbehave.**

Discipline means "to train"; the word "disciple" comes from the same root.

Then, what does **misbehavior** mean? What constitutes misbehavior?

Misbehavior – anything a student does that interferes with
- ☑ Your ability to teach and conduct class
- ☑ His ability to learn
- ☑ Others' ability to learn

If it is not one of these three, it might be a learning style issue or a medical issue. Can you teach or train the student to behave differently? (For example: a tactile-kinesthetic student tapping his pencil while he works might learn to tap on his knee or a mouse pad instead of the desk.)

Teacher Attitude--The Key to Success

The key to the success of any behavior management or discipline plan or method is <u>your</u> attitude.

Your choices are to be:
- ☑ Passive—"I'm afraid of you, so do whatever you want."
- ☑ Aggressive—"I'll make you pay for that!"
- ☑ Assertive—"I'm holding you accountable for the choices you've made."

Assertiveness is the only teacher attitude that works with discipline. If you are passive and too easy, you are shirking your responsibilities to maintain a fair and equitable classroom. Students will see you as weak and run over you. Students don't need you to be a buddy; they need you to be the teacher. If you are aggressive and mean, students will rebel and try to "get you." **Effective teachers exhibit** *compassionate assertiveness*. They are the *adults in charge*. You are responsible for the safety and learning for all of the children in your room. As my friend Sammye Henderson says in *Equine Essentials*, "Every group (class) will have an alpha dog." And I'm telling you that it had best be you, the teacher, or one of your students will take that role.

Discipline Management Intervention

When intervening, remember the 4 Fs:
Firm, Fair, Friendly, Focused

When a student misbehaves remember that you are to be <u>firm, fair, friendly,</u> and <u>focused on your goals</u>. Avoid yelling, using sarcasm or anger, raising your voice, making threats or rude comments. Remember: they are kids; you are the adult. Your job is to train them and model respect.

We can understand the idea by using the example of getting a speeding ticket. If I am speeding, I am breaking a law and should be held accountable. It is the highway patrolman's duty to do just that—if he's a good one. When he stops me, he usually reminds me of the law I've broken and asks if there are extenuating circumstances. "Mrs. Tucker, were you aware that the speed limit here is 60 mph? Do you have an emergency?" He's **fair**. Deciding my nail appointment did not qualify for an emergency, he checks my license and calmly begins writing the ticket, no matter what my excuses and pleas are. He's **firm** and consistent. He calmly hands me the ticket without yelling at me, making sarcastic remarks about my driving, or commenting about how great a driver my brother was. He's **focused** on his job, his duty. He doesn't apologize nor does he threaten to shoot me for having a bad attitude. He often finishes with a reminder about the goal and an encouragement. "Let's watch the speed and please drive safely. And thank you for visiting Travis County." He is **friendly** without being chummy or too familiar.

⑤ Mark the graph and describe under each how being firm, fair, friendly and focused reflects your classroom management.

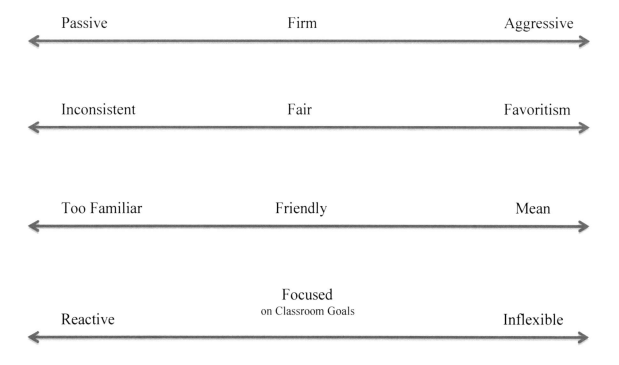

Standard Operating Procedure

When a student misbehaves, always intervene at the lowest possible level that stills holds the student accountable and allows you to continue teaching. Here is a common plan to live by every day. It is our SOP (standard operating procedure) when someone is off task or occasionally misbehaves. This is not the plan when there is an emergency or a major problem.

- ☑ <u>Ignore</u> the behavior if at all possible. If it stops—great!
- ☑ Make <u>eye contact</u> with the student. It says, "I see you; stop it."
- ☑ Use <u>proximity</u>. Move into his or her area.
- ☑ Drop student's <u>name</u> in the lesson. "Did you know, John, that India is…"
- ☑ Stop teaching and calmly ask the student if he or she knows what to do and <u>remind</u> student of the rule or expectation. "Jill, what are you supposed to be doing?" Wait. If the student knows and responds, say, "Do that now." If the student doesn't know, tell him and tell him to do that now.
- ☑ <u>Pause</u> and walk away. Wait for student to correct behavior.
- ☑ <u>Respond</u>, "Thank you," or assign consequences.

Suggestions:
- Don't get into an argument. Even if you win, you don't win.
- Refer to the **class goals** if a students asks, "Why can't I…" You can say, "Because one of our classroom goals is to be respectful. Your comment was not respectful." Or "Because when you sleep in class you cannot achieve our classroom goal of learning at high levels."

Important Reminder: When you need to intervene, always ask yourself these critical questions:

1. Does the student know <u>what</u> to do, <u>when</u> to do, <u>why</u> to do, <u>how</u> to do, and <u>where</u> to do what you want him to?
   - If the answer is "yes," then you must hold him accountable for not doing the right thing.
   - If the answer is "no," then teach him what, when, why, how, and where.
2. <u>Why</u> is the student misbehaving?
   - Discovering the reason for misbehavior is the beginning of changing that behavior and preventing future discipline problems.
   - Sometimes behaviors that look like discipline problems are something else entirely.

Selecting An Intervention Strategy

֍ For each of the scenarios below, consider the SOP from the previous page and suggest a teacher response that would (1) take little time and effort, (2) maintain a positive climate, and (3) not disrupt the lesson and those students who are on task.

A. You are presenting a new math concept. Five minutes into your presentation, you sweep-scan and observe Sammy pulling a comic book from his notebook and slipping it onto his lap. You…

B. You are leading students in checking last night's homework. You notice that Sally is paying more attention to construction outside your classroom window than to the paper before her. You…

C. Students are doing seatwork for the last 10 minutes of the period. You are sitting at your desk filling out a report the office just told you they needed yesterday. You look up, scan the room, and notice that Susan and Shane are making paper footballs in preparation for a "game." You…

D. You are explaining the procedure for filling out the top of achievement test forms, and students are supposed to be following your instructions. You observe that Leon is staring into space and has not put pencil to paper. You…

E. You are making a crucial point about the plot of *Romeo and Juliet* and notice that Paula and Raoul are passing notes. You…

F. You are covering key points of the Prussian War and observe Boone opening his briefcase, taking out a portable CD player, and slip an earphone into his ear. You…

G. As you monitor seatwork, you observe William taking out his wallet, checking his lunch ticket, and returning ticket and wallet to his pocket. You…

H. Although you have conferenced with Jamie twice about walking back from lunch and not running and shoving other students, you see him fly down the hall and tackle Rob. You…

I. For the fifth time in five minutes, Paula calls out an answer when you have called on someone else. You…

J. As students are passing papers to the front you observe Gary making an obscene gesture at another student's back. You…

K. During homeroom, Corrie enters late. When you comment on his tardiness, he snarls "So what!" at you. You…

L. Just as you begin presenting a new concept in the science lesson, you see Julie slip a packet of photos to Carlos, who begins to look at them. You…

M. While you are conferencing with a small group, you notice Sammy, who is supposed to be doing seatwork with the class, is once again up and meandering. You…

N. During a lab experience, Tony hooks up his Bunsen burner to the water line instead of the gas line, holds a lighted match over the burner, and turns the water on full force. Water squirts to the ceiling and drenches Tony and nearby students. You…

Adapted from <u>Classroom Organization and Management</u>, by C.M. Evertson

Understanding the Cause of Misbehavior
Why is the Student Misbehaving?

Behavior Analysis Activity

Think of one student you have who misbehaves.

☐ List the specific behaviors

☐ What is your reaction when the student misbehaves?
   How do you feel? What do you do?

☐ What is the result of your actions? Does the behavior stop, continue, get worse?

☐ What do you want the student to be able to do? What would be appropriate?

Linda Albert's *Cooperative Discipline*[11] suggests that students need to
- Feel <u>capable</u> of the tasks
- Believe they can <u>connect</u> with teachers and classmates
- Know that they <u>contribute</u> to the group

When these needs are not met, they misbehave in order to achieve one or more of **four goals**. In order to help them to make better choices, we must know why they are misbehaving.

Discovering the reason for misbehavior is the beginning of changing that behavior and preventing future discipline problems.

_____

[11] Linda Albert. *Cooperative Discipline*. AGS Publishing (December 1, 2002).

Four Reasons for Misbehavior
adapted from Linda Albert's Cooperative Discipline

Review the following information and develop a plan for dealing with the misbehavior you listed above.

Attention-Seeking: Their message is "Look at me!"

Some students misbehave to get extra attention. They want to be center stage all the time and constantly distract to gain an audience. They need attention whether it comes from negative or positive behavior.

Behavior: Active– Attention Getting Mechanisms (AGMs), disrupt class; Passive - dawdler

Interventions:
- Minimize the behavior – ignore, signals, proximity
- Clarify the behavior
- Legitimize the behavior-turn it into a lesson
- Distract the student
- Notice others' appropriate behavior

Don't:
Reward misbehavior with loud responses; that only reinforces it

Prevention:
- Catch them being good – 3 times more positive than negative feedback
- Teach them to get attention for doing the right thing

Power-Seeking Behavior: Their message is "You can't make me" or "Let's fight."

Some students misbehave in a quest for power. They try through words and actions to prove that they are in control.

Behavior: Active -- tantrums, lip, sass, lawyer syndrome "My dad knows the principal"; Passive -- noncompliance, hiding behind a label "I'm just lazy."

Intervention:
- Avoid escalating the situation by yelling, sarcasm, nagging,
- Remain calm and assertive
- Focus on the behavior, not the student
- Table it
- Allow student to save face
- Remove the audience (step away from other students)
- Acknowledge the student's power
- Use a fogging technique (agree, avoid, change subject, etc.)

Don't:
fight back or back them into a corner

Prevention:
- Allow voice and choice
- Grant legitimate power
- Delegate responsibility

Revenge-Seeking Behavior: Their message is "I'll get you or I'll get even."

Some students want to lash out to get even for real or imagined hurts. The target may be the teacher, other students, or both. It may not be about you, but it affects you. These students seem to sulk and scowl.

Behavior: Active—physical attacks and vandalism, psychological attacks, threats, suicide; Passive—sullen and withdrawn to hurt. Everything about them says "I hate you."

Interventions:

- Check the barometer at the door—watch for it, get help if needed
- Avoid escalating situation
- Ignore, if you can; report real threats
- Select reasonable consequences
- Use time out; walk it off

Don't:

Push or threaten back
Call their bluff

Prevention:

- Build caring relationships-you may be the only one for them
- Teach appropriate expression of feelings

Avoidance-of-failure behavior: Their message is "I can't, why try?"

Some students want to avoid repeated failure. They believe they can't live up to their own, the teacher's, their families' expectations. They choose withdrawal behaviors to compensate for this feeling. This is often missed or looks like another behavior.

Behavior: Active—frustration tantrum (implosion), clowning around to cover fear; Passive—procrastination, noncompliance, temporary incapacity, assumed disabilities.

Interventions:

- Modify instruction
- Provide tutoring
- Encourage positive self-talk
- Reframe "I can't"
- Teach procedures for becoming unstuck
- Make mistakes ok

Don't:

give up or give in

Prevention:

- Have an "I can" classroom
- Build trust

Adapted from Linda Albert's, *Cooperative Discipline*

 Go back to the analysis chart (p. 65) and think about which of these four might be the cause for the student's misbehavior. Jot down some interventions to try.

Look at the chart on page 60 and work on the 3rd and 4th columns.

Always Ask Why
John's Story

Sincere-from the Latin, *sincerus*. Ancient potters used to sell their wares at public markets. If their pottery was cracked or broken, it was worthless. Dishonest potters were known to fill the cracks in their broken pottery with wax, paint the pots to cover the cracks, and then sell them as whole. When the buyer used the pottery in cooking, the wax would melt and the pot would fall apart. Honest merchants began adding a sign over their pottery for sale: "*Sincerus*," meaning "Without Wax." It was a guarantee of the real thing. You could count on the integrity of the pottery; it would hold up even under fire. Sincere. The real thing. Integrity. When we do the right thing the right way for the right reason everyday, we are also *sincerus*.

I had a lesson in compassion seared on my heart several years ago. It was a lesson that changed my life, not just as a teacher, but also as a person. I had a student I'll call John, the last period of the day. That should tell you something about him already. To have a high school boy in an academic class last period meant that he wasn't involved in sports or other activities. John was from a hard-working, fairly poor, farm family. He was the oldest of three boys and three girls. Dad farmed; Mom kept the house and the garden; the kids all helped out.

The first few weeks of class, John was one of those "invisible" students. He came in, stayed quiet, and he left. When I recorded grades on the weekends, I would think, "I don't even remember seeing him this week, but here are his papers." I couldn't remember what he looked like. He was one of 180. But, by the end of the second six weeks, I knew what he looked like. He had started acting out, a little at first, then every day. I would be teaching my heart out (for the sixth time each day) about the wonders of some country and I would hear this sound or statement: "phhhhut! Yeah right." Or, "that's stupid!" Or, "this sucks!" I followed the ignore it first routine, then the eye contact routine, then the move into their space routine, then the redirect the inappropriate behavior routine. It only got worse. Daily. I hate to admit it to you, but I didn't like him – at all!

And as the fall wore on, that dislike turned to disdain. It got to the point that I would determine whether a day was going to be good or bad by whether he was in school or not. It was to the point that if someone said, "If you could get rid of one student and you know your life would improve 100%, who would it be?" John! No contest. I had dreams about him where I was hitting him in class. By the middle of November, I had sent him to the office three times. I never sent anyone to the office. I prided myself on being able to deal with any kid, any problem. Administrators placed troubled kids in my class because they knew I cared about them and would do whatever it took. But I couldn't deal with this one. I wanted him out of my class. It was interesting that John was not causing problems for any other teacher, just me.

After a particularly trying day with him, I approached him near the end of class, got in his face and said, "John, I've had it with you! If you do one more thing to irritate me, if you act up one more time, you're out of here! I will have your schedule changed, whatever it takes. I can't teach with you in here." He glared at me with an I-could-kill-you-look and stormed out. I felt pretty tough, pretty powerful. Macho-Teacher.

The next day, I had just started the lesson when John knocked everything off his desk and announced loudly with sarcasm, "Oh, excuuuse me!" He shot me a look that said, "Is that enough or shall I do more?" I was going to make good on my threat. I was almost glad he did it. I said, "That's it. You're out of here, Pal! Get your stuff and get to the office. I'll be there at the end of the period and we'll get your schedule changed. I don't have to put up with this." As he left, the rest of the class clapped.

After class I marched down to the office in my macho-teacher attitude. John slithered by me on his way out as I entered. I could tell he had been crying. "Yes! I made a big boy cry!" I was on a mission. The assistant principal met me in the hallway to his office and said, "Ginger, I'm sending John to your room to talk to you and…"

Before he could finish, I shrieked, "Not this time. I can't take it any more. I don't just want him to apologize. I want him out of there. I cannot teach with him in there. I want you to change his schedule!"

In his shock at my response he said, "Calm down, lady. Just go talk to him. After you've talked with him, we will get together to decide what to do next."

"All right." I said, heading out the office.

As I was going out the door, the person who really runs the school, you know…the secretary, quietly said to me, "Ginger, were you aware of what was going on with John's family?" She knew John's relatives through church and community.

"No," I said, a little put out that she insinuated that I, the great teacher, might have missed something.

"Well, you might just check with him." Oh, brother!

Well, I have to tell you that I had a very ugly meeting with myself on that long walk down the hallway to my classroom. I had always considered myself a caring, considerate, and compassionate teacher to my students all these years. Why, this very year I had helped a girl in this very class who was being sexually abused by a relative. And I was on the drug intervention team. And I tutored at-risk students after school. Why was I having this reaction? I realized that I was a fake! Sure, I was caring, considerate, and compassionate …to those I liked, or to those I thought worthy of my caring, consideration, and compassion. What a cracked pot! What a cracked pot filled with wax and painted over to cover the flaw!

I was having a face-to-face meeting with myself and I wasn't impressed with either person in attendance. I was reminded of Jesus' words to a shocked crowd when he raised the standard on relationships by commanding them to love not only their neighbors but also their enemies, "For if you love those who love you, what reward have you? Even the heathens do that." (Matthew 5:46) An inward battle was raging. I was going to have to go to my room and be caring, considerate, and compassionate to a kid I didn't like. To a kid I didn't want to like. And I didn't like that about myself.

I entered my room where John was sitting with his head bowed over his books at a student desk in the far corner of the room. I pulled up another student desk next to him and sat down, giving a big teacher sigh. Full of self-pity and self-righteousness, I said, "Okay, John, what is it? Is it me? Do you not like me?" Like, who could not like me? There was no response. "Is it geography?" Who could not like geography?" I was getting nowhere with my pitiful approach of avoiding the issue.

Then I said, "Tell me what's really going on with you. Is there something I need to know?" He glanced up at me with the saddest eyes I've ever seen, but said nothing. He bowed his head again as tears started to fall onto the desk. I can tell you I was not feeling like macho-teacher anymore. I touched his arm and said, "Tell me what's going on at home." This seventeen-year-old man-child simply said through sobs, "Momma left home and took the girls. Me and Dad don't know what to do."

For whatever reason his parents couldn't make it work; this young man's whole life had been torn apart and he had nowhere to turn for help. His mother had left his father about Halloween time after weeks of trouble. This family, which had always worked together to make a living, was suddenly in pieces, with a daddy who only understood farming, trying to take care of three boys who missed their mother.

As he told me about it, I sat there crying with him, wondering how he was even able get himself to school every day. "I don't know why I've been acting that way. I guess I'm just mad." I told him how sorry I was for his situation. We talked a long time about what could be done. In the long run, the nurse, counselor, and the assistant principal (whom I scared) were all involved in providing help and support for John. We talked about how he could overcome this sad, unfair situation and not let it be an excuse for failure or misbehavior.

I told him I was sorry that I had not known and had not been more sensitive to his pain. I wanted to fix it. I wanted to say, "This was probably my fault, along with the war in the Middle East; get your dad and brothers and come live at my house and I'll take care of you all to make up for what an uncaring person I've been." But I didn't and couldn't fix John's family. That wasn't my job.

My job was to be an adult who was aware of the huge impact I have on the lives of my students. My job was to treat every student with respect and to show compassion when they hurt, consideration when they mess up, and to care when they can't.

Why my class only? Why was I the only one he caused trouble for? Because he knew how I was with other students: caring, considerate, and compassionate; so he cried out for help in the only way he could.

While John was helped by our talk and the follow-up support, my life was changed by the incident. I had some cleanup to do. I had modeled for the rest of my class the obvious dislike I had for John, and it affected the way they viewed him. That would change beginning the next day. My role with John also changed from police-teacher to mother-teacher, one to which I am much better suited.

I learned something about myself that day that needed to change. I had become so consumed with my teaching that I forgot to care about those I taught. I had tasks to complete! Units to teach! I didn't have time for any diversions or slackers. I was so concerned about the content that I forgot the kids. I was so committed to the process that I forgot the people. How could I have forgotten how many people in my life had helped me, given me a chance, forgiven me? How could I not have shown the same compassion to another?

In reflection I asked myself when did it happen? When did I shift my focus from teaching my students the content to teaching my content to students? It's subtle, isn't it? I didn't just come to work one day and decide I didn't care about all students anymore. But I woke up one day and realized it had happened, more of a drift than a shift. We cannot educate for smarts at the expense of hearts.

My life changed because I was reminded that each person's life is precious. When a student is under my care, I can build his life up or tear it down. I realized that God loves every child sitting in my classroom, every teacher in my workshop at least as much as He loves me. The difference is that I believe He expects more of me. I'm a teacher. "Don't be in a rush to become a teacher, my friends. Teaching is highly responsible work. Teachers are held to the strictest standards." (James 3:1, The Message)

Some good friends of ours took us to a steak house in the large city where they live. They explained that it was the finest steak house in the city, maybe the state. The owner, a friend of theirs, has a philosophy of total commitment to customer service. He trains his employees diligently and is known to have the very best wait staff anywhere. Our friends explained his process: the wait staff is trained for two weeks in both the technical aspects of waiting tables and the people skills aspect. They are expected to perform at the level set before them. If they don't, they are returned to training for a second chance. If they don't meet expectations after that, they are let go. The owner explains his philosophy to them this way from the beginning: "I'm not paying you to have a bad day, be in a bad mood, or to exact justice. I am paying you to ensure that every customer who walks through that door, whether kind, rude, or indifferent, has the finest dining experience in this city." And they do.

What a great philosophy for me to remember as a teacher! I only need to change a few words. I am not being paid to have a bad day, be in a bad mood, or exact justice. I am not even being paid to like people or have them like me. I am being paid to ensure that every person who walks through the door of my classroom or workshop has the finest learning experience available. I am trained in the technical aspects; I am trained in the people skills. I can choose to treat people with love and respect, even if I don't feel like it. Real love is an action, not a feeling.

(Story from *The Heart of a Teacher: Sailing the High Cs,* by Ginger Tucker)

❧ What is your reaction to John's story?

❧ Which ideas or statements do you want to remember?

TIME-OUT SHEET

Who was involved?

What did I do?

How did it make me feel?

What could I have done differently?

What should my consequences be?

I state that this information is true.

_____   _____
Student's signature   Date

_____ _____ _____
Teacher's signature   Principal's signature   Parent's signature

** copy and use this sheet as needed

Problem Identification, Analysis, and Solution Worksheet

I. Identification

    A. Name the problem / issue.

    B. Describe the characteristics / attributes.

    C. Describe your feelings, reactions, and intuitions.

II. Analysis

    A. Root of problem:

        1. Brainstorm all possible causes.

        2. List possible deeper issues.

        3. Identify possible unmet needs.

    B. Effects of problem:

        1. List the negative effects of this problem.

        2. List the positive effects of this problem.

    C. Desired Outcome:

        1. Describe what you want, need, desire.

III. Solutions

    A. Brainstorm all possible solutions.

        1. Eliminate unworkable solutions.

        2. Select your top 3 choices.

    B. With each possible solution

        1. List positive outcomes.

        2. List negative outcomes.

        3. List resources needed.

        4. Plan time frame to implement / evaluate.

    C. Prioritize list of solutions.

    D. Implement. Take action.

    E. Evaluate actions.

DOCUMENTATION CHECKLIST

CLASS PERIOD _____

NAME OF STUDENT _____

DATE(S) OF INFRACTION _____

ACTION TAKEN _____

MINOR INFRACTIONS (warning, detention, office referral)

_____ Out of seat

_____ Excessive talking

_____ Failure to complete assignment

_____ Inappropriate comments / profanity

_____ Gum / Candy in classroom

_____ Failure to bring materials to class

MAJOR INFRACTIONS (Office referral)

_____ Disrespect toward teacher / students

_____ Refusal of a teacher request

_____ No goggles / apron during lab

_____ Unsafe lab procedure

_____ Failure to follow directions / lab procedures

_____ Horseplay in classroom / lab area

_____ Inappropriate use of lab equipment / chemicals

REMOVAL FROM CLASS INFRACTIONS (Office referral and removal)

_____ Endangerment of self or others

_____ Removal of equipment or chemicals from classroom

_____ Willful destruction or vandalism of equipment or school property

_____ Physical harm to teacher / faculty or students

_____ Any unauthorized lab performed or use of chemicals / equipment

COMMENTS _____

_____

DECISION – MAKING SHEET

Name_____

Date_____

1. What was happening before the problem occurred?_____

_____

2. What was your behavior when the problem began? _____

_____

3. How did you feel?_____

4. What other things could you have done? Name at least 4 that would have been more appropriate?

_____

_____

5. Which one of the 4 behaviors you listed in question # 4 would you like best? _____

_____

6. Why would you prefer to do that? _____

_____

7. What would have happened if you had chosen that behavior instead of the one you described in

question # 2? _____

_____

8. What has the problem behavior earned for you? _____

_____

9. How are you feeling now? _____

_____

10. Did you make any good decisions in spite of the problem? What were they? _____

_____

11. What can you do now to help yourself have a good day? _____

_____

_____

** Copy and use this sheet as needed

Quick Review & Reflection….

Describe each of the following in your own words:

Discipline—

Misbehavior—

Four Reasons for Misbehavior:

1.

2.

3.

4.

Reflection:

- How will I apply this information in my classroom?

- How will having a well-managed classroom benefit your instructional plan?

Chapter 5
Understanding Learning and the Learner

Good teaching requires that students have the opportunity to select and assimilate enough data to force them to challenge misconceptions and to create strong, accurate conceptions...
...The goal is to create explorers who have an idea of what they are looking for, who have a methodology with which to search, but who come with open minds so that, should they discover America, they will not assume they have landed in India just because that's where they intended to go.

--Cardellichio and Field

  Effective teachers facilitate classrooms that reflect their knowledge of students' learning needs and preferences.

 Teaching *for* Learning for *All*
- How will I describe what learning is and is not?
- How will I ensure high levels of *learning for ALL*?

Understanding the Learners' Brains
- What do I need to know about our amazing brains?
- How will I create and lead lessons in a brain-compatible style?
- How will I teach to all modalities every lesson, every day?
- How can I maintain a brain-friendly classroom environment?

Understanding Higher Level Thinking
- How will I teach for higher levels of thought?

Understanding the learners' unique personalities and strengths
- How can I apply the information on personality styles in my classroom?
- How does the research on multiple intelligences impact student learning?

 My Goals:

Ideas I want to explore further:

Teaching for Learning for All
What is Learning?

*Teaching for learning is **not** covering the material.*

Since the ultimate goal is **learning for all** students, before we begin planning and preparing our teaching material, we must first answer the basic question: What is learning?

Remember the bus trip analogy from Chapter One? We learned that the "learning trip" is not about getting the <u>bus</u> to the destination, but getting the <u>passengers there</u>. It may be the best bus that money can buy, traveling on the finest route know to man; but if the passengers don't get and stay on until they reach their destination, what's the point? You can have the best lesson plans and the finest classroom in America; but if the students aren't engaged and learning, what's the point?

Being exposed to something is not learning it. There is an immense difference between giving someone information and teaching for learning. Hearing is not learning. As we learn more and more about how the brain functions and learns, we are compelled as educators to incorporate that knowledge in our teaching. The field of brain research is exploding with new discoveries being made as you read these words. We know that people's brains are different, that people have unique personality styles, that individuals have distinct learning preferences, and that teaching for learning requires that we differentiate our instruction to meet those needs.

Learning is more than mere acquisition of information or facts. It must include the ability to understand, apply, explain, analyze, construct, and utilize, as well as recall the information or concepts being learned. This doesn't happen with a teacher "covering the material." Effective teachers make the learning experiences brain compatible if they expect learning to happen. They teach the way the brain learns.

Effective teachers plan from what they want in terms of learner outcomes. They assess, continually looking for the evidence and progress of learning. They facilitate lessons, knowing that brains are pattern-seeking and need relevance in order to make meaning of what is being learned. They connect the learning to something students already understand by using comparisons, analogies, and other brain-friendly strategies. They design lessons so that students experience the learning through simulation, role play, practice, and discovery. Effective teachers teach for learning.

According to William Glasser, author of <u>The Quality School,</u>
We Learn…
10% of what we <u>read</u>
20% of what we <u>hear</u>
30% of what we <u>see</u>
50% of what we both <u>see</u> and <u>hear</u>
70% of what we <u>discuss</u> with others
80% of what we <u>experience</u> personally
95% of what we <u>teach</u> someone else

Using The Nested Concept Organizer

The Nested Concept can help organize the aspects of a brain-friendly classroom. In order to accomplish *High Levels of Learning for All*, all three aspects of the *nest* must be considered. Start in the center with the number #1 question and work your way out. Each is dependent on the other; content (#1) can't be learned if the process (#2) or the environment (#3) are not brain-compatible.

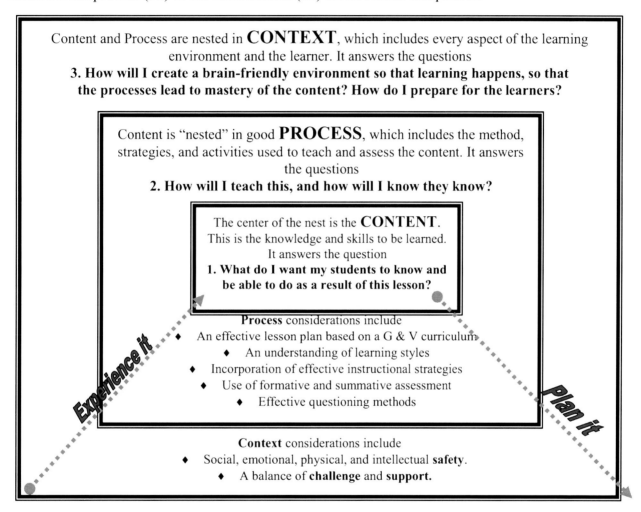

Content and Process are nested in **CONTEXT**, which includes every aspect of the learning environment and the learner. It answers the questions
3. How will I create a brain-friendly environment so that learning happens, so that the processes lead to mastery of the content? How do I prepare for the learners?

Content is "nested" in good **PROCESS**, which includes the method, strategies, and activities used to teach and assess the content. It answers the questions
2. How will I teach this, and how will I know they know?

The center of the nest is the **CONTENT**.
This is the knowledge and skills to be learned.
It answers the question
1. What do I want my students to know and be able to do as a result of this lesson?

Process considerations include
♦ An effective lesson plan based on a G & V curriculum
♦ An understanding of learning styles
♦ Incorporation of effective instructional strategies
♦ Use of formative and summative assessment
♦ Effective questioning methods

Context considerations include
♦ Social, emotional, physical, and intellectual **safety**.
♦ A balance of **challenge** and **support**.

Experience it

Plan it

🖑 **Discuss these ideas with a partner:**
Teachers plan from the inside out – Content-Process-Context—to achieve mastery.
Students experience it from the outside in – Context-Process-Content. Each can be a barrier to the next.

Add to this graphic as you study this chapter and chapter 6.

Understanding the Learners' Brains
Our Amazing Brains

The more we understand the brain, the better we'll be able to design instruction to match how it learns best...the brain matters because our children matter.
–Patricia Wolfe, in *Brain Matters*

These past thirty years or so have produced volumes of research and information about the brain—its structure, its functions, and its possibilities. We've learned so much in recent years mostly because of technology's enabling us to see inside the living brain instead of only being able to analyze a brain after one's death. These past years have also produced some challenges as people moved faster than research supported, making claims that, while exciting, were not proven. I think it is because we educators are so hungry to learn about what goes on inside the students' heads that we latch on to any bit of information that seems to give answers for behavior and learning. There is good research available and there are excellent sources to guide educators in the quest for "brain-friendly classrooms" as more is learned about our amazing brains. Among the reliable educational translators of brain research, I recommend Pat Wolfe, David Sousa, and Robert Sylwester. **The following sections are in no way intended to be a thorough exploration of current brain research. They are intended to whet your appetite for studying the experts and learning all you can about the several little brains sitting in front of you each day.**

Fast Facts about the Brain

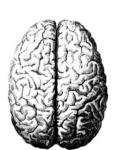

- The brain weighs about <u>1 pound</u> at birth, <u>doubling</u> in the first year, and weighs about <u>3</u> pounds in adulthood. It is about the size of a cantaloupe.
- The brain tissue is like the consistency of a ripe avocado.
- The brain has two distinct <u>hemispheres</u>, which communicate through a thick connection of nerves called the <u>corpus callosum.</u>
- The brain uses about 25% of the body's energy.
- Brain cells are called <u>Neurons.</u>
- Everyone is born with approximately <u>120 billion.</u>
- 30,000 neurons would fit on the head of a pin. Some neurons can be up to three feet long.
- Brain cells are different from other cells in the body. In most cases they don't <u>regenerate.</u>
- The brain and its functions are affected by internal and external stimuli—alcohol, air quality, music, lighting, water, stress, food…

Brain Cells

Nerves are what make up the brain. Each nerve is made up of many single nerve cells called **NEURONS.** Each neuron has a cell body and a cell nucleus, called the **soma.** Each neuron also has a long thin **axon**, which electrochemically carries messages from the cell body to other neurons. Some axons are wrapped in a white fatty substance called **myelin**, which acts as an insulator, allowing signals to move faster along the axons. Branching out from the cell body are little branches called **dendrites**, which means "trees." Messages travel from the axon of one neuron to the dendrite of another neuron by crossing a gap called a **synapse**. The message-containing chemicals "dock" in a receptor site on the dendrite of the receiving 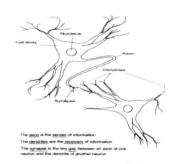 neuron. Each neuron has thousands of receptor sites, which can receive many different messages at once and then determine whether to pass the message on. Neurons are surrounded by **glial cells**, which insulate and protect neurons. They also carry nutrients to the neurons. *Glia* is Greek for "glue." Most scientists agree that brains don't regenerate new neurons, except possibly in some regions of the midbrain. So, with the brain, it is *use it or lose it.*

The Neuron

Look at the diagram of the neuron on the right. Can you see why neuro-anatomist Dr. Marion Diamond called them the "magic trees of the mind"? The more we learn, the more our brain is stimulated and the more "branches are in our trees." The more branches you have, the more you can have. That, in the simplest terms, is what makes us smarter—more dendrites receiving more messages across more synapses.

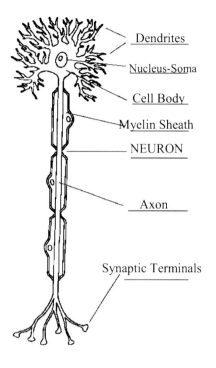

- ◆ Cell body - has a nucleus, also called soma
- ◆ Dendrites - Greek for "tree"
  Tens of thousands of branches per neuron
  We grow more dendrites as we learn
  Receive electrical impulses from other neurons
  Transmit impulses along the axon to other neurons
- ◆ Axon
  One long fiber from the cell body
  Impulses travel from the dendrites down the axon
  An impulse can travel the length of a 6-foot body in 0.2 of a second.
- ◆ Neurotransmitters – the brain's chemical messengers
  Chemical molecules processed by the neuron and released across the synapse to attach to a receptor on another neuron's dendrite.
  Scientists have identified more than 50 neurotransmitters.
  These chemicals stimulate, inhibit, or modulate the actions of the receiving neuron.
  Examples are dopamine, serotonin, and endorphin.
- ◆ Myelin sheath - Surrounds each axon
  Glial cells that act like wax to insulate the axon and increase the speed of the impulse
  Repetition increases myelin and so does sufficient sleep
  The last two hours of sleep are critically important to memory by laying down myelin.
- ◆ Synapse
  Greek word for "to join together"
  Neurons never touch each other.
  They send out electrical impulses down the axon, out the synaptic terminal, and into the synapse where chemicals are released from the sacs at the end of the axon.
  Synapse is 1/1,000,000th of an inch
  The chemicals or neurotransmitters stimulate the neurons around it.
  Learning occurs by changing the synapse so that connections are made.
- ◆ Glial cells – Greek for "glue"
  Support neurons and hold them together
  Act as a filter or vacuum cleaner as we sleep
  Albert Einstein's brain showed many more glial cells per neuron than the average brain

---

⚡ **Application:** Draw a diagram on a blank page of your arm from the elbow to your fingertips. With your fingers representing the dendrites and your elbow the synaptic terminal, label the parts of a neuron on your diagram. With a partner, use your "manipulative" (your arm) to explain the parts of the neuron brain cell. With everyone at your table, demonstrate what a neural network might look like. (Elbow to fingertips to elbow to fingertips, etc.)

Brain Geography

This section will give you a brief overview of the regions of the brain, the function of each, and the impact of anger, fears, and stress on the brain. The diagram below shows you a sagittal view of the right hemisphere. The brain has two hemispheres which are connected by the corpus callosum, a thick band of approximately 200 million myelinated axons. These connections are how the integrated brain communicates and performs functions across the hemispheres.

We can loosely think of the brain as having three major regions each with several structures and functions: the outer brain, the inner subcortical system, and the cerebellum.

☞   Color-code each structure as you read. Draw a symbol in the margin to help you remember the function.

Outer brain –
*   **Cerebrum** (Latin for *brain*) - the outer layer of cells, the cerebral cortex, and the underlying network of connections, sometimes called the white matter. The cerebrum makes up about 85% of the weight of the brain.
*   **Cerebral Cortex** (Latin for *bark*) – the thin outer layers of cells that process conscious sensory, thought, decision, and motor functions. It is deeply wrinkled and only about 1/32 of an inch thick and is composed of six layers of neurons. If you spread the cerebral cortex out flat, it would be about the size of a pillowcase (Wolfe), or of a stack of six 12x18 inch pages of construction paper (Sylwester). It is divided into two distinct hemispheres and four distinct areas (lobes) with separate functions: the occipital, parietal, temporal, and frontal.
*   **Central brain structures–**
    In 1952 Paul MacLean coined the term *limbic system* to describe the structures beneath the cerebrum and above the brain stem that were erroneously thought to be the seat of emotion. Many scientists include some or all of these structures in the cerebrum; some include them in the subcortical system. *We will look at them separately here with the understanding that they do not comprise a region or a system.* Remember that these are pairs, one in each hemisphere.

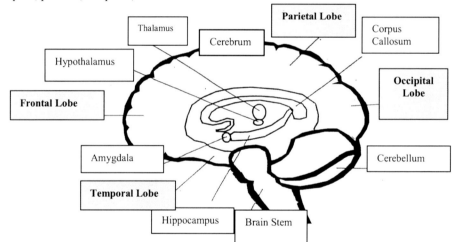

    *   **Thalamus** (Greek for *chamber*)– This small plum-shaped structure located in the center of the brain can be thought of as the relay station of the brain. It relays all sensory information except smell to the cortex for processing.
    *   **Hypothalamus** – This small cherry-sized structure is located just below the thalamus and controls body temperature, heart rate, hunger, thirst, sex drive, aggressive behavior, and pleasure. It is also responsible for the responses to the stress response.
    *   **Amygdala** (Greek for *almond*)– This almond-shaped structure is located at the base of the temporal lobe and is thought to be the source of emotions and emotional memories. It can be thought of as the brain's central alarm system.
    *   **Hippocampus** (Greek for *seahorse*) – This curved structure located deep within the temporal lobes plays a key role in the formation and retrieval of long-term declarative memories. People whose hippocampus has been removed or damaged are unable to form new declarative memories. Alzheimer's disease is thought to involve the progressive degeneration of the hippocampal neurons (Sylwester).

Inner subcortical system –

♦ **Spinal cord** – The bundle of nerves that runs from the base of the brain down to the middle of the back is an extension of the brain. The role of the spinal cord is to carry messages between the brain and body through ascending and descending pathways.

♦ **Brainstem** – The brainstem is made up of three main parts: the mid-brain, the pons, and the medulla oblongata. Often called the reptile brain, its primary function is survival. It controls autonomic functions like breathing, heartbeat, respiration, and other basic functions.

Cerebellum (Latin for *little brain*)– In mammals, the cerebellum is the key to balance, maintenance of body posture, and coordination of muscle functions. The cerebellum takes over control of the complex motor activities as we become proficient, leaving the conscious mind free to do and think about other things. Once thought only to control balance and motor memory, new research indicates that the cerebellum is intricately involved with the rest of our brain.

Lobes of the Brain – The Basics

Occipital Lobes– Located at the central lower back of the brain, this is the primary brain center for processing visual stimuli, also called the visual cortex. Touch the back of your head and think of a teacher with "eyes in the back of her head."

Temporal Lobes– Located just above the ears, the temporal lobes' main function is processing auditory stimuli. Put your hands over your ears and think of listening to music with big earphones.

Parietal Lobes– Located at the top of the brain, these plate-like lobes handle spatial awareness and orientation. The front part of the lobes is a strip of cells called the somatosensory cortex, whose primary function is to receive incoming sensory stimuli, such as touch and pain. The rear part of the parietal lobes is responsible for spatial awareness, where each part of the body is at all times and in relation to its surroundings. Touch the top of your head, say, "ouch!" and think of touching the top of your head.

Frontal Lobes – These lobes account for the largest part of the cortex and perform the most complex functions, such as problem-solving, decision-making, higher-level and critical thinking. Tap you forehead and decide which colors you will use on the brain diagram below and what symbols you will draw as function reminders for each.

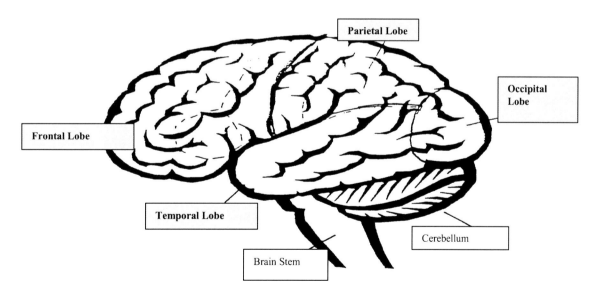

🖎 **Kinesthetic Practice:** In a group of four, let each person represent one of the lobes. Demonstrate your understanding of the **location** and **function** of the brain's lobes by forming a hemisphere and doing some action that demonstrates the function. You may add two more to represent the brainstem and cerebellum.

Brain Geography Review

Reflect on your learning journey and see how much you can remember. Write your responses to the questions and prompts below. Stand and compare your answers with others, one at a time, to see if their answers match yours. Edit and refine your answers as you choose. Prepare to share the last four with your team or whole group.

Define Neuron.	Use your arm to describe the parts of a neuron.	Name the 4 lobes of the brain and show their location.	Define and give an example of a neurotransmitter.
Describe where the cerebellum is and give an example of its function.	Which structure is the seat of the emotions? Think of a memory link.	Describe 4 facts about the cerebrum.	Why is the hippocampus important?
Explain the major role of the brainstem.	How do the hemispheres communicate?	Compare and contrast the geography of the brain with world geography.	Use the metaphor of a tree to describe the parts and functions of a neuron.
What is the most interesting thing you learned?	What else do you want to learn?	What difference will this knowledge make to you?	What do you plan to do with this knowledge?

Brain Friendly Classrooms

Even with only the basic elementary knowledge of the brain and how it learns, we can make decisions about creating classrooms that are conducive to learning. What you will find is that the more we learn about the brain and brain-compatible classrooms, the more we see that, for the most part, it is what excellent teachers have always done. Science is confirming good practice. You may want to add these to your Nested Concept graphic organizer as we start with…

Establishing a Positive Learning Environment
12 Factors that Influence How the Brain Learns

One of the most exciting new discoveries from research on the brain is that our brains can continue to grow connections throughout our lives. Our brains are shaped by our interaction with the environment and, in turn, we impact our environment with our thoughts and actions. A basic concept is that many of the same principles that create and maintain strong bodies apply to creating and maintaining strong minds, including nutrition and exercise. Use it or lose it! This section will examine 12 factors, organized into 3 categories, which influence our brains. Think of how these impact you and your learners. Look for the things you can and cannot influence as a teacher and learner. Remember that of all environmental factors influencing students, the most important factor is YOU!

1. Positive Emotional Environment

Emotional Safety
When our brains sense danger, whether in the form of a physical, emotional, or intellectual threat, they instinctively regroup to protect us. This action has been called "downshifting" because the blood flow changes from our thinking brain to our emotional brain and brainstem. When this happens, we cannot think clearly because our body is utilizing the energy to protect itself (fight or flight syndrome). When we are in this state, new learning cannot happen.

Laughter
Laughing increases the flow of neurotransmitters that relieve stress, suppress pain and improve the immune system. Laughter is truly good medicine. Humor can increase learning retention.

Positive expectations
When classrooms operate like a family (a functional family), students feel safe to learn and are able to focus on gaining concepts and skills, rather than surviving. An environment of respect among all adults and students creates a bond and motivates students to put forth effort.

Rituals…expectations need to be taught
Classrooms that are well-managed with clear and reasonable expectations for all students are places where students feel safe and understand what is expected of them. Even when they choose to misbehave, they understand the expectations—they are fair and there are no surprises. Opening and closing rituals help students cooperate with the teacher's plans.

2. Enriched Physical Environment

Lighting
Natural lighting is best. Incandescent is next best. Fluorescent lighting raises the cortisol level in the blood and suppresses the immune system. In recent studies with elementary children, it actually made them sick.[12]

Aromas & Air Quality
Certain scents have shown to either stimulate or calm neural activity. Neural stimulators are mint, lemon, and cinnamon. Relaxing scents include vanilla, lavender, Rose of Sharon, and chamomile. Be careful to think about students with allergies. Our brains seem to be stimulated when the air is negatively charged, like it is after a rain. Fresh air breaks are critical to good brain activity.

Color
Color has either a stimulating or soothing effect on our brains. Red and orange are excitatory and create energy. Dark colors (blue, greens) are soothing and calming. There are some studies that suggest working on a table with a deep purple background increases the brain's ability to focus. Try a tablecloth or place mat and see what the results are.

3. Mentally Engaging Environment

Music
This one could go in all three categories. Music appears to have some major influences on our brains. It can be used to energize or relax us. Use positive faster beats before learning to energize; low volume Baroque to soothe (such as Vivaldi); classical before analytical tasks (Mozart). Music also is a terrific carrier for learning. An example is the alphabet song ("Twinkle, Twinkle, Little Star"). Our brains love rhythm, rhyme, and music. Brains encode things learned with music in long-term memory more easily. The other function of music is that it has been shown in some studies to boost intelligence in some tasks under certain conditions. Listening to certain selections before certain tasks may prime the neural pathways and make learning easier.

Visuals
"If these walls could talk…" Walls might not talk, but they can teach! Using visuals to create interest and reinforce learning is essential to the brain's ability to make sense and meaning of content.

Movement
Movement increases the flow of blood, thus increasing oxygen to our brains. Exercise releases chemicals in our brain that suppress pain, lower stress, lower blood pressure, and increase enjoyment. Using movement to learn content increases the ability to remember.

"Mobility is central to everything that's cognitive…whether the movement is physical or mental. Misguided teachers who constantly tell their students to sit down and be quiet imply a preference for working with a grove of trees and not a classroom of students."   -- Robert Sylwester

---

[12] http://ec.europa.eu/health/ph_risk/committees/04_scenihr/docs/scenihr_o_019.pdf

"Through movement the brain is getting itself in better condition for sustained use."--William Greenough (neuroscientist)
"Movement activates the brain to wake up, to take in sensory information from the environment…movement anchors all learning."   --Carla Hannaford, (neurophysiologist) in Smart Moves

Stimulation - High challenge & low stress builds confidence

Our brains need stimulation to grow. An enriched environment for the brain is one that is challenging, yet safe. Novelty excites the brain to learn. Learning in the same way all the time bores the brain and decreases the capacity to learn.

Feedback and Processing

Our brains need constant feedback from the environment, others, and ourselves to make meaning of what we are learning. Research indicates that our brains were not meant to focus for extended periods of time without down time for processing. The time our brains can be expected to pay attention is one minute per year of age up to twenty; for a 10-year-old, teaching cycles need to include processing time every ten minutes. Sitting through long lectures of details and data is not what the brain was designed to do. Processing can include thinking, writing, speaking, and moving.

Other Factors that Influence the Brain:

Rest and Sleep

Our brains need deep rest and power napping. Our bodies and brains are busy repairing themselves while we sleep. If we deprive ourselves of enough quality sleep time, we cannot expect to function at our best. It seems that the last few hours of sleep are especially crucial to our brain's repairing itself and creating strong connections. Adults need 7-8 hours of sleep per night. Children need more.

Nutrition

Protein is critical as are unsaturated fats and complex carbohydrates. Foods good for the brain include eggs, wheat germ, salmon, nuts, dark green vegetables, apples, bananas, lean meats, and other vitamin and mineral-rich food and supplements. Water is critical to our brain's function. Dehydration is a common problem linked to poor learning. Water is a conductor of the electrical energy in our brains. When we do not consume enough water over time, our brains send messages that we are dehydrating and our body responds. A rule of thumb for amount needed is one's body weight divided by three equals the number of ounces of water needed daily. Drugs and alcohol are detrimental to our brain's function. Especially tragic are the effects on the fetus from alcohol consumption by pregnant mothers.

🍎 **Application:** Using the graph below, brainstorm how you can apply the 12 factors that influence the brain in your classroom.

The Principles of a Brain-Friendly Classroom

Let's boil down all the ideas, research, and suggestions into some basic **principles** and **enduring understandings.** Lynn Erickson defines *principles* as "key conceptual relationships that are always true and have significant roles in a discipline." **Enduring understandings**, or generalizations, are the deep essential ideas that come from facts. They may not always be true in every case. We will call the principles our Four Main Brain Things. If you are from Texas, as I am, it rhymes.

This page will provide an **overview** of the principles with enduring understandings; the following pages will give an in-depth view of each.

Ginger's 4 Main Brain Things…Overview

Principle 1. Learners have **modality preferences** for learning and learn best when new information is given and received through that modality.

Enduring Understandings:
- The more senses used in learning, the greater the potential for learning and remembering.
- Learners learn best when involved in activities where they have the opportunity to say, hear, see, touch, and do.
- Learners' brains are strengthened through opportunities to practice, using all or some of their weaker modalities.

Principle 2. Brains learn best when content is in **small chunks** with **down time for processing**.

Enduring Understandings:
- Teaching must involve chunking content into smaller "bite-size" segments followed by processing activities that give the brain time to catch up and make sense and meaning of the input.
- Learners learn best with time to "chew " on the content in one or more of the following ways: stop and think, stop and talk, stop and write, stop and move, stop and perform.

Principle 3. Brains are pattern-seeking and learn best when **connections are made** and/or when **learning is experiential**.

Enduring Understandings:
- Teaching must involve the use of examples, models, role-play, stimulation, stories, analogies, and demonstrations.
- Learners learn best by connecting new content and skills to something relevant.

Principle 4. Rehearsal (practice) is the means for moving knowledge and skills from short-term to long-term memory.

Enduring Understandings:
- Elaborative rehearsal is best for learning cognitive skills (math facts, vocabulary).
- Rote rehearsal works best for learning motor skills (playing piano, keyboarding).
- Learners learn best when engaged in activities where they make meaning of the content/skill and can practice in a variety of ways, including using movement, rhythm, rhyme, and music.
- The brain that works is the brain that learns.

Application: Talk with a partner about your thoughts regarding these principles and understandings. About which are you anxious to learn more?

Learning Modalities

Principle 1. Learners have **modality preferences** for learning and learn best when new information is given and received through that modality.

Modalities are the sensory channels through which our brains send and receive messages. Individuals have one or more learning modality preferences.

 AUDITORY LEARNERS

Auditory learners perceive their experiences through sound. They process information best through hearing it and saying it. They
- o Understand verbal instructions
- o Need to discuss to absorb information
- o Remember names, not faces
- o Talk to self and others
- o Are easily distracted by noises
- o May have difficulty with silent reading, written tests

STRATEGIES FOR AUDITORY LEARNERS
- ☑ Use tape recorder
- ☑ Use marker to keep place when reading
- ☑ Give verbal instructions
- ☑ Read aloud from books and slides
- ☑ Provide time for discussion
- ☑ Have them repeat instructions

VISUAL LEARNERS

Visual learners perceive their experiences best through their eyes.
Their attention is given to visuals in their environment. They
- o Understand written instructions
- o Like graphs, charts, maps
- o Remember faces, not names
- o Doodle or draw while listening
- o May have difficulty with verbal instructions, visual distractions

STRATEGIES FOR VISUAL LEARNERS
- ☑ Use flash cards
- ☑ Use pictures
- ☑ Outline notes
- ☑ Make charts, graphs of information
- ☑ Write instructions
- ☑ Diagram concepts
- ☑ Provide time for writing notes
- ☑ Allow time for them to outline information from reading

TACTILE – KINESTHETIC LEARNERS

Tactile refers to touching and feeling. Kinesthetic refers to moving. T-K learners learn by doing, touching, moving, and manipulating. They

- o Tend to be active
- o Use entire body to communicate
- o Remember what was done, not heard or seen
- o Tend to fidget, move around
- o May have difficulty sitting

STRATEGIES FOR TACTILE – KINESTHETIC LEARNERS
- ☑ Use hands-on activities, manipulatives
- ☑ Have lab activities
- ☑ Role-play situations
- ☑ Provide markers, highlighters
- ☑ Give a "big picture" overview
- ☑ Use mnemonic devices
- ☑ Make lessons relevant; tell why it is important

Key ideas:
- When people don't have the opportunity to learn new content and skills through their modality preference, they are less likely to be successful.
- The more senses used in learning, the greater the retention.
- Students can build modality strength through opportunities to practice.

۞ **Extension:**

Label the columns for the modalities based on the characters depicted. List characteristics and strategies for each. Analyze a recent lesson and list the activities in the chart based on the modalities they targeted. Research the percentages of your students' modality preferences.

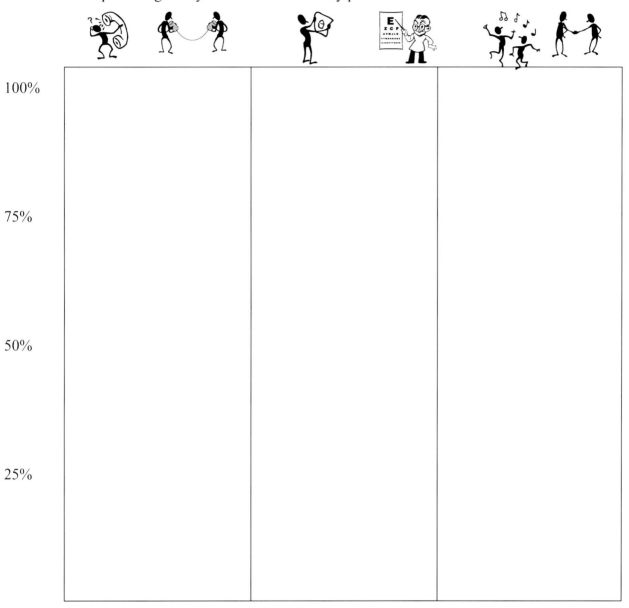

۞ **Challenge:** Design lessons that intentionally integrate **all modalities every lesson**, **every day**.

◌ Application:

You are observing the following middle school colleagues and will give them feedback on incorporating activities that will meet all learning modalities in their lessons. Analyze the differences in the way these teachers give directions and integrate the activities. How does each impact the students' potential to be successful? How does each model teaching to all modalities? What feedback and advice will you give?

Teacher A

Mrs. Thomas begins class by asking students to turn in their homework papers, get out their notebooks and a pen, and open their books to page 48 in chapter 7. While most students are still getting out their books, she begins discussing the day's lesson by asking several students to answer questions. Many students are still getting ready; some are asking others what to do. Mrs. Thomas reprimands the class for not listening and for not being responsible.

Teacher B

As students enter Mr. Scott's class and are seated, many look at the color-coded directions on the board and copy those into their class notebooks. Mr. Scott begins class by pointing to and reading aloud the directions on the board and waiting while students write the assignment in their notebooks. He then asks them to check with their partner to make sure both understand the assignment to create a foldable for taking notes on today's lesson. When he gets the all- ready signal from every pair, he tells the students they have one minute to prepare their foldable with a partner's help if needed. When all foldables are visible, Mr. Scott begins the lesson.

Teacher C

As students enter Miss Garcia's room, they comment on how great it smells…like oranges! After the opening class rituals, including students writing the learning targets in their notebooks, Miss Garcia gives each team of four students an orange for each person and an instruction sheet for the activity. She explains that they will use the orange to better understand the earth as a spheroid and examine what causes map distortion. The team leader reads the instructions aloud as the team recorder writes the group's "I'm wondering…" questions. Miss Garcia moves from group to group as the students complete the assignment. Students cut the orange in two hemispheres; some eat the fruit; some toss it. Students flatten the orange halves in order to create a flat "map" from the spheroid. Sounds of, "Wow!" and "Cool!" are heard as students discover the gaps in the orange peels…

Teacher D

Mr. Jacobsen begins class by taking roll and giving the answers to last night's homework. He then begins to talk about map distortion from notes in an outline on the board. When students have finished copying the notes, he distributes a worksheet to be completed by the end of the period, using the textbook. While students complete the assignment, Mr. Jacobsen records their homework grades….When the bell rings at the end of the period, he assigns a chapter to be read for homework.

Processing Time

Principle 2. Brains learn best when content is in **small chunks** with **down time for processing**.

How would you like to go have a steak dinner later today? I'm buying! Let's say we meet for the dinner at a fabulous restaurant. The décor is stunning, the atmosphere is pleasant, and the staff is attentive. You order the best steak on the menu and are excited to savor it. How would you feel if, at the moment it arrived, I inform you that I have some special requirements for eating the steak because I'm busy and have to move on to other things? What if I say: "This is how I need you to eat this beautiful steak. Lean your head back, open wide, and eat the whole steak at one time. If you try to spit it out, I will push it back in. You must get the steak eaten."

How would that dining experience be? What's wrong? Isn't it a good steak? Don't you like steak? Are you not a motivated steak eater...shall we try chicken?

Even though the steak is great and you like steak (or, at least you used to like steak), the way I tried to make you eat it made it inedible and the entire experience horrible. Think about what would have made the dinner enjoyable and the steak delicious. Would you like to have time to enjoy your meal? Would you like to cut your steak into bite-size pieces and then have time to chew each piece thoroughly before swallowing? Would you like to enjoy the other items on your plate with the steak? Would you like to celebrate the completion of your dinner with a big thick slice of cheesecake? Sound better?

Now, **let's make the transfer to teaching**. It is the same with learning—I've seen many a student who looks as if he's just had a steak crammed in his mouth. He can't chew, he can't swallow, he can't even ask for help. Content has to be delivered in a manner that allows time for processing, not in one whole indigestible piece. The brain is not designed to pay attention to and be able to remember incoming sensory data for long, extended periods of time. The brain needs down time for processing if it is going to learn. The content needs to be cut into bite-size pieces with time for chewing and swallowing it. How big should the chunks be? It depends on how much the learner can chew.

The formula for how long the brain can focus before it needs to process is about one minute per year of age up to about 20. For example, if I teach 10-year-olds, I need to stop and process after 10 minutes of instruction with new material or skills. How long should the processing time be? It depends on what you want students to do. A quick Think-Pair-Share could take 30 seconds. A journaling activity might take 15 minutes. Effective teachers' instructional plan includes breaking content into "bite-size" pieces and designing "chewing" time.

Make a wave with your hand, up and down, up and down. Think of that being the way the brain learns and the way the lesson needs to be designed, representing teach time and down time, and say, "Process time, teach time, process time," etc.

teach-process-teach-process

The process time can and should include a variety of activities. Here are a few examples:
- Reflection / journaling / drawing
- Restating or paraphrasing to a partner
- Writing an answer or a summary
- Giving an example
- Highlighting key ideas in notes
- Demonstrating your answer to a partner
- Using a strategy like Mix - Match, involving movement

Processing Activities:

Here are some examples of processing activities to incorporate in your lessons.

Mix-N-Match (works well for questions with one correct answer; i.e., country-capital, math facts, vocabulary, etc.)
- ☑ Teacher prepares cards or gives instructions for partners to write a question on one card and the answer on another. Make enough for each student to have a card.
- ☑ Have the class stand, mix around the room and trade cards with as many people as possible until the signal is called.
- ☑ Call "freeze" and tell class to find the matching card and then move to the outside of the room to debrief.
- ☑ Debrief, involving all students in checking the matches: agree, not sure, or disagree.
- ☑ Options: mix and try again or have each student make his own set for individual practice after the whole group practice.

Mix-Pair-Discuss (works well for reciprocal teaching, gathering data, discussing current events, checking homework, etc.)
- ☑ Group mixes around room without talking.
- ☑ Tell them to pair with nearest person at your signal.
- ☑ Give them a topic to discuss.
- ☑ Mix again and repeat.

Think-Pair-Share (works well for a quick check or summary statement)
- ☑ Teacher asks question or gives problem.
- ☑ Teacher asks partners to think about it.
- ☑ Partners take turns sharing with each other for designated time.

Round Robin
- ☑ Team members number off (1-2-3-4).
- ☑ Teacher assigns task, asks question or gives problem.
- ☑ Teammates answer question in turn.
- ☑ Teacher leads a whole group check or debrief.

Showdown
- ☑ Teacher prepares one set of cards per team with questions or problems.
- ☑ Students number off from 1-2-3-4.
- ☑ Game is played when #1 Flips over card with problem or question, then reads it out loud.
- ☑ All answer on scratch paper <u>Solo</u>: No Talking.
- ☑ When everyone is finished or time is up = Signal Thumbs Up.
- ☑ #1 Calls out "<u>Showdown!</u>" and all show their answers.
- ☑ #1 Leads in checking answers / praise / correction / help.
- ☑ Pass deck to #2. Repeat.

Team Meeting (Numbered Heads Together)
- ☑ Students number off (1-2-3-4).
- ☑ Teacher gives problem or asks question.
- ☑ Teacher calls for individual think time (no talking).
- ☑ At signal the teammates put their "heads together" to come up with answer (All must know answer).
- ☑ Teacher calls time and selects a team or individual at random to answer.

There are dozens of easy checking and processing activities available. In addition to Marzano's work, Marcia Tate, Spencer Kagan, and others have great resources for whole group, team, and individual activities.

Making Connections

Principle 3. Brains are pattern-seeking and learn best when **connections are made** and/or when **learning is experiential**.
It was DYNAMITE!

What did your mind do when you read that statement?
Depending on your age and your experiences, your brain may have created one of the following images:

The explosive TNT   It was great!   JJ Walker's DI-NO-MITE!   Napoleon Dynamite

Because the brain is pattern-seeking, it is always striving to make sense and meaning of incoming sensory data. If the data is not complete, the brain will complete it with prior experiences and knowledge, sometimes erroneously.

Research on learning says that the brain cannot learn anything new without one or both of two things happening. Can you predict what they think those two things are?

1. The new information or skill must <u>connect to prior learning</u> or stored knowledge.
    Example: comparing/contrasting, metaphors
    Using a football grid to understand the geographic grid, comparing eating a steak to learning
2. The learner must <u>experience </u>the new concept concretely.
    Example: providing a tangible example or a model.
    Turning the classroom into a geographic grid, using a hand to teach the cell

🖐 Try the following strategy to demonstrate both connections and experience:
Four Corners
1. Ask students to think about their favorite soft drink from the choices you give: Coke, Pepsi, Dr. Pepper, Other (or any topics you choose, such as holidays, characters, etc.)
2. Write the choices on large cards and tape in the four corners of the room. Ask students to stand in the corner that matches their choice without talking.
3. Ask them to share with a partner why they made this choice or what they like about it. Then tell them about today's lesson on fractions. Tell them you were wondering what fraction chose Pepsi, etc.
4. Ask them to get with their partner and determine what steps need to be taken to solve this problem. Take responses and, using a chart or the board, demonstrate finding the common denominator and the numerator. Ask if any can be reduced and do that.
5. Form a bar graph: Give enough pieces of colored paper to each corner group for each person to have one. Use a different color for each group. Form a bar graph by asking students to form lines, one in front of the other from the wall, with the front person holding the corner label. After debriefing questions, have them lay the papers on the floor, forming a bar graph. Debrief.
6. Form a pie graph: Ask each corner group to stand shoulder to shoulder and form a circle with the entire class representing the whole. Take ribbons or crepe paper strips of different colors. Holding all the ends in your hand, stand in the middle of the circle. Give the other end of each ribbon to the first and last person representing each corner, creating a pie graph. Ask processing questions about the data.

🖐 How does this strategy model Principle #3? What about Principles #1 and #2?
Think of a concept you teach or will teach that is very difficult for most students to grasp. How can you connect it to prior learning and create an experience with the learners so that they can learn?

Sense and Meaning

In order for learning to transfer, it must make sense and have meaning to the learner. If he understands the concept, it makes sense. If he knows <u>how</u>, <u>why</u>, and <u>when</u> to use it, it has meaning. It is our job to make those connections and to provide the opportunity for the learning to make sense and have meaning. The chart below shows the outcomes.

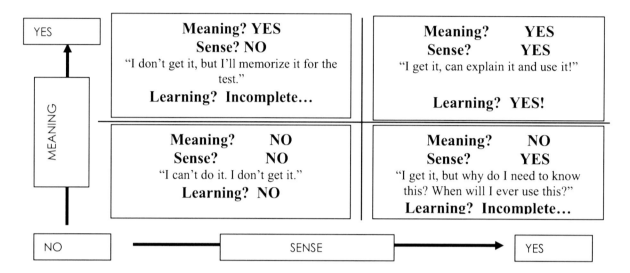

When the learner makes <u>**sense**</u> of the learning, he understands the concept--it is comprehended. "I get it!" "I see!" "2 apples and 2 oranges equals 4 pieces of fruit, or 2+2=4!"

When the learning has <u>**meaning**</u> to the learner, it has application--he knows how and when to use the learning. "When will I ever use this?" "Why do I have to know this?" are questions that show us that there is no meaning.

Something can make sense and have no meaning—trivial bits of data.
Something can have meaning and make no sense—memorizing terms for a test without understanding the definition.

If either of these is the case, learning is incomplete and not applicable.

▸ Learning is the process by which we acquire <u>knowledge and skills</u>.
▸ Memory is the process by which we <u>retain</u> it.
▸ Retention is the process whereby long-term memory preserves learning in such a way that the memory can be <u>located</u>, <u>identified</u>, and <u>retrieved</u> accurately in the future.
▸ Retention requires sense (understanding) and meaning (relevancy).

Practice Makes…Permanent

Principle 4. **Rehearsal (practice)** is the means for moving knowledge and skills from short-term to long-term memory.

Complete the following: "In fourteen hundred and ninety two…"

Did you say, "Columbus sailed the ocean blue?" Did you say it with a cadence? Where did that come from? Did you practice it earlier today? No? Where was it? Think of other commercial jingles, songs, or sayings that you could repeat in response to a stem without much conscious thought. How is it that you can hear a song from your high school prom that you haven't heard for decades and be instantly transported to the place and time, experiencing the same emotions? Why do you know the Beverly Hillbillies' theme song but can't name the Secretary of State or remember the capital of Canada? Or, where did I place my keys…?

Those things were drawn from long-term memory, your permanent storage of knowledge, skills, and emotions.

I will borrow loosely from David Sousa's model to provide a very simple and basic understanding of the process of learning and memory. For a thorough treatment of this subject, please study his books, especially *How the Brain Learns*.

1. Think of your brain as having shutters that either allow or prevent incoming sensory (from your 5 senses) data from going to your conscious memory. The shutters close when the incoming data is perceived as unimportant, or if the brain is occupied with survival instead of learning. When the brain has to choose between breathing and critical thinking…it always chooses surviving.

2. After an instantaneous trip to the thalamus, and if emotional, to the amygdala, the incoming sensory data goes into **short-term memory**, which lasts about 18 seconds. Think of this as a dry erase marker board or a clipboard for quick notes. If it isn't used or practiced, it is gone. For example: looking up and dialing a phone number, then forgetting it. There are two major exceptions: 1) when the data is extremely emotional or traumatic in nature: for example, September 11. In those cases brain chemicals sear those events in long-term memory; and, 2) when the data is unique or unusual in nature or pattern. For example, if the phone number were 555-444-3333, it would be recalled more easily. Remember: the brain loves to store data with patterns.

3. If the data from short-term is used or rehearsed, it goes to **working memory,** or mid-term memory, which lasts for about 48 hours. Think of this as your desktop with all the files you have open and are currently working on. If that information is not used, most of it will be gone, leaving only vague traces. For example: cramming for a test by memorizing trivial information, making an A, and then forgetting the information a few days later.

4. If the information from working memory is rehearsed and used, it can go to **long-term memory**, or permanent memory storage, which can last forever. (Example: In 1492…)
Think of this memory as a system of filing cabinets, with drawers for different types of memory: episodic, procedural, semantic, emotional, etc. Every time we are learning something new, our brain searches those files and tries to make a connection to something in our long-term memory (MBT #3). One way to think of it is that our brains try to find the folder in which to store the page with new data. If there is not a folder, the data can be lost or stored in the wrong place, making retrieval difficult. That new information has a greater chance of being stored permanently when it is associated with prior learning. That's one of many reasons concept-based learning is so powerful. Concepts are the tabs on the folders of our brains. When we grasp the concepts, we have organized our "brain files" to receive and store more incoming data. Also, the more background knowledge I have means more folders in my filing cabinets, and the more places for learning to attach. Think of your students, some with very sparse filing cabinets…not many folders, not many tabs.

Learning Flowchart

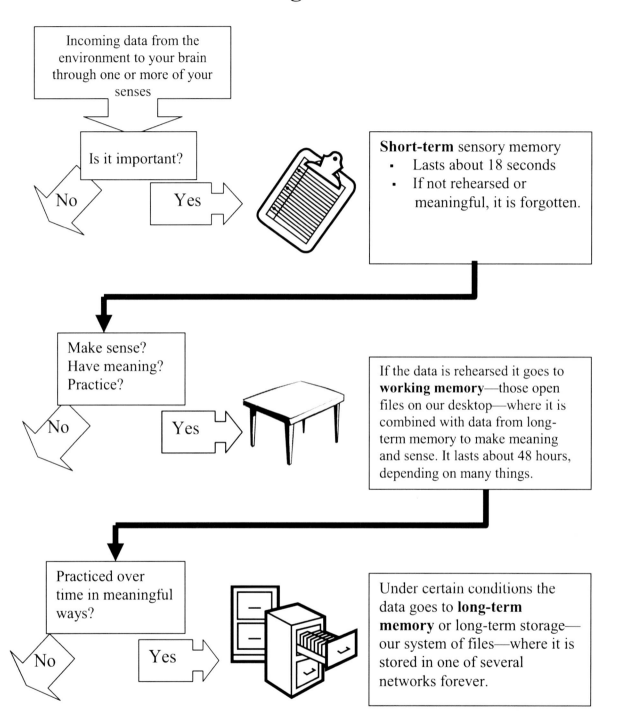

Incoming data from the environment to your brain through one or more of your senses

Is it important?

No

Yes

Short-term sensory memory
- Lasts about 18 seconds
- If not rehearsed or meaningful, it is forgotten.

Make sense?
Have meaning?
Practice?

No

Yes

If the data is rehearsed it goes to **working memory**—those open files on our desktop—where it is combined with data from long-term memory to make meaning and sense. It lasts about 48 hours, depending on many things.

Practiced over time in meaningful ways?

No

Yes

Under certain conditions the data goes to **long-term memory** or long-term storage—our system of files—where it is stored in one of several networks forever.

Sources: David Sousa and Pat Wolfe

Big Idea: Rehearsal - Forming Strong Memories

When learning, the strongest memories formed tend to be those that
- Are learned to rhythm, rhyme, music (remember, the brain is pattern-seeking and loves patterns and cadences)
- Have a strong emotional tie – that's why storytelling is so powerful
- Are relevant to the learner
- Use the most senses in learning – MBT Principle #1
- Allow time or processing – MBT Principle # 2
- Make sense and have meaning – MBT Principle #3
- Have been rehearsed in a meaningful way - MBT Principle #4

Rehearsal or practice is the process of moving learning from short-term to long-term memory. Rehearsal is the process of attaching sense and meaning to new learning.

There are two categories of rehearsal:
- **Rote rehearsal** is doing the same thing over and over the same way. It is the best kind of practice for learning motor skills (procedural memory) and becoming proficient in skills like keyboarding and playing golf. You would never be able to ride a bicycle by reading a book and working on vocabulary about biking.
  - What are other skills that require rote rehearsal?

- **Elaborative rehearsal** is practicing something in different ways, using music, rhythm, higher levels of thought, paraphrasing, drawing, explaining, summarizing, teaching, and demonstration. This type of practice is best for increasing semantic (factual) memory
  - What other skills require elaborative rehearsal?

- **Application:** Consider something you need your students to have in long-term memory.

Describe how you will teach that concept with MBT Principle #4 in mind.

Revise one of your lessons with all 4 MBT Principles.

Teaching for Thinking

INCREASING THE LEVEL OF THINKING

One of the goals of teaching is to increase the level of thinking required. Complex level thinking skills can be increased by the way questions are framed. We do not want learners who memorize facts and data only, but who can think critically, creatively, and solve problems.

One of the ways to increase the level of thought is to use the work of Dr. Benjamin Bloom: Bloom's Taxonomy of thinking levels.

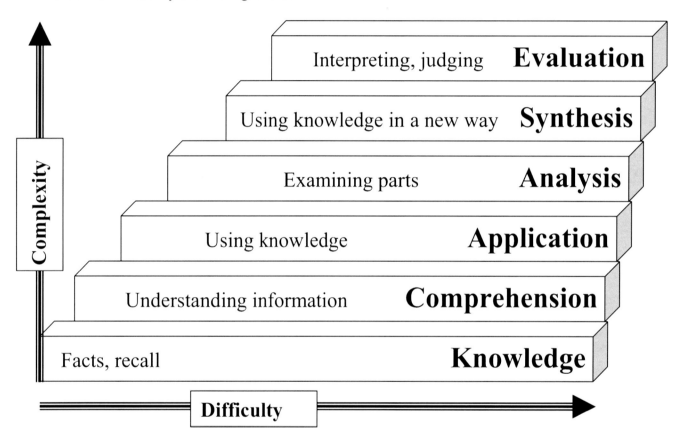

Interpreting, judging	**Evaluation**
Using knowledge in a new way	**Synthesis**
Examining parts	**Analysis**
Using knowledge	**Application**
Understanding information	**Comprehension**
Facts, recall	**Knowledge**

Complexity (vertical axis)

Difficulty (horizontal axis)

Revised Bloom's Taxonomy

Dr. Lorin Anderson, a former student of Bloom's, and his colleagues published an updated version of Bloom's Taxonomy that takes into account a broader range of factors that have an impact on teaching and learning today. This revised taxonomy differentiates between "knowing what," the **content** of thinking, and "knowing how," the **procedures** used in solving problems.

The **Cognitive Process Dimension** is the "knowing how" dimension. It has six skills with sub-skills. They are listed here from simplest (remembering) to most complex (creating).

Remembering	**Producing the right information from long-term memory**.
Recognizing	Example: *Identify a noun in a sentence.*
Recalling	Example: *Write the multiplication facts.*
Understanding	**Ability to make meaning from educational material such as reading and teacher explanations.**
Interpreting	Example: *Draw a diagram of the digestive system*
Exemplifying	Example: *Name a mammal that lives in your area.*
Classifying	Example: *Label numbers odd or even.*
Summarizing	Example: *Write a sentence that captures the key ideas of the article.*
Inferring	Example: *Discuss the motivation of the character in the story.*
Comparing	Example: *Explain how the heart is like a pump.*
Explaining	Example: *Diagram how the water cycle works.*
Applying	**Using a learned procedure either in a familiar or new situation.**
Executing	Example: *Add a column of two-digit numbers*
Implementing	Example: *Design an experiment to see how plants grow in different kinds of soil.*
Analyzing	**Breaking knowledge down into its parts and thinking about how the parts relate to its overall structure.**
Differentiating	Example: *Create a Venn diagram of the two main characters' qualities.*
Organizing	Example: *Draw a diagram showing how plants and animals interact.*
Attributing	Example: *Determine the author's point of view from an article.*
Evaluation	**Making judgments based on criteria and standards.**
Checking	Example: *Review a project to see if all the necessary steps are included.*
Critiquing	Example: *Judge how well a project meets the criteria of a rubric.*
Creating	**Putting things together to form something new or recognize components of a new structure.**
Generating	Example: *Create an alternative hypothesis based on the criteria.*
Planning	Example: *Outline an essay.*
Producing	Example: *Put on a play based on a chapter from the novel.*

✍ Compare and contrast this revised list to Bloom's original taxonomy.
Discuss with a partner how this knowledge will increase your ability to teach students to think and function at higher levels.

The **Knowledge Dimension** is the "knowing what" dimension and it has 4 categories. Each level of knowledge can correspond to each level of cognitive process. For example, a student can **remember** factual or procedural knowledge and can **understand** factual or conceptual knowledge, etc.

Factual Knowledge Basic information	Conceptual Knowledge The relationships among pieces of a larger structure to make them function together	Procedural Knowledge How to do something	Metacognitive Knowledge Knowledge of thinking in general and your thinking in particular
-Knowledge of terminology Ex: Vocabulary terms, math symbols	-Knowledge of classifications and categories Ex: species of animals, geological eras	-Knowledge of subject-specific skills and algorithms Ex: procedure for solving quadratic equations, serving a volleyball	-Strategic knowledge Ex: ways of memorizing facts, reading comprehension strategies
-Knowledge of specific details and elements Ex: names of continents, major WW II battles	-Knowledge of principles and generalizations Ex: Newton's Laws of motion, principles of democracy	-Knowledge of subject-specific techniques and methods Ex: literary criticisms, analysis of historical documents	-Knowledge about cognitive tasks Ex: differences in writing with email and a business letter
	-Knowledge of theories, models, and structures Ex: DNA model, economic theories	-Knowledge of criteria for determining when to use appropriate procedures Ex: standards for different genres of writing	-Self-knowledge Ex: knowing one's learning style needs

Anderson, L. W. & Krathwohl, D. R. (2001). A *Taxonomy for learning, teaching, and assessing*. New York: Longman.

.

Questioning Using Different Levels Of Thinking

❧ Think of the questions you normally ask when checking for understanding and on your assessments. What level are most of your questions? The following verbs can be used to develop questions from the levels of thinking taxonomy:

Remembering	**Understanding**	**Applying**
State	Interpret	Apply
Define	Exemplify	Construct
List	Classify	Read
Identify	Summarize	Write
Name	Infer	Translate
Find	Compare	Solve
	Explain	Model

Analyzing	**Evaluating**	**Creating**
Compare	Check	Generate
Differentiate	Judge	Design
Examine	Justify	Propose
Contrast	Criticize	Construct
Categorize	Decide	Organize
Analyze	Conclude	Produce

Question Samples: Secondary social studies

R   1. What is the capital of Texas?
U   2. Describe the function of the governor.
Ap   3. Predict what the population makeup of Texas will be in 2050.
An   4. Compare and contrast the Coastal Plains and the Panhandle Plains.
E   5. Based on the article, judge the validity of the argument for border control.
C   6. If Texas were to become an independent country, decide how the new states should be organized. Propose a new form of government.

Kindergarten   "Little Boy Blue"

R   1. What is the name of the main character in the story?
U   2. Discuss why Little Boy Blue needed to blow the horn.
Ap   3. Translate the story into a picture or draw a picture of the rhyme.
An   4. Compare Little Boy Blue and Little Red Riding Hood: how were the two alike, and how were they different?
E   5. What do you think the farmer should do since Little Boy Blue let the cows get in the corn?
C   6. Write a story about what would happen if Little Boy Blue had forgotten his horn; how would he get the cows out of the corn?

🍎 Teaching for Thinking Activity

Part I
Write 3 questions to check for understanding on something you teach.
1.

2.

3.

Part II
Analyze those questions for the level of thinking required.

Part III
Write six questions, one from each of the six levels of Bloom's.
1.

2.

3.

4.

5.

6.

Part IV
Check with a partner.

Understanding the Learner's Unique **Personalities and Styles**

In order to make sense of our world, we all have unique and specific mental qualities through which we perceive and order the world around us. There are four basic styles which account for our points of view, mind sets, values, and basic personalities. We have been looking at style differences since the time of Hippocrates. According to Dr. Anthony F. Gregorc's Mind Styles, perception and ordering are mind qualities found within four basic mediation channels which help us to relate to the world. Those mediation channels are Concrete Sequential, Concrete Random, Abstract Random, and Abstract Sequential. According to Don Lowry's True Colors, the four styles are Green, Gold, Blue, and Orange. While there are some differences in lining up True Colors with Mind Styles exactly, basic similarities are noted below. The **intent** of learning about diverse styles is to understand and appreciate oneself and others. Following is a brief overview of the four styles:

Concrete Sequential	Abstract Sequential	Abstract Random	Concrete Random
Gold	Green	Blue	Orange
practical	visionary	emotional	action oriented
linear	future oriented	perceptive	risktaker
time conscious	analytical	intuitive	impulsive
dependable	conceptual	relationships	competitive
orderly	intellectual	colorful	physical
stable	verbal	creative	now oriented

As people learn more about their own and others' styles, conflicts can be avoided, stress reduced, and strengths recognized and valued. Each of the styles has particular positive and negative characteristics. Individual analysis of one's style is determined by taking the instruments designed for that purpose.

The teacher's role in reference to styles is to be prepared to meet the needs of all styles in the learning environment, processes, and content. For example, Gold learners need you to be organized, start on time, and to have a purpose. Green learners need you to be knowledgeable, current, and cause them to think. Blue learners need a personal connection, opportunities to work with others and a safe setting. Orange learners need relevance, application, and active learning.

The following pages give detailed information about these styles from Gregorc and True Colors. To order resources for True Colors, visit www.truecolorsintl.com. For Anthony Gregorc's resources, visit www.gregorc.com.

Attributes of Different Styles
Gold (Concrete Sequential)

General Attributes

Motto is "Be Prepared"
Loves to plan
Detail oriented
Service oriented
Values family traditions
Helpful and trustworthy
Conservative and stable
"Shoulds" and "should nots"
Never breaks the speed limit
Strives for a sense of security
Punctual, predictable, precise
Value order and the status quo
Duty, Loyalty, Useful, Responsible
There is a right way to do everything
Tends to be left-brained and analytical
Strong belief in policies, procedures, rules
Most comfortable with a formal environment

IN THE LEARNING ENVIRONMENT
Needs:
Classify
Categorize
Construct models - solar system, maps
Textbook sources
Evaluate via quiz
Worksheets
Make graphs, charts
Organize and plan experiments, activities
Prefer:
Objective clearly stated
Scheduled time-frame
Structured / organized
Discipline - assigned seats
Visual aids
Prefer small groups
Reinforce content
Give individual attention
Specific step-by-step directions
Wants other students and teacher to be on task
Need time schedule for deadlines
Desire question / answer periods and instant feedback
Likes re-teaching and review
Environment: quiet, orderly, uninterrupted
Learning must have a meaning or purpose
Opportunity to practice
Recognition for a job well done

Gold may see self as:

Stable
Providing security
Dependable
Firm
Always have a view
Efficient
Realistic
Decisive
Executive type
Good planner
Organized person
Punctual, expects same
Goal oriented
Finish what I started
Good at sorting, weeding out

Others may see Gold as:
Rigid
Controlling
Dull, boring
Stubborn, pigheaded
Opinionated
System-bound
Unimaginative
Judgmental
Bossy, controlling
Limiting flexibility
Uptight
Sets own agenda
Predictable
Rigid idea of time
End justifies the means
Limited-not able to do many things at once
Throws away good items needlessly

From True Colors™

Attributes of Different Styles
Green (Abstract Sequential)

General Attributes
"Should be able to"
"Why"
Intellectual
Theoretical
Idea people
Philosophical
Very complex
Perfectionists
Standard setters
Visionaries, futurists
Can never know enough
Cool, calm, and collected
Work is play – play is work
Often not in the mainstream
Abstract, conceptual, global
Need for independence and private time
Explores all facets before making decisions
Knows how to spell and pronounce "big" words
Approaches interpersonal relationships in a logical manner

IN THE LEARNING ENVIRONMENT
Green Learners…
Need:
Guided imagery / specific focus
Films showing origins
Create new models
Lecture
Library research
Individual study, research
Analyze graphs, charts
Develop teaching posters
Deductive reasoning
Debate

Prefer:
Quite and uninterrupted
Neat and orderly
Mental activity supersedes environment
Brief overview, then focused learning
Logical presentation
Leave me alone to think about it
Don't waste time, get to it
Opportunities for in-depth independent exploration

Green may see self as:
Superior intellect
98% right
Tough-minded
Efficient
Powerful
Creative, visionary
Original, unique
Eminently reasonable
Rational
Calm, not emotional
Under control
Precise, not repetitive
Able to find flaws
Objective
Task, goal focus
Holding firm to policy
Seeking justice
Assuming things will be well done
Firm-minded, able to reprimand
Great planner

Others may see Green as:
Intellectual snob
Arrogant
Heartless
Doesn't care about people
Ruthless
Unrealistic
Eccentric, weird
Emotionally controlled
Ignores people values
Cool, aloof, unfeeling
Afraid to open up
Covers subject from all angles
Critical, fault finding
Not on my side
Devaluing relational aspects
Having limited ability to see obvious differences
Lacking mercy, unfair
Unappreciative, stingy with praise
Nasty, hatchet man
Doesn't consider people in plans

From True Colors™

Attributes of Different Styles
Blue (Abstract Random)

General Attributes

Mediators
Optimistic
Caretakers
Passionate
Peacemakers
True romantic
Cause oriented
Need to feel "special"
Always has a kind word
Enjoy symbols of romance
Strong sense of spirituality
Sensitive to needs of others
Peace, Harmony, Relationship
Motivate and encourage others
Cooperative rather than competitive

IN THE LEARNING ENVIRONMENT
Blue Learners…
Need:
Guided Imagery
Group Work, Reports
Group Discussions
Poems, Essays, Reports
Written Descriptions
Illustrate, Draw, Paint
Collect Items
Library Reading
Cooperative Learning
Prefer:
Environment safe, secure, non-threatening
Warmth, Friendliness
Displays of student work
No study corrals
Small group circles
One-on-one with a blue teacher
Active participation
Positive reinforcement
Hands-on activities with interaction
Variety
Flexible time frame
Relevance to own life
Praise / feedback with acknowledgement
Personal interaction
Informal situations
Talk time

Blue may see self as:
Warm, Caring
Compassionate
Romantic
Spiritual
Creative
Idealistic
People person
Willing to work tirelessly for a cause
Unselfish
Empathetic
Affirming
Expressive, expansive
Caretaker
Promoting growth, well-being
Social interaction expert
Able to see need for exceptions
Conscious of past relationships
Likes to please people
Sympathetic
Great communicator
Trusting
Wanting harmony
Individualized personal values

Others may see Blue as:
Over-emotional
"Bleeding Heart"
Mushy
Other-worldly
Flaky, unrealistic
Hopelessly naïve
Too tender hearted
Easily duped
Too "Touchy- Feely"
Just pathetic
Too nice
Naïve, too trusting
Smothering
Teaching non-essentials
Slick, manipulative
Ignores policy, creates chaos
Stuck in / lives in the past
Groveling, fawning, soft
Obscures the issues
Talks too much
Illogical, incomprehensible
Individualized personal values

From True Colors™

Attributes of Different Styles
Orange (Concrete Random)

General Attributes

Playful
Energetic
Charming
Risk-taker
"Just Do It"
Test limits
Quick-witted
Master negotiator
Creative, inventive
"Let's make a deal"
A natural entertainer
High need for mobility
Visual and kinesthetic
Pushes the limits
Natural non-conformist
Thrives on competition
Likes tangible rewards
External locus of control
Stimulates the economy
Impulsive and spontaneous
Appreciates immediate feedback
Tends to be left right brain integrated
Most productive in informal environments

Orange Learners...
Need:
Field trips
Independent study
Brainstorm
Synthesize
Link abstracted and concrete science-poetry
Create new systems
Problem solving
Debate
Manipulatives
Contests, competition
Prefer:
Active environment
Teacher is active
Teacher is facilitator
Hands-on
Animated, entertaining
Variety is the spice of life
No dittos
No busy work
Independent work
Be a part of planning
Don't talk down to us
Negotiated rules within a framework
Purposeful learning

Orange may see self as:
Fun-loving, enjoys life
Spontaneous
Flexible, adaptable
Carefree
Proficient, capable
Hands-on person
Practical
Problem-solver
Good negotiator
Here and Now person
Do many things at once
Eclectic
Can deal with chaos
Curious, welcomes new ideas
Superior ability to discriminate among
options, see shades of gray

Others may see Orange as:
Irresponsible
Flaky
Wishy-washy
Not serious
Spends time at things they enjoy
Not interested in ideas
Unimaginative, dull
Disobeys rules
Manipulative, not to be trusted
Turn off to past-oriented blue and future-
oriented green
Not able to stay on task
Scattered, cluttered
Uncontrollable, resists closure or decision
Indecisive

From True Colors™

STUDENT LEARNING EXPECTATIONS

ORANGE students need...
Direct Application of Knowledge
Competitive Instruction
Opportunities to Discover by Doing
Recognition for Immediate Application
Physical, Fun Activities / Simulations
Variety of Instructional Strategies
Content-Applied Learning

GOLD students need...
Structure With Clearly Defined Goals
Traditional Instruction
Opportunities to Share Responsibility
Recognition for Being On-Task
Foundation of Subject Established First
Routine, Rules, Directed Instruction
Specific Content Learning

BLUE students need...
Open, Interactive Atmosphere
Group / Cooperative Learning Environment
Opportunities for Self-Esteem / Reassurance
Recognition for Being an Individual
Imaginative / Creative "Sharing" Activities
Open-Communication Approach to Instruction
Conceptual and Content Learning

GREEN students need...
Theory Investigation
Independent Instruction
Opportunities to Explore New Knowledge
Recognition for Competence
Immediate Challenge
Beyond Text Instruction
Conceptual Learning

TEACHING STYLE MODELS

ORANGE tendencies...
Unstructured Discipline
Spontaneous
Hands-on Immediacy
Expects Student Variety
Strong Use of Innovative Approaches
Learning Linked to "Here and Now"
Variety of Action Experiences
Emphasis on Relevancy

GOLD tendencies...
Firm Discipline
Organized Routine
Outlined Lectures
Expects Students Accountability
Strong Use of Text / References
Learning Linked to Past Traditions
Detailed Lesson Plans / Syllabi
Emphasis on Traditional Content

BLUE tendencies...
Fair / Democratic Discipline
Nurturing Format
Individualization / Cooperative Learning
Expects Student Initiated Learning
Strong Use of Variety of Materials
Learning Linked to Individual Needs
Adjustable Lesson Plans Per Student Needs
Emphasis on Application and Ownership

GREEN tendencies...
Discipline Expected Due to Interest
Sharing of Instructor Research
Lecture / Discussion
Expects Critical Thinking
Strong Use of Outside Materials
Learning Linked Answering Questions
Logical But Changing Lesson Plans
Emphasis on Futuristic Application

Physical Environment

☞ Use this space to describe and design a classroom that would meet the needs of all four personality styles.

Teaching With Style

☞ Use this space to plan a lesson that meets the needs of all four styles. Explain how the learners' needs are met.

Different Kinds of Smart

Not how smart are you, but *HOW are you smart?*

That is the question Howard Gardner has been asking educators to consider. In his theory of **Multiple Intelligences**, which is based on decades of biological and cultural research, Gardner describes eight (and, maybe more to come) intelligences—ways of thinking and doing. Individuals exhibit varying levels of intelligence in one or more areas and can increase skills in others through experiences. Schools tend to value only a few of these and primarily focus on and measure two ways of thinking: Logical/Mathematical and Linguistic intelligences. As you consider these Multiple Intelligences, think about how your classroom can value and tap into these *ways of being smart.*

Logical-Mathematical *Body Smart* The ability to detect patterns, reason deductively, and think logically.	Linguistic *Word Smart* The ability to effectively use language to express oneself and to remember information.	Spatial *Picture Smart* The ability to manipulate and create mental images in order to solve problems.	Musical *Music Smart* The ability to recognize and compose musical pitches, tones, and rhythms.
Bodily-Kinesthetic *Body Smart* The ability to use one's mental abilities to coordinate one's own bodily movements.	Interpersonal *People Smart* The ability to notice distinctions among others: moods, temperaments, and intentions.	Intrapersonal *Myself Smart* The ability to access one's own feelings and emotions and to draw on that to understanding and guide one's behavior.	Naturalist *Nature Smart* The ability to recognize, categorize, and classify plants, animals, and things in the human environment.

❧ **Apply:** Think about your classroom and your lessons. How will you tap into the strengths and meet the needs of students with these multiple intelligences? Analyze one of your lessons for activities that match and/or build the 8 intelligences. Revise the lesson to incorporate any you didn't consider.

Research: Find Gardner's resources and learn more about the intelligences and how to incorporate MI strategies in your classroom.

Go to http://www.howardgardner.com to learn more or http://literacyworks.org/mi/assessment/findyourstrengths.html to take an online assessment.

Review and Reflection…

1. Think about all you have learned so far about learning, the brain, and brain friendly classrooms. Write essential learning statements (important truths or concepts) about your learning using the acrostic below.

B-

R-

A-

I-

N-

F-

R-

I-

E-

N-

D-

L

Y

Share with a partner. Combine best ideas.

Chapter 6
Teaching for Learning for All

*The greatest enemy of understanding is **coverage**. As long as you are determined to cover everything, you actually ensure that most kids are not going to understand. You've got to take enough time to get kids deeply involved in something so they can think about it in lots of different ways and apply it—not just in school but at home and on the street and so on.*
Howard Gardner

Effective teachers plan, prepare, facilitate, and assess student learning in a way that leads to mastery.

Teaching *for* Learning for *All*
- How will I ensure high levels of *learning for ALL*?

The *Teaching for Learning House* ™
- What are the design elements in the house metaphor?
- What is a guaranteed and viable curriculum?
- What are the attributes of an effective curriculum?

Deciding What to Teach
- What are the components of an effective curriculum?
- What planning format should I use?

Planning How to Teach - Instruction
- What are the best strategies to use?
- How will I utilize interactive strategies?
- How will I teach for higher levels of thought?
- Do I know how to correctly use cooperative learning?
- How will I differentiate instruction for all learning levels?

Assessing Learning
- Do I understand the purpose of assessment?
- What is the difference in summative and formative assessment?
- Which assessment strategies will I use?

My Goals:

Ideas I want to explore further:

Teaching for Learning for ALL

The question is not, Is it possible to educate all children well? But rather, Do we want to do it badly enough? –Deborah Meier

Over the past couple of decades, education has been moving away from simply covering content and hoping something sticks to someone long enough for a test to be passed, to authentic teaching, learning, and assessment. The frustration for many educators is that while we know what needs to be done in order to achieve high levels of learning for all children, barriers prevent achieving that goal on a broad scale. You, the new teacher, are the hope for our future. What you do with what you are given will have enormous impact on our civilization. In order for our civilization to prosper and thrive, we must continue to produce educated, moral citizens who can think and perform at high levels, communicate effectively, solve problems, and cooperate with others.

After studying schools that are committed to, and are achieving, high levels of learning for all students, many researchers and educators have challenged us to do the things that effective schools are doing. Makes sense, doesn't it? Richard DuFour and others assert that schools and teachers will never achieve the results they seek unless they can effectively answer some essential questions in the context of the **BIG question**:

What knowledge and skills does a successful graduate possess?

Essential Questions:

1. What do we want <u>all</u> students to know and be able to do?
- ❖ What do we expect students to learn <u>exactly</u>?
- ❖ Solution – A *Guaranteed & Viable Curriculum* utilizing *Effective Instructional Strategies* is the answer. If every teacher knows exactly what is supposed to be learned and uses strategies that work in his class, students can be successful.

2. How will we know when <u>each</u> student has acquired the essential knowledge and skills?
- ❖ Where is each student compared to where he/she needs to be?
- ❖ Solution – Effectively using *Formative and Summative Assessment* to measure the progress and product lets students and teachers know if learning <u>has</u> happened and *is* happening and to what extent. Effective teachers use a variety of assessment methods to measure what matters—learning; they don't simply give grades for completion of tasks. Grades reflect learning, not task completion.

3. What happens in our school when <u>a</u> student does not learn?
- ❖ What systemic response do we have to ensure success?
- ❖ Solution – Effective teachers and effective schools plan and execute *Effective Intervention* strategies for students who need help. Those strategies include help for students who can't learn and for those who won't attempt the work or cooperate. These interventions include classroom strategies, grade level strategies, and whole-school strategies. They are proactive—used at the first sign of trouble so that students <u>don't</u> fail; they are not held back for remedial use when it is often too late.

Other researchers have added this important 4th question...

4. <u>What</u> happens when they do learn?

- ❖ What plan is in place if they already know it?
- ❖ Solution – Effective schools plan and use strategies for *Differentiation and Acceleration*. Allowing students to move forward (upward and onward) when they have mastered the required concepts is vital to student motivation and morale. Effective teachers plan for and use strategies that extend learning without punishing students for already knowing something.

A deeper answer to these essential questions is what Chapter 6 is all about! As you continue to learn and grow professionally, use these questions to guide your thinking and planning.

❧ You might not be able to answer for your school or grade level yet,
but how would you answer the four questions for yourself and your classroom?

The business of schools is to produce work that engages students, that is so compelling that students persist when they experience difficulties, and that is so challenging that students have a sense of accomplishment, of satisfaction—indeed of delight, when they successfully accomplish the tasks assigned. –Phil Schlechty

Ginger Tucker's
Teaching for Learning for ALL House ™

Think of the purpose of school as a house. If our job is learning for all, then certain elements must be included in the design. In order for students to achieve at high levels,

☑ Our house must have a solid **foundation** – representing the attributes of a guaranteed and viable curriculum. That's where we will focus in this chapter.

☑ That foundation is secured by strong **underpinnings** – representing our beliefs about teaching and learning. We discussed beliefs in Chapter 1.

☑ There are 3 load-bearing walls or **pillars**. The house would crumble if any of these pillars were missing – those represent our written, taught and tested curriculum. Each of those walls has critical attributes and components. We will explore each of these in this chapter.

☑ This house is covered and protected by a **roof** – representing the overarching mission, vision, values and goals we have for student and professional learning and behavior. Chapter 7 will explore the roof.

☑ As with actual houses where each person decorates and lives in his house based on his culture and personal taste, classrooms will reflect the individual teacher while still guaranteeing that all students learn.

❖ Ideally, your house will be located in a **professional learning community** filled with houses all dedicated to a shared mission, vision, values, and goals. In such a community, you would know exactly what students should know and be able to do when they come to your house, and you will know exactly what they need when they leave your house for the next. Chapter 8 will examine PLCs.

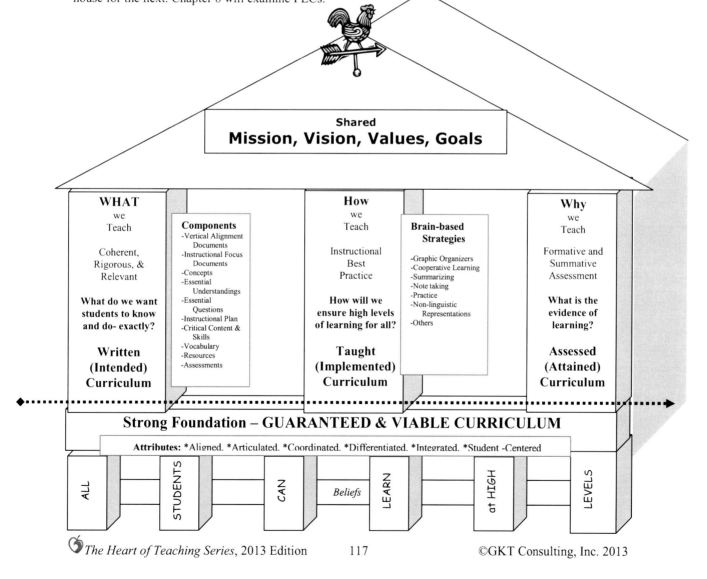

A Strong and Secure Foundation

A great teacher once taught a parable about two men who built their houses with very different results. The wise man built his house on the solid rock; the foolish man built his on the sand. While these houses may have looked good and solid at first glance, the truth about their foundations became apparent when the winds blew and the storms came. The house secured to the solid rock survived the storms, and the house built on the sand crumbled. (Matthew 7: 24-27) Even though this master teacher's point was eternal, the example serves us well when we consider the task before us. A strong, solid foundation secured by inspiring beliefs provides the support for learning for all.

As with any construction, the *Teaching for Learning House* begins on a strong foundation, with secure underpinnings. Our foundation is a **guaranteed and viable** curriculum, secured by the belief that all children can learn at high levels.

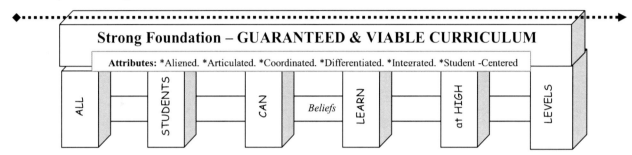

❖

Guaranteed – assurance that all students are taught and learn at high levels the **intended** curriculum, no matter which teacher the student has or what the student's background is.
- When teachers don't teach the curriculum, students leave without the essential knowledge and skills required for the next level. They have holes and gaps unless they are "lucky" enough to have a good teacher.
- Schools must provide teachers with a standards-driven curriculum, not just a curriculum that "matches" the standards. Standards are the starting point.
- In a guaranteed curriculum, every teacher knows exactly what to teach and when to teach it. Every teacher also knows what others are teaching and how the skills and knowledge fit together.
- A guaranteed curriculum says, "I promise you will have what you need to be successful and to go to the next level!"

❖ **Viable** – the curriculum is coherent, pertinent, alive, and relevant. It can be taught and learned with the time and resources available.
- Teachers have the time and opportunity to teach for mastery the concepts, knowledge, and skills in the curriculum.
- Students are learning a curriculum that is useful and applicable.
- A viable curriculum says, "This is important…you will need it and use it!"

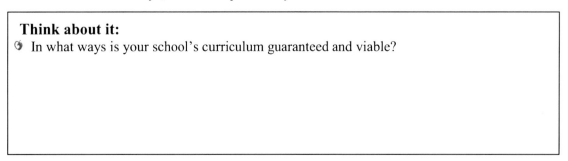

Think about it:
❧ In what ways is your school's curriculum guaranteed and viable?

An effective guaranteed and viable curriculum has the following attributes:

☑ **Aligned** – Alignment between the written, taught, and tested curriculum is the only assurance for student success. I have observed many classrooms where what teachers were doing in the classroom had nothing to do with what they were supposed to be teaching and what was going to be tested. No wonder the students couldn't achieve the desired results. Look at the **arrow** on the diagram of the house. It pierces the what, how, and why. Think of a student

who has the misfortune to be in a classroom where the teacher teaches only his "love units" and not the required curriculum. Let's say this social studies teacher's special love is the Native American unit, because he has visited historic sites and served as a missionary to a western tribe during his college days. He has slides and posters and artifacts. The students love this unit! The problem is that this teacher's assignment is not American History; it is World History. The Native American unit is in the previous grade level's curriculum. The students have already studied this content. These students will face a comprehensive exam over the World History standards, not western Native American culture. This teacher's curriculum is not aligned. He is not teaching what he is supposed to be teaching and what is going to be tested. The first diagram below represents an unaligned curriculum; the second shows alignment. Think back to the house. Without the center load-bearing wall, the house will sag and eventually fall.

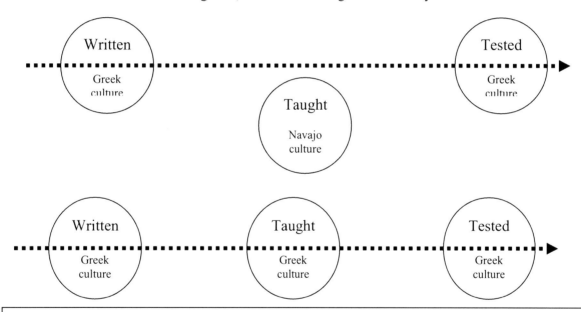

❧ **Question:** How do I demonstrate that my instruction is aligned with the written and tested curriculum?

☑ **Articulated** – When the skills and knowledge, including vocabulary, are spiraled from one grade to the next (from K-12), teachers can build on previous learning. Articulation includes content knowledge, skills, and vocabulary. Teachers should know <u>exactly</u> what students who are coming to them have been taught and what they are expected to teach students before sending them to the next level. Picture a group of social studies teachers, one from each grade level and subject, in a district with a G&V curriculum. The kindergarten teacher knows exactly where students need to be by the end of the year and what a successful graduate who mastered the social studies curriculum looks like at grade 12. The first grade teacher knows exactly what her students will bring to the first grade and where her students need to be at the end of first grade. And so on. Now let's look at that Native American guru from the alignment example in the K-12 lineup. Do you see a crimp in the chain? It's not that he is teaching anything bad or teaching badly; it's just that he isn't teaching what he is supposed to be teaching. His students are missing a "chunk" of their content and being placed at risk. I'm thinking— change his assignment—use that passion and expertise in American History! Think of an articulated curriculum as a slinky—spiraled and connected as a whole. It can "walk the stairs" and stay in one piece. Now think of a curriculum without articulation as a slinky cut into thirteen smaller pieces. It is no longer capable of doing the things a slinky is designed to do—it is not a slinky anymore.

🍎 **Questions:**

What is the evidence that I understand the skills and knowledge students coming to me have learned and the knowledge and skills they are expected to learn by the time they leave me?

How do I fill in the gaps for transfers and those who are behind?

☑ **Coordinated** – All teachers who teach the same content/grade level should plan together to assure that all students gain the essential knowledge and skills. Oh, boy! This one brings up some bad memories. When I was department chair for a high school social studies department, we decided to follow the 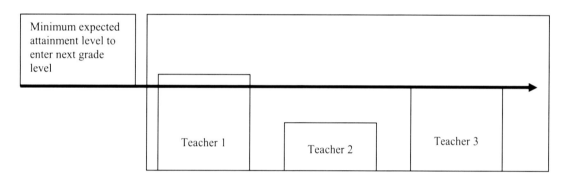 advice to work smarter, not harder. I was the geography expert; another had more experience in history, another in government, etc. Each of us decided to work in an area and then share lesson plans and resources. We would all give the same exams and then compare results. When it came time to share exam results, two of the geography teachers declined to share their results. When pressed for the reason, they admitted that they had not followed the lessons and had given only parts of the exams. When further pressed, they shared that they didn't understand some of the content, so they didn't teach it. Aaaack!!! Those students went to the next level with gaps in their learning. **Effective teams of teachers plan together, teach, and analyze student data for gaps and growth. They share a deep understanding of the meaning of the standards.** It doesn't mean that everyone has to be on the same page on the same day or even do the exact same activities; it means that all students have the same opportunities for learning the curriculum. A receiving teacher should never be able to say, "I can certainly tell which teacher you had last year," for any reason other than personality. It puts everyone at risk when a teacher receives a group of students who are deficit in skills and knowledge because of the previous teacher they had. If you are the receiving teacher of the students from the three teachers depicted on the graph, what challenges will you face?

Minimum expected attainment level to enter next grade level			
	Teacher 1	Teacher 2	Teacher 3

🍎 **Questions:**

How does everyone who teaches the same subject plan together and analyze data together?

How can you use the data to improve instruction?

☑ **Integrated** – Brain research continues to support that learning is best when concepts, content, and skills across subject areas are integrated into lessons so that students connect learning. Think of our poor students who have 7 or 8 different subjects and different teachers during the day. Primary teachers who teach all subjects may not realize how many times per day they integrate learning concepts and skills for students or how important that is. When they teach all students every subject, they know and can connect to previous learning and concepts across the curriculum, throughout the day, even on the playground! "Remember…in math we talked about…" Integration also means that skills are integrated into content: technology, process skills, etc.

Question: How do I integrate the concepts in the other subjects that my students are learning and show how mine relates?

☑ **Differentiated** – Students should have the opportunity to learn the required curriculum through a variety of strategies and levels. Students are different and learn in different ways. When teachers know exactly what students must know and be able to do, they are able to design instruction around the essential concepts, knowledge and skills required. With struggling students, teachers can focus on the essentials; with advanced students, teachers can lead them beyond the essentials. Teachers can differentiate instruction and assessment based on the learner's learning styles, needs, and strengths. One of the greatest disservices we do to the advanced student is requiring him to complete mundane tasks in areas where he is already competent, resulting in boredom and low achievement (and sometimes misbehavior). Effective teachers use formative and summative assessment data to differentiate for all students. (More on differentiation in chapter 5)

Question: How do I demonstrate that I understand how my students learn and how can I differentiate their instruction and assessment?

☑ **Student-centered** – All curricular decisions are based on what students need. When I first started teaching, curriculum (if we could call it that) was teacher-focused. I was evaluated on what I did or didn't do; student performance had no impact on my evaluation. I taught what I wanted to teach, the way I wanted to teach it. If I was talking and the students were quiet...I received good feedback. If students learned…good. If they didn't…too bad. If they wanted to be successful, they would have to try harder to learn the way I taught. It was teacher-focused. Then the shift toward learning occurred. Now classrooms are not about the teaching, but about the learning. If students aren't learning, I must adapt my teaching. I am evaluated based on what the students can do as a *result of what I do*, not just what I do. It is learner-focused.

Question: In what way is my instruction focused on the needs of my students?

◑ Process: Select <u>two</u> of the following activities to complete:

1. Draw symbols for the 6 attributes on the house diagram.

2. Develop a mnemonic chain to help you remember the 6 attributes:

     A-

     A-

     C-

     D-

     I-

     S-

3. Using a metaphor other than the house, depict the comprehensive elements of the teaching for learning curriculum.

Deciding What to teach
The *What* Pillar

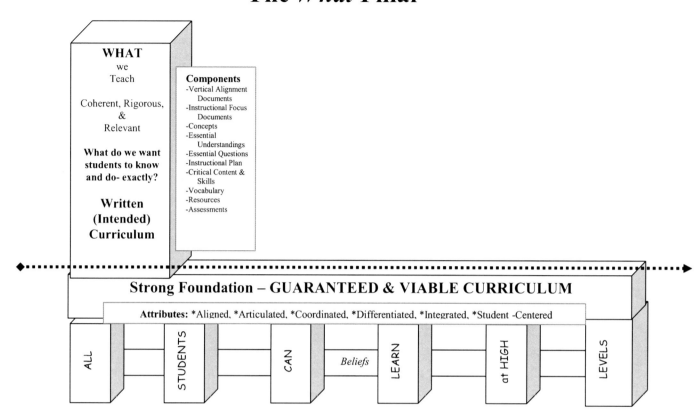

The answer to deciding what to teach is found in answering the questions,

"**What** do we want all students to know and be able to do?" "What do we expect students to learn <u>exactly</u>?" Effective schools determine WHAT should be taught based on knowledge and skill standards and provide a resource-rich written curriculum for each teacher. In today's standards-based curriculum world, **individual teachers should never have to determine <u>what</u> to teach**. Each teacher should know exactly what is expected of his students and what he can expect his students to come to class with from the previous teachers. That frees teachers to concentrate on <u>how</u> to teach.

Components of a Guaranteed &Viable Curriculum

In order for a standards-driven curriculum to be aligned, articulated, and coordinated, it must have *at least* the following components. The works of Fenwick English, Lynn Erickson, John Crain, and others form the research base for these components.

Vertical Alignment Documents – These documents represent the standards aligned across all grade levels. Because state standards are only a framework on which to build the curriculum, alignment requires that all essential knowledge and skills are clarified and articulated K-12. Think of the power of this document for teachers who have precious little time to teach the curriculum. It delineates exactly what every teacher must teach and spirals all essential knowledge and skills across the grades. Vertical alignment documents provide the big picture for a content area and the map for vertical teams.

Instructional Focus Documents or **Unit Maps**– These documents organize the clarified standards that have been "unpacked" and "bundled" into a logical sequence for instruction. In older curriculum terms, this is the "scope and sequence." These documents give a teacher the standards, including the performance indicators, which are taught in a grading period. To create these documents, the standards must be "unpacked," meaning they are taken apart to identify the essential contents and skills and reorganized or "bundled" into coherent sets of what Wiggins and McTighe call "power standards." or enduring, essential understandings. This is the only way teachers can teach the curriculum in the time allotted!

Units** – The units are the teacher's blueprints. Quality units have the following components:
- ♦ **Concepts** – mental constructs that are broad, abstract, timeless, and universal. Concepts facilitate deep understanding and allow transfer of knowledge, not just memorization. Concepts are not topics, like "The American Revolution," but are organizing ideas like "conflict" or "revolution." Concepts are the big ideas to be remembered when all else is forgotten.
- ♦ **Essential Understandings** – these are sometimes called generalizations and are conceptual statements of the essential knowledge and enduring understandings. Statements may begin with, "Students understand that…"
- ♦ **Guiding or Essential Questions** – these are open-ended, thought-provoking questions that probe the actual and conceptual understanding. These are developed by turning the generalizations into questions. For example, look at the third grade geography standard: *The student understands the concepts of location, distance, and direction on maps and globes.* A guiding question might be: *How is a scale used to determine the distance between places on maps?*
- ♦ **Instructional plan** (lessons) – using a researched-based format (more on lesson plans later)
- ♦ **Resources** – materials, technology, textbooks, supplies needed to complete activities
- ♦ **Vocabulary** – the terms to be learned for the unit.
- ♦ **Assessments** – formative and summative assessments to measure whether learning is happening and has happened.

** Even if your school doesn't provide a written curriculum, you can still build great units with the above components and find many resources online.

Planning Lessons

Chapter 2 included the background on lessons planning and examples of formats. See pages 24-38. This chapter focuses on the 5E Instructional Framework.

The 5 E Model

The **5E Instructional Framework** is most often associated with the constructivist learning design, a theory where learners *construct* new ideas or concepts based on their current and past knowledge. It is a learner-centered model, rather than an instructor-centered model of instruction. The 5E Model has been familiar to science teachers across the nation as an effective instructional process for many years. Other content areas began to embrace this format as an effective tool for planning and instruction with high levels of student involvement. The 5E Model guides the planning of an instructional cycle.

Benefits of the 5E Model:
- Applies to units or single lessons; it isn't linear.
- Uses a hands-on approach .
- Does not assume prior knowledge, but provides opportunities to build knowledge.
- Allows for teacher creativity in response to student needs.

Overview - Phases of the 5E Model:
- **Engage**

Activities are designed to generate interest in order to focus the student in the learning task and connect to past and future activities.
    - Example: Read partial story; have students generate what they know so far and what they want to know on a KWL chart.

- **Explore**

Activities are designed so that all students have common, concrete experience upon which they build concepts, processes, and skills.
    - Example: After reviewing guiding questions, students read story and begin to formulate theories.

- **Explain**

Concepts, processes, and skills are presented clearly, simply, and directly by students and teacher.
    - Example: Students take notes and depict concepts on a graphic organizer as teacher shares content and vocabulary in small chunks. Students pair and share summary statements following each content chunk.

- **Elaborate**

Activities that provide time and experiences contribute to learning. Students are applying and extending learning.
    - Example: Students use graphic organizer to write an accurate version of the original story.

- **Evaluate**

Students demonstrate an understanding of concepts and skills through formative and summative assessment.
    - Example: Students in teams answer essential questions and complete KWL chart before taking a unit test.

These phases are not linear and might represent one lesson or a series of lessons.

Practice: Think of a lesson you have recently taught and use the 5E Model to plan it.

An In-Depth Look at the 5E Instructional Model

[Descriptions of the 5E Model are based on the constructivist model and adapted from description by Cornel University, 2005]

Engage

- The first phase is to **engage** the student in the learning task. The student mentally focuses on an object, problem, situation, or event. The activities of this phase should make connections to past and future activities. The connections depend on the learning task and may be conceptual, procedural, or behavioral.
- Asking a question, defining a problem, showing a discrepant event, and acting out a problematic situation are all ways to engage the students and focus them on the instructional activities. The role of the teacher is to present a situation and identify the instructional task. The teacher also sets the rules and procedures for the activity.
- The activity should…
  - Generate interest
  - Make connections between past and present learning experiences
  - Organize students' thinking toward the learning outcomes
  - Anticipate activities
  - Access prior knowledge
  - Connect to past knowledge
  - Set parameters of the focus
  - Frame the idea

The Student…
- Asks questions such as:
  - Why did this happen?
  - What do I already know about this?
  - What can I find out about this?
  - How can this problem be solved?
- Shows interest in topic.
- Responds to questions demonstrating his own entry point of understanding.

The Teacher…
- Raises questions and problems.
- Elicits responses that uncover students' current knowledge about the concept/topic.
- Generates interest.
- Generates curiosity.

Your Examples –

Explore

- Once students are engaged in activities, they need time to explore their ideas. Exploration activities are designed so that all students have common, concrete experiences upon which they continue building concepts, processes, and skills. This phase should be concrete and meaningful for the students. The aim of exploration activities is to establish experiences that teachers and students can use later to formally introduce and discuss content area specific concepts, processes, or skills. During the activity, the students have time in which they can explore objects, events, or situations. As a result of their mental and physical involvement in the activity, the students establish relationships, observe patterns, identify variables, and question events.

- The teacher's role in the exploration phase is first and foremost to select activities that lead to *substantive concept building*. The teacher's role, then, is that of facilitator or coach. The teacher initiates the activity and allows the students time and opportunity to investigate objects, materials, and situations based on each student's own ideas and phenomena. If called upon, the teacher may coach or guide students as they begin constructing new explanations.

- Exploration activities provide students with a common base of experiences in which current concepts, processes, and skills are identified and developed.
  - Experience key concepts
  - Discover new skills
  - Probe, inquire, and question experiences
  - Examine their thinking
  - Establish relationships and understanding

The student...
- Thinks creatively within the limits of the activity
- Tries alternatives to solve a problem and discusses them with others
- Suspends judgment
- Conducts activities, predicts, and forms hypotheses or makes generalizations
- Becomes a good listener
- Shares ideas and suspends judgment
- Records observations and/or generalizations
- Discusses tentative alternatives

The Teacher...
- Elicits responses that uncover students' current knowledge about the concept/topic
- Raises questions and problems
- Acts as a facilitator
- Observes and listens to students as they interact
- Asks good inquiry-oriented questions
- Generates interest
- Generates curiosity

Your Examples –

Explain

- Explanation means the act or process in which concepts, processes, or skills become plain, comprehensible, and clear. The process of explanation provides the students and teacher with a common use of terms relative to the learning experience. In this phase, the teacher directs student attention to specific aspects of the engagement and exploration experiences. First, the teacher asks the students to give their explanations. Second, the teacher introduces explanations in a *direct and formal manner*.

- Explanations are ways of ordering and giving a common language for the exploratory experiences. The teacher should base the initial part of this phase on the students' explanations and clearly connect the explanations to experiences in the engagement and exploration phases of the instructional model. The key to this phase is to present concepts, processes, or skills briefly, simply, clearly, and directly; and then continue on to the next phase.

- This phase also provides opportunities for teachers to
  - Connect prior knowledge and background to new discoveries
  - Communicate new understandings
  - Connect informal language to formal language

The Student...
- Explains possible solutions or answers to other students
- Listens critically to other students' explanations
- Questions other students' explanations
- Listens to and tries to comprehend explanations offered by the teacher
- Refers to previous activities
- Uses recorded observations in explanations
- Uses previous observations and findings
- Provides reasonable responses to questions

The Teacher...

- Formally provides definitions, explanations, and new vocabulary
- Uses students' previous experiences as the basis for explaining concepts
- Encourages students to explain their observations and findings in their own words
- Provides definitions, new words, and explanations
- Listens and builds upon discussion from students
- Asks for clarification and justification
- Accepts all reasonable responses

Your Examples –

Elaboration

- Once the students have an explanation of their learning tasks, it is important to involve them in further experiences that apply, extend, or elaborate the concepts, processes, or skills. Some students may still have misconceptions, or they may only understand a concept in terms of the exploratory experience. Elaboration activities provide further time and experience that contribute to learning. The teacher should provide opportunities for students to practice their learning in new contexts.
- Elaboration activities challenge and extend students' conceptual understanding and skills to...
  • Develop deeper and broader understanding, more information, and more adequate skills through new experiences
  • Apply new learning to a new or similar situation
  • Extend and explain concept being explored
  • Communicate new understanding with formal language

The Student...
• Applies new labels, definitions, explanations, and skills in new, but similar, situations
• Uses previous information to ask questions, propose solutions, make decisions, design experiments
• Draws reasonable conclusions from evidence
• Provides reasonable conclusions and solutions
• Records observations, explanations, and solutions

The Teacher...
• Expects students to use vocabulary, definitions, and explanations previously provided in new context
• Encourages students to apply the concepts and skills to new situations
• Reminds and refers students of alternative explanations
• Uses previously learned information as a vehicle to enhance additional learning
• Encourages students to apply or extend the new concepts and skills
• Encourages students to use terms and definitions previously acquired

Your Examples –

Evaluate

- At some point, it is important that students receive feedback on the adequacy of their explanations. Informal evaluation can occur from the beginning of the teaching sequence. The teacher can complete a formal evaluation after the elaboration phase. As a practical educational matter, teachers must assess educational outcomes. This is the phase in which teachers administer formative or summative evaluations to determine each student's level of understanding. This also is the important opportunity for students to use the skills they have acquired and evaluate their understanding. This is also the time when the teacher determines whether students have met the performance indicators and decides how to evaluate student progress.
- Evaluation activities encourage students to…
  - Assess their understanding and abilities
  - Demonstrate understanding of new concept by observation or open-ended response
  - Apply within problem situation
  - Show evidence of accomplishment

The Student…
- Demonstrates an understanding or knowledge of concepts and skills
- Answers open-ended questions by using observations, evidence, and previously accepted explanations
- Evaluates his or her own progress and knowledge
- Asks related questions that would encourage future investigations
- Provides reasonable responses and explanations to events or phenomena

The Teacher…
- Assesses students' knowledge and skills
- Observes students as they apply new concepts and skills
- Looks for evidence that students have changed their thinking
- Allows students to assess their learning and group process skills
- Asks open-ended questions such as, Why do you think…? What evidence do you have? What do you know about the problem? How would you answer the question?
- Encourages students to assess their own learning

Your Examples –

A quality written curriculum is only words on paper or on a website without considering ***How We Teach***.

Planning *How* to teach - Instruction

*Research has proven that the single greatest determinant of learning is
not socioeconomic factors or funding levels.
It is instruction.* -Mike Schmoker

The *How* Pillar

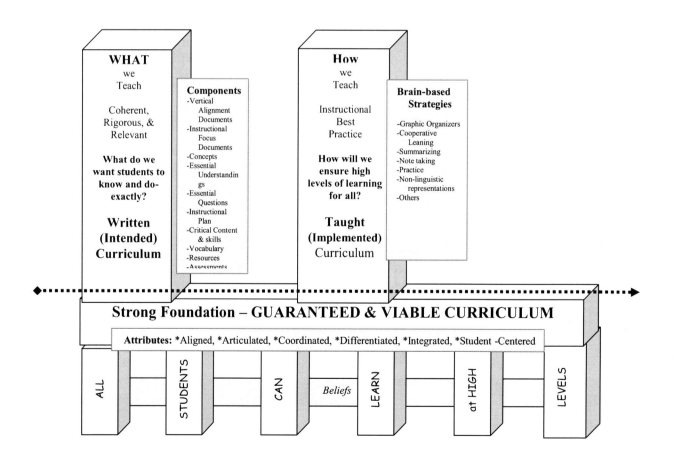

One of the characteristics of effective teachers is the ability to use effective instructional strategies. Think of these strategies as your tools-of-the-trade. You began filling your toolbox during your first year; now you begin the process of assessing the tools you have and continue adding effective tools throughout your career. One of the keys is knowing which tools to use in each circumstance.

The books and articles on classroom instruction would fill a school gymnasium. The **intent** of this small chapter is to give you some chunks of content with examples in order to familiarize yourself with the instructional knowledge and skills, and to inspire you to dig deeper into the research and resources available from experts in the field. The foundational research for this chapter is Patricia Wolfe's work, including *Brain Matters*, the meta-analysis on effective instruction found in Robert Marzano's *Classroom Instruction That Works* and *The Art and Science of Teaching,* and the many others found in the resources section of this book.

WHAT
we
Teach

Coherent,
Rigorous, &
Relevant

**What do we
want students to
know and do-
exactly?**

**Written
(Intended)
Curriculum**

Components
-Vertical
  Alignment
  Documents
-Instructional
  Focus
  Documents
-Concepts
-Essential
  Understandin
  gs
-Essential
  Questions
-Instructional
  Plan
-Critical Content
  & skills
-Vocabulary
-Resources
-Assessments

How
we
Teach

Instructional
Best
Practice

**How will we
ensure high
levels of learning
for all?**

**Taught
(Implemented)
Curriculum**

**Brain-based
Strategies**

-Graphic Organizers
-Cooperative
  Leaning
-Summarizing
-Note taking
-Practice
-Non-linguistic
  representations
-Others

Strong Foundation – GUARANTEED & VIABLE CURRICULUM

Attributes: *Aligned, *Articulated, *Coordinated, *Differentiated, *Integrated, *Student -Centered

ALL | STUDENTS | CAN | *Beliefs* | LEARN | at HIGH | LEVELS

Instructional Strategies

Robert Marzano's *Classroom Instruction That Works* is a thorough meta-analysis of instructional strategies. The study looks at instructional strategies that have the highest potential to have impact on student learning. Marzano warns that these categories are only a starting point. There are many other strategies that can be very effective, and there are also other factors that determine whether or not the strategies are effective. In 2009 Marzano and colleagues published the results of the impact of the following high impact strategies. [13]

15 Impactful Instructional Strategies

The range of percentage gain (projected average student learning gains in classrooms where the strategy is used effectively) is shown in parentheses following each strategy. Anything above 0% is good.

- Advance organizers (2%)– involves providing students with a preview of new content.
- Building vocabulary (17-20%) – involves use of a complete six-step process to teaching vocabulary that includes teacher explanation, student explanation, student graphic or pictographic representation, review using comparison activities, student discussion of vocabulary terms, and use of games.
- Effort and recognition (12-14%)– involves reinforcing and tracking student effort and providing recognition for achievement.
- Feedback (4%)– involves providing students with information relative to how well they are doing regarding a specific assignment.
- Graphic organizers (11-13%)– involves providing a visual display of something being discussed or considered; e.g., using a Venn diagram to compare two items.
- Homework (13-15%)– involves providing students with opportunities to increase their understanding through assignments completed outside class.
- Identifying similarities and differences (18-20%)– involves the identification of similarities and/or differences between two or more items being considered.
- Interactive games (18-20%)– involves use of academic content in game-like situations.
- Nonlinguistic representations (15-17%)– involves providing a representation of knowledge without words; e.g., a graphic representation or physical model.
- Note taking (15-17%)– involves recording information that is considered to be important.
- Practice (13-14%)– involves massed and distributed practice on a specific skill, strategy, or process.
- Setting goals/objectives (22-25%)– involves identifying a learning goal or objective regarding a topic being considered in class.
- Student discussion/chunking (14-17%)– involves breaking a lesson into chunks for student or group discussion regarding the content being considered.
- Summarizing (16-19%)– involves requiring students to provide a brief summary of content.
- Tracking student progress and scoring scales (31-34%)– involves the use of scoring scales and tracking student progress toward a learning goal.

❧ These are listed in alphabetical order. Create a graph or make a chart that lists them by percentage gain.

[Page 175-177 gives Marzano's *Comprehensive List of Strategies that Relate to Effective Teaching*]

---

[13] Mark W. Haystead & Dr. Robert J. Marzano. *Meta-Analytic Synthesis of Studies Conducted at Marzano Research Laboratory on Instructional Strategies.* Marzano Research Laboratory Englewood, CO. August, 2009.

Marzano offers the following nine instructional *categories* of instructional strategies that have the highest potential to have impact on student learning.

General Instructional Category	Strategy Example	Tool/ Activity Example
Identifying similarities and differences	-Comparing and contrasting -Metaphors and analogies	Venn Diagram
Summarizing and Note taking	-Student-generated verbal and written summaries -Students revising notes	2-column notes
Reinforcing effort and providing recognition	-Celebrating progress toward goals during and at the end of a unit	Effort and achievement charts
Homework and practice	-Specific feedback on all homework -Purposeful homework -In-class practice of skills	Partner assignment folders
Nonlinguistic representations	-Construct graphic organizers -Draw, depict -Physical or mental models -Mind maps	Concept maps
Cooperative Learning	-Students learning together on specific tasks	Chapter jigsaw
Setting objectives and providing feedback	-Essential questions -Student self-assessment	Student rubrics
Generating and testing hypotheses	-Problem solving tasks -Inquiry tasks	Case studies
Questions, Cues, and Advance Organizers	-Pre-assess knowledge -Thinking organizers	KWL chart Guiding questions

The following pages will give you a description of each of the *categories* with sample activities. Keep in mind that some classroom activities might involve several of the categories. For example, I might have my students use a **graphic organizer** to **compare and contrast** systems of government and then work in a **cooperative group** to produce a product that reflects the **summary** of key concepts. This activity connects to at least four of the categories.

❧ **Practice:**
Design a lesson using as many of these categories as possible. Share with a partner.

What will you do with this knowledge?

1. Identifying Similarities and Differences

The ability to break a concept into its similar and dissimilar characteristics allows students to understand complex problems by analyzing them in a simple way. These can be teacher-presented, student-generated, and/or shown on a graphic representation.

Four Strategies to identify similarities and differences are:

- **Comparing**
  - Identifying similarities and differences between and among things or ideas
  - Tools: Venn diagrams, matrices, graphs, T-charts, Line-up activities
  - Example: Use a Venn Diagram to compare and contrast apples and oranges

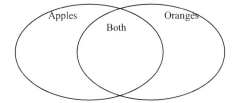

- **Classifying**
  - Grouping things that are alike based on their characteristics
  - Tools: Graphs, charts, double-bubble, four corners activity,
  - Example: Create a chart to classify the information of the brain's lobes.

Lobe	Occipital	Temporal	Parietal	Frontal
Location	Back of head	Sides of head	Top of head	Front of head
Main Function	Vision	Hearing	Movement	Thinking

- **Using Metaphors**
  - Identifying the common pattern in two dissimilar things or ideas
  - Tools: stories, analogies, graphics
  - Example: Remember our steak dinner example from page 95?

Eating a Steak	Abstract	Learning new content

- **Using Analogies**
  - Identifying the relationships between two concepts
  - Tools: graphics, stories, formula-A:B::C:D (A is to B as C is to D)
  - Example: In geographic landforms:

    A <u>strait</u> is to <u>water</u>

    as

    An <u>isthmus</u> is to <u>land</u>

Application:
  What are you already doing in this category?
  What will you add?

2. Summarizing and Note taking

These skills promote greater comprehension by asking students to analyze a subject to expose what's essential and then put it in their own words. When our brain summarizes, it has to pull all the data from different parts of the brain's short- and long-term storage to the frontal lobe to make sense of the information. That is terrific for the learning and memory process. Cornell Note taking and its many variations combine both aspects of this category. In 1986 Walter Pauk developed what is known as the Cornell note taking technique to help Cornell University students better organize their notes. The six steps to the system are

1. Record as many facts and ideas as you can in the details column.
2. Reduce important facts to key words, ideas, depictions, and questions in the main ideas column.
3. Recite out loud and in your own words the facts and ideas you are trying to learn.
4. Reflect on the information with questions that help you connect to other knowledge.
5. Review and recite your notes several times during the week.
6. Summarize the main ideas of your notes in your own words at the bottom of the note page. Summarize each page of notes and then the entire section.

Cornell Note taking example	
Main Ideas (diagram, symbols, drawing)	Details (Text)
Key words Questions	➤ Record facts and ideas ○ Fact ○ Fact ○ Idea ○ Idea ➤ Reduce to key words, ideas, depictions, and questions ➤ Recite ➤ Reflect with questions that help you connect to other knowledge. ➤ Review and recite ➤ Summarize
Summary statement: *the main ideas of your notes in your own words*	

❧**Process:** How will you use this strategy?

Two Column Notes

Main Ideas (diagram, symbols, drawing)	Details (Text)

Summary statement:

3. Reinforcing Effort and Providing Recognition

Teaching students the connections between effort and achievement changes their beliefs and attitudes. Recognition enhances achievement and increases intrinsic motivation. Make rewards and recognition personal.

In *Growth Mindset*[14], author Carol Dweck describes two distinct ways individuals view intelligence and learning. The chart provides an overview of each.

Fixed Mindset	Growth Mindset
Believe intelligence is an inborn trait Value looking smart Are afraid to risk performing poorly Do not like effort Believe that if you have ability, everything should come naturally Don't handle setbacks well • Become discouraged and defensive • Decide to withdraw effort	Believe you develop intelligence over time View challenging work as opportunity to learn Value effort Believe that even geniuses have to work hard to develop abilities Handle setbacks by trying new strategies and using different resources

Dweck asserts that meaningful work teaches students to
- learn academic content
- love challenges
- be resilient
- enjoy effort
- value their own improvement

Teachers support a growth mindset culture in the classroom by
- praising students for effort, strategies, choices, and persistence.
- emphasizing that fast learning is not always deepest or best.

Building a growth mindset requires teachers to
- emphasize challenge, not just "success."
- give a sense of progress toward mastery, possibly with pre-assessments.
- grade for growth using "not yet," rather than absolute failure.

Brainstorm the following with a partner:

➤ How can we recognize and celebrate progress toward learning goals during a unit?

➤ How can we recognize and reinforce effort?

➤ How can we recognize and celebrate progress toward learning goals at the end of a unit?

Research connection: Student Engagement

A recent survey of high school students reveals that they are mostly bored with school and that they don't see the value in the work they are being asked to do. Sixty-six percent indicated that they are bored every day. *Charting the Path from Engagement to Achievement: A Report on the 2009 High School Survey of Student Engagement* [15] asked 42,000 high school students to respond to questions such as, Are you challenged academically in your classes? If you've been bored, why are you bored? Does your work in high school contribute to your growth in thinking critically? Writing and speaking effectively? Reading and understanding challenging materials? Learning independently? Acquiring skills to work after high school? Solving real world problems?

The report also indicates the work that does engage most of them: discussion and debate, group projects, technology, role-play and drama. Teacher lecture receive the highest "not at all" votes.

"I am glad in an emphatic way that I took this survey; this survey allowed me to let go of some of my anger and allowed me to express who I am in a very unique and special way. I am glad that there are people that really care (and I do hope you people do care, I honestly hope so)." — HSSSE 2009 Student Respondent

---

[14] Dweck, Carol S. (2006) *Mindset: the New Psychology of Success.* Random House.
[15] Yazzie-Mintz, E. (2010). *Charting the path from engagement to achievement: A report on the 2009 High School Survey of Student Engagement.* Bloomington, IN: Center for Evaluation & Education Policy.

4. Homework and Practice

When used effectively, these practices can provide students with opportunities to deepen their conceptual understanding and skills. Homework can be one the best strategies or it can be the worst. Much has been written about the attributes and value of homework in recent years.

Keys to effective homework:
  ➢ Homework should be purposeful. Homework should be for the purpose of practice, preparation, or elaboration. It should never be used as punishment or for inflating grades.
  ➢ Parents need to understand the homework procedures and policy. Involve and inform parents about how they can support their child. Parents should not help or do the homework, only coach and encourage.
  ➢ Homework should be meaningful and reasonable. Consider how unreasonable it would be for the 7 to 8 teachers of a middle or high school student to give 30 minutes to one hour of homework each night—that's four to eight hours of after-school work. We encourage cheating and copying when such assignments are made.
  ➢ Homework amount should vary by age. Some research says no more than ten times the grade level of the student. So, for a third grader, no more than thirty minutes total.

Movement can be used to lift energy by associating it with rehearsal[16].

Rehearsal refers to repeating important information in a way that helps students remember it. For example, a teacher who has noticed her students are having difficulty recalling units of measurement might ask them to represent the largest of the units by standing straight up, the smaller measurements by bending over, and the smallest measurements by kneeling down.

Mnemonic Devices Can Aid Effective Practice

Mnemonic devices are helpful ways of committing data to memory. These are only helpful if the learner understands the content. It would serve no purpose to memorize a list of things and have not a clue what the list meant! These are a few examples of mnemonic devices:

Acronyms:
  ➢ **HOMES**: Huron, Ontario, Michigan, Erie, Superior (the Great Lakes in North America)
  ➢ **FACE**: Notes representing the spaces on the treble clef

Acrostics:
  ➢ **My Very Excellent Mother Just Served Us Nine Pizzas:** the planets in order --Mercury, Venus, Earth, Mars, Jupiter, Saturn, Uranus, Neptune, Pluto--Now that Pluto is apparently out, we will have to learn another…We could change "nine pizzas" to "nachos."
  ➢ **Kings Play Chess On Finely Ground Sand:** taxonomy in biology (Kingdom, Phylum, Class, Order, Family, Genus, Species)
  ➢ **Please Excuse My Dear Aunt Sally:** order of operations (Parenthesis, Exponents, Multiplication, Division, Addition, Subtraction)
  ➢ **Aunt Alice Ate Apples Nearly Every Saturday:** the 7 continents

Rhymes and Jingles:
  ➢ In 1492 Columbus sailed the ocean blue
  ➢ I before E except after C or when it says "a" as in neighbor or weigh
  ➢ ABC song to *Twinkle, Twinkle Little Star*

❧ **Application**: How can you incorporate mnemonic devices in your lessons?

---

[16] Marzano, R. J., & Pickering, D. (with Heflebower, T.). (2010). *The Highly Engaged Classroom* (p. 25). Bloomington, IN: Marzano Research Laboratory.

5. Nonlinguistic Representations

Knowledge is stored in two forms—linguistic and visual. The more we use both forms, the better we are able to think about and recall knowledge. The more students use both, the more they will achieve. When used effectively, these strategies can transform teaching and learning.

Strategies include
- Creating graphic representations
- Using graphic organizers
- Creating thinking maps
- Generating mental images
- Making physical models
- Drawing pictographs and pictures
- Engaging in kinesthetic activities
- Using mnemonic devices to aid memory

Non-linguistic representations should **elaborate** on knowledge. For example, a student can elaborate on his knowledge of fractions when he constructs a model of how a fraction might appear in concrete form. The process of generating non-linguistic representations leads students to deeper understanding with easier recall of information.

Using Graphic Organizers

The following pages give you examples of graphic organizers you may copy and use in your classroom.
David Hyerle's book, *Visual Tools for Constructing Knowledge*, identifies **six graphic organizers** with great utility in the classroom because they correspond to six common patterns with which information can be organized. Select one of the following to include in a lesson:

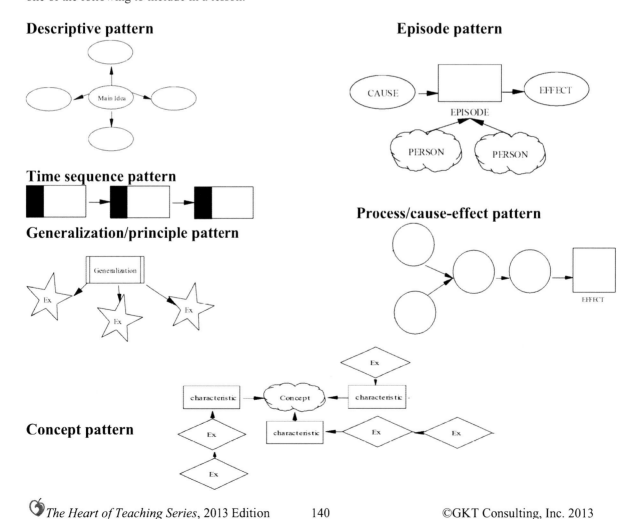

Descriptive pattern

Episode pattern

Time sequence pattern

Generalization/principle pattern

Process/cause-effect pattern

Concept pattern

Who, What, When, Where, Why, and How

Who

What

When

Where

Why

How

Brainstorming Web

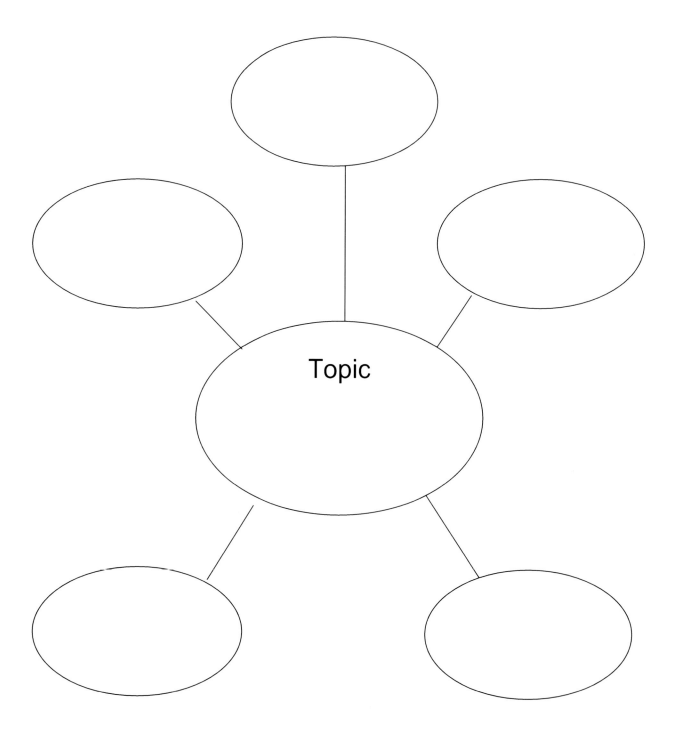

Topic

Sequence Organizer
Beginning - Middle - End

Beginning

Middle

End

Facts Chart

Part 1	Part 2	Part 3
Main Ideas	Main Ideas	Main Ideas
Supporting ideas	Supporting ideas	Supporting ideas

Alphabet Organizer
Fill in as many ideas and facts as you can remember in each space that begins with that letter.

A	B	C	D
E	F	G	H
I	J	K	L
M	N	O	P
Q	R	S	T
U	V	W	X
Y	Z		

Triple Venn

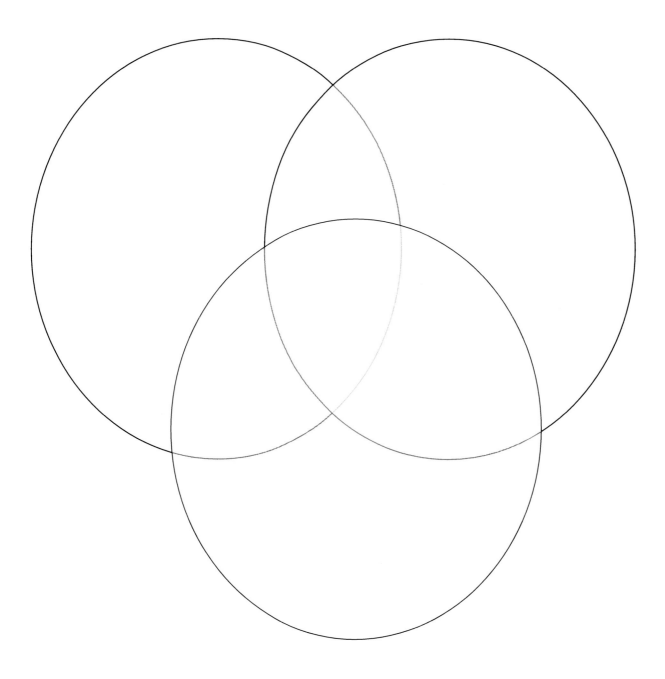

Analogy Organizer

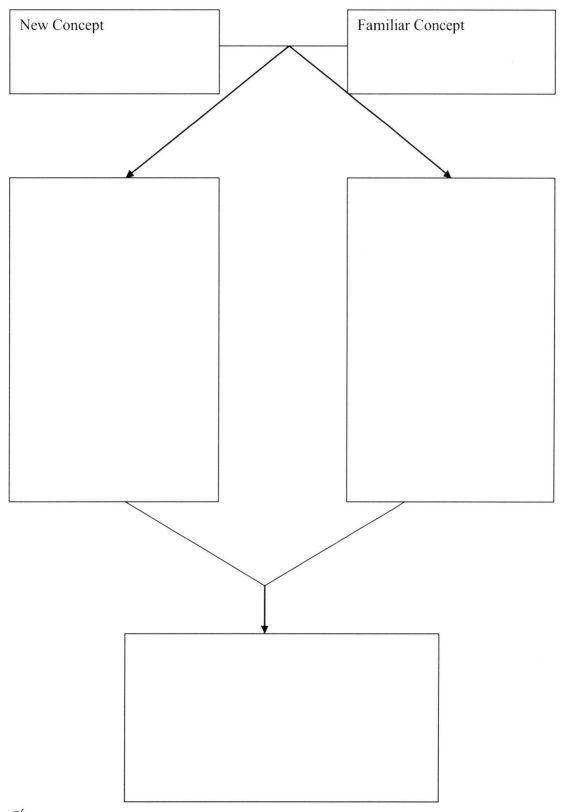

KWL Chart

What I Know	What I Want to Learn	What I Learned

6. Cooperative Learning

Cooperative Learning may be the single most misunderstood concept in education. Simply put, it is ***Learning Together in order to Perform Alone***.

- Cooperative Learning is not just group work.
- Cooperative learning is not one student doing the work for another.
- Cooperative learning is teacher-directed and structured.
- Students are in heterogeneous teams of 3-4 for a period of 3 to 6 weeks.
- Cooperative learning involves social, cognitive, and communication skill building.
- Culture-building activities are an essential part of cooperative learning.

Key Principles:

 Teamwork – creating a win-win spirit. Everyone is needed to do the tasks and when one wins, the team wins. The only competition in cooperative learning is against a class or team goal, not against another team or individual. In learning, everyone can win.

 Each person is responsible for his own performance. There are no group grades in cooperative learning. We learn together; I perform alone. I can only give a student a grade based on what he knows and can do, not on what someone else did or didn't know or do.

 All participate. Create equal participation by having students take turns or timing them. If you don't, one will dominate; one will do nothing. We have to teach teamwork.

 Maintain a high percentage of involvement. Create activities where the percentage of active involvement at one time is the highest possible. In pairs, it's 50%; in teams, it's 25%. Remember: the brain that works is the brain that learns!

Kagan Cooperative Learning describes these 4 principles of cooperative learning that are essential: **P-I-E-S**
- Positive Interdependence- creating a win-win spirit
- Individual Accountability-each person responsible for learning
- Equal Participation-involving all by taking turns or timing
- Simultaneous Interaction-the highest percentage of active involvement possible

Johnson and Johnson's elements of cooperative learning can be remembered with the mnemonic **PIGSFace:**
1. Positive Interdependence – sink or swim together
2. Individual and group accountability
3. Group Processing and reflection
4. Small group interpersonal skills
5. Face-to-face interaction – learning together

The Three-Step Interview on the next page is an example of a cooperative learning activity.

❧ Strategy – **Three-Step Interview**

Purpose: To gather and synthesize data and information from all students in the class on selected essential questions. To promote skills of listening, interviewing, writing, drawing, speaking, comparing, categorizing, synthesizing, and presenting.

Instructions: These instructions are for a class of 24. Make adjustments for larger or smaller groups.

Prepare the 6 essential questions you want students to use in the interviews. Make four copies of each question sheet. To make facilitation easier, use four different colors of paper, one for each question. For the last step, have a graphic organizer that has space for each team's report. Place the chairs/desks in 4 rows of 6 so that rows A & B face each other almost knee-to-knee and rows C & D face each other. Leave a side space of at least two feet between each chair so that the partners facing each other can hear without interference from those next to them. Place the colored sheets in the chairs so that the same colors start in the same position in each row. (Question 1 on green paper in row A is facing Question 1 on green paper in row B; question 2 on yellow paper in row A is facing question 2 on yellow paper in row B, etc.)

Begin: Ask students to bring a pen and their notebook for backing to write on; select a seat and give instructions below.

Row ∩ ∩ ∩ ∩ ∩ ∩ **A-**
Row ∪ ∪ ∪ ∪ ∪ ∪ **B-**

Row ∩ ∩ ∩ ∩ ∩ ∩ **C-**
Row ∪ ∪ ∪ ∪ ∪ ∪ **D-**

Procedure:

Step 1—The Interview
- ☑ You will be interviewing everyone in the row across from you one at a time, gathering data from responses to the questions on your sheet. You will keep the same sheet for the entire activity.
- ☑ Everyone with the same colored sheet has the same questions.
- ☑ At my signal, the people in rows A & C will have 2 minutes to ask the person facing them (rows B & D) the questions and record the responses in the space provided.
- ☑ The person across from you will then have 2 minutes to interview you and record your responses.
- ☑ After that, the people in rows A & C will stand up and shift one seat to the right. The person on the end will come to the empty seat at the other end.
- ☑ You will then repeat the process of interviewing the new partner, who will ask you a different question.
- ☑ This will be repeated until all have been interviewed and you are back facing your original partner.

Step 2—Processing the data
- ☑ You will next meet with everyone who had the same questions (same color) you had to compare responses.
- ☑ Take turns sharing the data you collected, listening for similarities.
- ☑ Discuss the data and find commonalities, categories, and themes.
- ☑ Write a summary statement of the key and supporting ideas.
- ☑ Prepare a chart that depicts your findings and be prepared to report out.

Step 3—Report
- ☑ Determine how you will make your 2-minute presentation involving everyone on your team.
- ☑ Report your findings in 2 minutes or less.
- ☑ Record the team's findings on the graphic organizer provided, comparing the summaries to your original ideas.

Teacher tips:
- ➢ I have used this activity with as few as 8 people (2 rows of people x 4 questions) and with as many as 110 (10 rows of people x 10 questions, with an observer in each group).
- ➢ Use a whistle or some other signal and a timer.
- ➢ If the time seems too long, adjust it.
- ➢ If you have an odd number, buddy people up.

Cooperative Strategies To Increase Involvement

The following strategies are brain compatible ways to check for understanding, involve all learners, and provide participants the opportunity to rehearse learning. Some of these strategies have been adapted from Johnson and Johnson CL and from *Kagan Cooperative Learning*. (www.kaganonline.com.)

Corners
- ☑ Announce 4 (more or less) categories that are on cards located in the corners.
- ☑ Tell class to think of response; write choices.
- ☑ Tell class to go to corners they chose.
- ☑ In pairs, assign topic to discuss, using partners share or Timed- Pair- Share.

Inside-Outside Circle
- ☑ Have class write a question on one side of a card and the answer on the back.
- ☑ Tell them to form a circle, facing in and number off 1-2-1-2.
- ☑ Tell the two's to move inside and face the #1's.
- ☑ Question / Answer Round: #1s Ask, #2s Answer; then #2s Ask, #1s Answer.
- ☑ Trade cards and have inside circle rotate to a new partner.

Line Ups
- ☑ Give the class a topic/sequence. (birthday, spelling words, number sequence, events)
- ☑ Ask them to line up in correct sequence.
- ☑ Process the activity by: talking with partner, making a graph, round robin share

Jigsaw
- ☑ Select the content to be learned: articles, chapters, problems, etc.
- ☑ Divide content into 4 equal parts.
- ☑ **Solo work**: Assign each teammate one of the parts to read, highlight, and make notes.
- ☑ Send teammates to **expert groups** (those from other teams who read the same part.)
- ☑ Expert groups **share and prepare** critical points, and each creates a visual to take back to teach.
- ☑ Teammates go back to their home teams where they will **teach** each other in order, while teammates take notes or fill in organizer.
- ☑ Whole group check: either ask questions randomly or give a short individual worksheet or quiz.

Thinking Levels Jigsaw
- ☑ Number team members 1-2-3-4.
- ☑ Team members move to same-number groups (all #1s together, etc.)
- ☑ Each group develops questions at the level assigned on the topic. (For example: #1s write remember-level questions, #2s write understand-level questions, #3s write application-level, and #4s write analysis-level questions, etc)
- ☑ Members return to their original team to answer questions together.

Rotating Role Round Robin
- ☑ Prepare cards with content questions – use lower and higher level questions.
- ☑ Step 1: #1 Fans the cards and says, "Pick a card, any card."
- ☑ Step 2: #2 Reads question (Give wait time; count to 5).
- ☑ Step 3: #3 Answers.
- ☑ Step 4: #4 Praise / Correct / Check
- ☑ Rotate and Repeat.

7. Setting Objectives and Providing Feedback

Objectives provide students with a direction for their learning. Feedback is a powerful practice for enhancing learning. Goals and objectives should be personalized and stated behaviorally. Feedback should be corrective and timely.

Strategies:
- Set specific learning goals at the beginning of each unit.
- Lead students in setting their own learning goals at the beginning of units.
- Provide feedback throughout the unit.
- Have students track their progress on learning goals.
- Provide summative feedback at the end of a unit.
- Have students assess themselves at the end of a unit.

Here is an activity that can be designed to include both setting objectives and providing feedback.

Rotating Feedback

Teams or individuals display projects or other work on charts or table areas. Other teams rotate through, giving feedback. Divide the class into teams according to the number of products to review. Teams prepare one chart with the group or individual work and post them around the room. Chart might include concepts learned, stories written, drawings, topics, issues, problems, etc. Students may write the aspect on which they wish to receive feedback.

Each team is numbered off and assigned to a chart to begin. Each team has a different colored marker (so you can monitor who is giving what feedback to whom.)

1. At your signal, each team begins reading or reviewing the work at a designated chart. Depending on the work, allow about 3-5 minutes at each chart.
2. Student #1 on each team is the scribe who **records** the team's feedback on the chart.
3. At the next signal, ask #1 to pass the marker to #2, who will be the new scribe. The teams **rotate** to the next chart. Teams **read and discuss** what the previous team(s) wrote, agreeing with a ✓, questioning with a **?**, and disagreeing with an **✗**. (Each team member can respond individually or the team can come to consensus and give one response.)
4. The team then brainstorms its responses and adds to the list.
5. At the signal, the team passes the marker, rotates, reads the new chart, responds, and adds to the list. Repeat until the teams are back at the chart where they started.
6. The teams have 4-5 minutes to review the feedback. The report out can be held as a gallery walk (where teams on their own preview the charts) or as a whole group activity.
7. Teams or individuals take the feedback, deciding what they wish to edit or add to their product.
8. Variations:
   Carousel Brainstorming: Students follow the same procedure to rotate through the charts, responding or brainstorming solutions to issues or problems.
   Rotating Review: Follow the same procedure except use topics on charts for review. As teams rotate, they list everything important about that topic in the time allotted.

8. Generating and Testing Hypotheses

This skill applies to a variety of tasks in many subjects. Students should be able to explain their hypotheses and conclusions.

Strategies:
- Problem solving
- Historical investigation
- System analysis
- Invention
- Inquiry
- Decision-making

Team Problem-Solving Activity with Class Input

This activity combines cooperative learning with generating and testing hypotheses.
- ☑ Divide the class into teams of 3-4 or into pairs. Each team decides what problem it will attempt to solve or what issue it will investigate. Teachers may choose to assign topics.
- ☑ Teams identify and write their goal on form provided. Legal size paper, at least.
- ☑ Teams brainstorm, describe, and list the barriers to solving the problem.
- ☑ Teams identify possible solutions and then hypothesize which solutions will work.
- ☑ Teams write one question on which they would like to receive input from the other teams.
- ☑ Teams then place the following items in a Ziploc bag or large envelope:
  - The form with their stated problem, barriers, solutions, and hypotheses
  - The specific question for input written on a large card
  - Role cards: leader, timekeeper, recorder, reporter
  - Rubber bands, paper clips, blank cards or scrap paper or sticky notes (lots!)
- ☑ Number the teams. Each team sends its packet to the next team in numerical order.
- ☑ Instruct the groups to take out the role cards and distribute them. They will keep these roles for the entire activity.

Process: Instructions
1. Leader reads the input question to his small group and then reads the problem, barriers, solutions, and hypotheses.
2. All team members **silently** brainstorm and respond to question on individual slips of paper. (one idea per sheet) (2-3 minutes)
3. Each reads his responses round robin. – (2 minutes)
4. Group selects the top 5 (or whatever number you choose) ideas. – (2 minutes)
5. Rubber band each of those ideas together. (Keep all of the cards.)
6. Clip the extra ideas together and put one rubber band around all of them.
7. Put everything back in the bag except the role cards.
8. On the facilitator's signal, pass the bag to the next group.
9. Repeat steps 1-5 **without** looking at previous group's responses. (8-9 min.)
10. Look at previous group's top five ideas and combine with yours. (3-5 min.)
11. Select five new top ideas. (2 min)
12. Rubber band the top five together.
13. Clip the extras together.
14. Put everything back in the bag except the role cards.
15. On the facilitator's signal, pass the bag to the next group.
16. Repeat steps 10-16 until groups have their original packet back.
17. Teams look at the top five categories and all the others. Select solutions to try or hypotheses to prove.
18. Teams try out the solutions.
19. Teams prepare to report on whether hypotheses were correct or not, along with the next steps.

9. Questions, Cues and Advance Organizers

These tools help students use what they already know about a topic to enhance further learning. These tools are used prior to new content to link previous learning and organize new learning. They should be used to focus on important concepts and ideas, not unusual information.

Strategies
➢ Graphic organizers, like KWL charts
➢ Guiding questions
➢ Folded paper manipulatives

Dinah Zike[17] termed those little student-made paper manipulates *Foldables* and changed the face of note-taking by increasing memory and creating fun for teachers and students across the country. By tapping into the modality strategies that work for students (and adults), these folded devices can be a learning insurance policy for those hard-to-reach tactile-kinesthetic learners. As with any strategy, it can be overused and become redundant. Remember: the brain loves novelty, so even a great new strategy can become old and boring if overused. See her resources for a thorough treatment of creating and using Foldables.

This strategy is very effective for note-taking, for creating non-linguistic representations, and for advance organizers. These can be notebook paper size or chart paper size.
Here are a few samples for you to incorporate into your lessons. I've selected ideas that connect to our curriculum attributes, to brain principles, and to Marzano's Categories of strategies.

⊙ Basic Ideas and instructions– Write your ideas beside each one.

Half-Books – created by folding paper in half, lengthwise (hotdog) or widthwise (hamburger).

Folded Books – created by folding paper in half twice, hot dog, then hamburger. It makes a booklet with four small pages and can be opened to show four more spaces.

Three-Quarter Books – created by cutting off the left tab of a two-tab book. Several can be glued together. Sketch or glue a graphic to the left; write questions on the right tabs with answers and information under the right tab.

Tab Books – created by hotdog-folding a paper in half and then a hamburger fold. Open the hamburger fold and cut along the crease to the fold. Tab books can have as many tabs as needed for the content. This is a great way to organize the "chunks" of content in a lesson or unit. **Concept Map Tab-Book** – these demonstrate relationships between ideas by dividing complex ideas into smaller parts.

---

[17] www.dinah.com

Pocket Books – created making a hamburger fold, opening it and folding up two inches along the lengthwise edge. Glue or staple the outer edges of the pockets. These look like smaller versions of pocket folders. This works well to show a topic of study or concept on the front of the booklet, with vocabulary, details, etc., on small cards in the pockets. This could be used as a KWL by having one pocket labeled What I Know and the other labeled Need to Know. As students master content, the cards are move from one pocket to the other.

Shutter Books – created by creasing the paper in a hamburger fold and then bringing the edges to the fold. This can be used for comparing, for charting. Other graphics and booklets could be glued to the shutter fold booklet or poster.

Tri-fold Books – created by folding paper into thirds. This works well when making charts with three columns, Venn diagrams, comparing or reporting on three people or events.

Layered Flipbook – created by stacking half as many sheets of paper as the topics needed. Stagger the pages so that the sheets are about one inch (or less depending on number of pages) apart. Fold the papers together so that all the tabs are the same distance apart when folded. Glue or staple the pages together. Use the tabs to label the topic; use the inside for details, vocabulary, and graphics.

Envelope – created by folding paper into envelope shape. Concepts can be labeled on the outside flaps with details on the inside, or this can be glued like a real envelope to hold cards with vocabulary or definitions on a topic.

"Blooming" Action Verbs for Questioning

The description of Bloom's Taxonomy is on pages 100-104. These verbs will assist you in developing questions at all levels.

KNOWING (Knowledge): Knowledge is defined as the remembering of previously learned material. This may involve the recall of a wide range of material, from specific facts to complete theories, but all that is required is the bringing to mind of the appropriate information. Knowledge represents the lowest level of learning outcomes in the cognitive domain.

RELATED ACTION VERBS

Acquire	Group	Name	Record
Choose	Identify	Outline	Repeat
Count	Indicate	Pick	Reproduce
Define	Know	Point	Select
Distinguish	Label	Quote	State
Draw	List	Read	Tabulate
Fill-in	Locate	Recall	Trace
Find	Match	Recite	Underline
Follow directions	Memorize	Recognize	Write

UNDERSTANDING (Comprehension): Comprehension is defined as the ability to grasp the meaning of material. This may be shown by translating material from one form to another (words to numbers), by interpreting material (explaining or summarizing), and by estimating future trends (predicting consequences or effects). These learning outcomes go one step beyond the simple remembering of material, and represent the lowest level of understanding.

RELATED ACTION VERBS

Account for	Draw	Group	Reorder
Associate	Estimate	Infer	Reorganize
Change	Expand	Illustrate	Represent
Classify	Explain	Interpolate	Retell
Conclude	Express in other	Interpret	Reword
Compare	terms	Measure	Rewrite
Contrast	Extend	Outline	Restate
Convert	Extrapolate	Paraphrase	Show
Demonstrate	Fill in	Predict	Simplify
Describe	Find	Prepare	Suggest
Determine	Generalize	Put in order	Summarize
Define	Give in own	Read	Trace (on map or chart)
Differentiate	words	Rearrange	Transform
Distinguish	Give examples	Recognize	Translate

APPLYING (Application): Application refers to the ability to use learned material in new and concrete situations. This may include the application of such things as rules, methods, concepts, principles, laws, and theories. Learning outcomes in this area require a higher level of understanding than those under comprehension.

RELATED ACTION VERBS

Apply	Discuss	Keep records	Produce
Calculate	Distinguish	Locate	Prove (in math)
Choose	between	(information)	Put into action
Classify	Employ	Make	Put to use
Collect information	Estimate	Manipulate	Put together
Complete	Examine	Model	Record
Compute	Expand	Modify	Relate
Construct	Experiment	Operate	Restructure
Construct using	Express in a	Organize	Select
Convert (in math)	discussion	Participate	Show
Differentiate	Find (implies	Perform (except	Solve
between	investigation)	in math or in	Track (in development,
Demonstrate	Generalize	public)	history, process)
Derive	Graph	Plan	Transfer
Determine	Illustrate	Practice	Translate
(calculate)	Interpret	Predict	Use
Develop	Interview	Prepare	Utilize
Discover	Investigate	Present	

ANALYZING (Analysis): Analysis refers to the ability to break down material into its component parts so that its organizational structure may be understood. This may be relationships between parts, and recognition of the organizational principles involved. Learning outcomes here represent a higher intellectual level than comprehension and application because they require an understanding of the content and the structural form of the material.

RELATED ACTION VERBS

Analyze	Differentiate	Identify	Search
Break down	Discover	Illustrate	Select
Categorize	Discriminate	Infer	Separate
Classify	Distinguish	Inspect	Simplify
Compare	Divide	Make inferences	Sort
Contrast	Draw conclusions	Order	Subdivide
Criticize	Examine	Outline	Survey
Debate	Formulate	Point out	Take apart
Deduce	Form	Put into	Transform
Detect	generalizations	(categories)	Uncover
Determine	Examine	Recognize	
Diagram	Group	Relate	

EVALUATING (Evaluation): Evaluation is concerned with the ability to judge the value of material (statement, novel, poem, research report) for a given purpose. The judgments are to be based on definite criteria. These may be internal criteria (organization) or external criteria (relevance to the purpose) and students may determine the criteria given them. Learning outcomes in this area are highest in the cognitive hierarchy because they contain elements of all of the other categories, plus conscious value judgments based on clearly defined criteria.

RELATED ACTION VERBS

Appraise	Criticize	Grade	Select
Argue	Critique	Judge	Standardize
Assess	Decide	Justify	Summarize
Award	Defend	Interpret	Support
Choose	Describe	Measure	Test
Compare	Determine	Rank	Validate
Conclude	Discriminate	Rate	Verify
Consider	Distinguish	Recommend	
Contrast	Evaluate	Relate	

CREATING (Synthesis): Synthesis refers to the ability to put parts together to form a new whole. This may involve the production of a unique communication (theme or speech), a plan of operations (research proposal), or a set of abstract relations (scheme for classifying information). Learning outcomes in this area stress creative behaviors, with major emphasis on the formation of new patterns or structures.

RELATED ACTION VERBS

Arrange	Devise	Originate	Rearrange
Blend	Develop	Organize	Reconstruct
Build	Document	Perform (in	Relate
Categorize	Explain	public)	Reorganize
Combine	Form	Plan	Revise
Compile	Formulate	Predict	Rewrite
Compose	Generalize	Prepare	Specify
Constitute	Generate	Prescribe	Suppose
Construct	Imagine	Present (an	Summarize
Create	Integrate	original report or	Synthesize
Deduce	Invent	work)	Tell
Derive	Make up	Produce	Transmit
Design	Modify	Propose	Write

Differentiation

Differentiation is a philosophy that enables teachers to plan strategically in order to reach the needs of diverse learners in classrooms today to achieve targeted standards. Differentiation is not a set of tools but a philosophy that a teacher embraces to reach the unique needs of every learner.
-Gayle H. Gregory and Carolyn Chapman, in *Differentiated Instructional Strategies*

Differentiation is an organized yet flexible way of proactively adjusting teaching and learning to meet kids where they are and help them achieve maximum growth as learners.
-Carol Ann Tomlinson, *The Differentiated Classroom*

Differentiated instruction considers where the learners are and offers challenging and appropriate options to achieve success for all students.

Carol Ann Tomlinson[18] suggests that there is not one right way to create a differentiated classroom; such classrooms are built on the premise that learners differ in important ways and that effective teachers begin where students are and move them to high levels of learning. Tomlinson says such effective teachers
- Engage students in instruction through different learning modalities, by appealing to differing interests, and by using varied rates of instruction, with varied degrees of complexity.
- Provide specific ways for each individual to learn as deeply and as quickly as possible.
- Work diligently to ensure that struggling, advanced, and in-between students think and work harder than they meant to and achieve more than they thought they could.

Tomlinson's Principles for Differentiated Classrooms:
- **The Teacher Focuses on the Essentials**
  - The teacher carefully designs instruction around the essential concepts, principles, and skills of each subject.
  - The teacher ensures that struggling students learn the essential concepts without getting bogged down in the peripheral and that advanced students are challenged to dig deeper rather than repeating what they already know.
- **The Teacher Attends to Student Differences**
  - The teacher unconditionally accepts students as they are and expects them to become all they can be.
- **Assessment and Instruction are Inseparable**
  - Assessment is formative, ongoing, and diagnostic. "It is today's means of understanding how to modify tomorrow's instruction….it has more to do with helping students grow than with cataloging their mistakes."
- **The Teacher Modifies Content, Process, and Products**
  - Teachers may adapt one or more of the curricular elements (content, process, products) based on one or more of the student characteristics (readiness, interest, learning profile) at any point in a lesson or unit.
- **All Students Participate in Respectful Work**
  - The teacher shows respect for learners by honoring both their commonalities and differences, not by treating them alike.
- **The Teacher and Students Collaborate in Learning**
  - The classroom is student-centered; students are the workers. Teachers coordinate time, space, materials, and activities.
- **The Teacher Balances Group and Individual Norms**
  - Assessment, instruction, feedback, and grading take into account both group and individual goals and norms.
- **The Teacher and Students Work Together Flexibly**
  - The teacher draws on a wide range of strategies that help focus on individuals, small groups, and the whole class.

---

[18] Tomlinson, Carol. (1999). ***The Differentiated Classroom: Responding to the Needs of All Learners.*** ASCD.

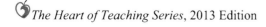

Effective Teachers:

Differentiate Content – focusing on the amount and essentials struggling students must learn; enriching for the advanced students.

Differentiate Instructional Strategies – using effective strategies in this chapter and applying knowledge of how the brain learns, multiple intelligences, levels of thought, cooperative learning.

Differentiate Assessment – varying the types and amounts of performance tasks and other assessment.

Application

Think of the three pillars of our *Teaching for Learning House*. Each of those walls can be differentiated and still be "load-bearing." This chapter offers several ways to differentiate instruction. Scan back through the chapter and highlight ideas for differentiation.

Use the nested organizer to brainstorm ways to differentiate the 3 aspects of the classroom.

CONTEXT - Environment

PROCESS – Instruction and Assessment

CONTENT – Knowledge and Skills

Reflect and discuss with a partner:

The teacher in a differentiated classroom is like a coach, because _____.

The *Why* Pillar

The most powerful single innovation that enhances achievement is feedback. The simplest prescription for improving education must be 'dollops' of feedback.
—John Hattie, from a review of 7,827 studies on learning and instruction

This is the ***results*** aspect of our coherent curriculum and aligned instruction.

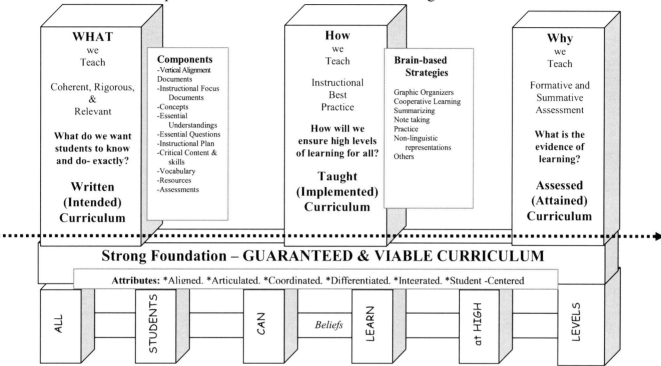

Assess comes from the Latin *assidere*, a word that literally means *to sit beside,* as in the one who sat beside the judge who evaluated and determined the amount of tax or levied a fine. Today it means **to evaluate and to determine standing or status, usually in reference to a standard.** With today's high-stakes, standards-based accountability systems, based on student performance on state or national tests, assessment can erroneously be thought of only in terms of the big, once-a-year "assessments."

Let's think of it here as **Measuring What Matters**—student learning. In this chapter we will talk mostly about classroom assessment and measuring <u>as</u> students are learning, rather than focusing on measuring the end result or district or state assessments.

Many times uninformed teachers and parents will complain that, "all schools do today is teach to the test." I would like to respond, "Good!..."or "I wish!" Think about it. If assessments (tests) measure the evidence of what students know and can do, don't we want teachers to teach to those targets? In order to be successful, all students should know what is expected for them to learn, and they should have the instructional opportunities to learn those things. DuFour says, "Schools may <u>teach more</u> than they test, but they should <u>test only</u> what they teach." Now, if a teacher were teaching the test and nothing else, we would all complain. When a valid assessment reflects what is to be learned, in an aligned curriculum, teachers teach to what will be tested.

❧ **Read the following statement and discuss with a partner:**
> *Used with skill, assessment can motivate the unmotivated, restore the desire to learn, and encourage students to keep learning, and it can actually create—not simply measure—student achievement.*
> -- Rick Stiggins

Organize Your Thinking

Complete the *K&W* on the KWL chart and use it to organize your thinking as you learn about classroom assessment:

What do you **KNOW** about Classroom Assessment?	What do you **WANT** to learn?	What have you **LEARNED**?

Classroom Assessment – Overview

Research indicates that the score a student receives on a test is more dependent on <u>who</u> scores the test and <u>how</u> they score it than it is on <u>what</u> the student knows and understands. (Robert Marzano)

Like most things in education, while classroom assessment is known to enhance student achievement, it only does so under certain conditions. Marzano summarizes those conditions with the following:

---

4 Generalizations about the Effectiveness of Classroom Assessment
1. Feedback from classroom assessments should provide students with a clear picture of their progress on learning goals and how they might improve
2. Feedback from classroom assessment should encourage students to improve.
3. Classroom assessment should be formative in nature.
4. Formative classroom assessments should be quite frequent.

ᘓ Read the following quote from Rick Stiggins in *Classrooms Assessment for Student Learning: Doing it Right, Using it Well*. Highlight the key concepts, looking for the **five indicators** of his *Sound Classroom Assessment Practice*.

> Quality classroom assessment produces accurate information that is used effectively to maximize student learning. Accurate information comes from clearly defining learning targets for students, clearly understanding the purposes for which information about student learning is being gathered, using a variety of assessment methods well, and designating assessments that cover important aspects of a learning target and that avoid circumstances that might bias results.
>
> Effective use includes using assessment results to plan instruction, using assessment information and materials to involve students in their own assessment, and communicating assessment results clearly and in a way tailored to the user's needs.

Stiggins' **Indicators of Sound Classroom Assessment Practice** are organized around these five questions:

Stiggins' Indicator	More about it…	My application…
1. Purpose: Why Assess? Assessment processes and results serve clear and appropriate **purposes.**		
2. Targets: Assess What? Assessments reflect clear and valued student learning **targets.**		
3. Assess How? Learning targets are translated into **assessments** that yield accurate results.		
4. Communicate How? Assessment results are managed well and **communicated** effectively.		
5. Involve Students How? **Students** are involved in their own assessment.		

ᘓ **As you study this section on assessment, fill in the chart with details and application.**

1. What is the Purpose of the Assessment?
Is it **before** instruction to assess prior knowledge and skill?
Is it **during** instruction to assess progress?
Is it **after** instruction to assess whether learning happened?

Stiggins and others classify the **two purposes for assessment** as

Summative Assessment = Assessment **OF** Learning	**Formative Assessment =** Assessment **FOR** Learning
Assessments used to determine how much students have learned at a particular point in time in order to report status and to plan for curricular changes. ♦ An example might be a state performance exam or teacher's semester exam. ♦ The data from summative assessments is valuable for future curriculum planning—for identifying gaps, but is of little value in affecting the present learning of the one tested. ♦ Measures many things infrequently.	All activities undertaken by teachers and by their students that provide information to be used as feedback to modify the teaching and learning activities in which they engage. (Black & Wiliam) ♦ An example could be a district-wide benchmark, a grade-level common assessment, student-teacher conference, or a student's self-assessment. ♦ Measures a few things frequently.

The determining factor of whether it is formative or summative is how the data is used.

Generally, *formative assessment occurs <u>while</u> knowledge is being learned; summative assessment occurs at the <u>end</u> of a learning episode.* (Marzano)

The following analogy from Stiggins is an easy way to understand the difference:
<u>Summative</u> is to <u>Formative</u> as <u>Autopsy</u> is to <u>Checkup</u>.

Data from an autopsy, while important in learning why someone died and useful in preventing future deaths of others, has zero impact on the health and wellness of the victim.

Formative Assessment
- Formative Assessment is the gathering of information in order to adjust our behavior to improve student learning.
- Formative classroom assessment is **ongoing** – beginning immediately within a learning episode and spanning its entire duration. It can be **formal** (paper-pencil test) or **informal** (discussion, observation). It is this type of assessment that has a powerful impact on student learning.
- Assessment expert W. James Popham, in his book, *Transformative Assessment*, defines formative assessment formally and succinctly in the following ways:
- *Formative assessment is a planned process in which assessment-elicited evidence of students' status is used by teachers to adjust their ongoing instructional procedures or by students to adjust their current learning tactics.*

- Or plainly:
- *Formative assessment is a planned process in which **teachers** or **students** use assessment-based evidence to **adjust** what they are currently doing.*

To use our bus example (loosely): It is the difference in making sure students stay <u>on the bus</u> during the entire trip or waiting until the end of the trip to see if they are on the <u>bus and have finished the trip</u>.

2. **Designing Assessment**
What is being assessed? What do grades represent?

In his research, Marzano describes one of the problems with curriculum is that there is too much content and there is a lack of **unidimensionality**. Assessments tend to give one grade on an assignment or test that represents multiple learning targets. That grade doesn't necessarily represent a student's mastery of the various learning targets.

"**Unidimensionality** means that a single score on a test represents a single dimension or trait that has been assessed." (Marzano)

Example - Imagine that an art student who is learning about Impressionism is required to: <u>understand</u> vocabulary and historical events, <u>identify</u> famous works of art and the artists, <u>describe</u> the characteristics of the method, and <u>produce</u> an example of impressionistic art. There are at least *four* different **dimensions** in the learning requirements. How could one grade on a test show whether the student mastered each of the dimensions and to what degree each was mastered?

❧ **Practice:**

1. Look at this high school geography standard and <u>underline</u> the unique knowledge and skills. How many "dimensions" would be taught and assessed? What would an assessment look like?

> Geography. The student understands the concept of region as an area of Earth's surface with related geographic characteristics. The student is expected to:
> - (A) identify physical and/or human factors such as climate, vegetation, language, trade networks, political units, river systems, and religion that constitute a region; and
> - (B) describe different types of regions, including formal, functional, and perceptual regions.

2. What would the following geography assessments communicate to a student who is supposed to be able <u>to know the countries and capitals</u> and to <u>identify features on a map</u>? On which of the two dimensions has the student shown mastery? Does the scoring method communicate that? On which dimension does the student need tutoring/reteaching?

Sample 1   **60**

Geography Test – Unit 3 – Europe
Fill in the blank with the country's capital city.

1. France *Paris*
2. Spain *Madrid*
3. Italy *Rome*
4. Austria *Australia (ha-ha)* **X**
5. Belgium *Brussels*
6. Norway *Oslo*

Identify the following features on the map.
- Rhine River   <u>32</u> **X**
- Alps   <u>27</u>
- English Channel   <u>19</u> **X**
- Mediterranean Sea   <u>23</u> **X**

---

3. Look at the difference in Sample 2 at the validity of the score when the teacher reorganizes the assessment to align with the principle of unidimensionality. This method of scoring informs student and teacher regarding instruction.

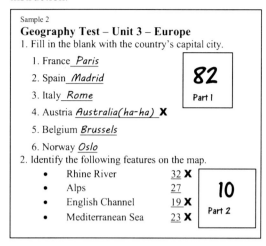

4. The teacher might want to communicate to students whether they have reached mastery or have "not yet." Thus, the scoring might look like Sample 3. The student and teacher both know the targets that have been mastered and those for which tutoring are needed.

5. The teacher might also have pre-determined that identifying features on a map is more important than matching countries and capitals and assign different value to the two dimensions. Instead of each question being worth 10% of the total grade, the mapping items are worth 80% of the grade and the fill-in-the-blank are worth 20%, making the grade on Part One a 97.

❁ **Application:** Design an assessment using the Blueprint. Decide the following:
- Which targets will be assessed (dimensions) based on the learning objectives?
- What value will be assigned to each?
- How many questions in each dimension?   (We will add the method later.)

Common Assessment Blueprint			
Key Understandings/ Learning Objectives	Number of Items	% of total	Assessment Method

3. Assessment Methods

How do you know they know? How are you going to evaluate student learning? What do they know and what can they do? There are many choices of assessment methods. Whether it is done with paper and pencil or on a computer, objective testing is a quick and easy way to assess knowledge and comprehension. However, it is not always the best way to really know whether learning is happening and has happened. The method needs to be appropriate for the learning target and the level of skill and knowledge required. To make any type of test more valid, vary the types of questions, including diagrams, writing, and examples instead of always using multiple choice and true-false.

Here are the methods that Stiggins[19] suggests with some examples. See his book for a thorough treatment of each method.

- Selected response (multiple choice, fill-in-blank, matching)
- Extended written response (essay)
- Performance assessment (product, skill performance)
- Personal/ oral communication (interview, portfolio presentation, performance)

Think back to the art example on page 165. This chart is just a sample that indicates which methods would be more appropriate for each learning expectation. Some could fit more than one method. The teacher can design the assessments with the appropriate methods in mind.

Selected Response Multiple choice, fill-in-blank, etc.)	Extended Written Response	Performance Assessment	Personal/Oral Communication
understand vocabulary and historical events	describe the characteristics of the method	produce an example of impressionistic art	identify famous works of art and the artists

Working with Multiple Choice Questions
Since much of the testing today is in multiple choice format, here are a few reminders as you design student assessments.

A multiple choice item consists of **three parts**: 1. The stem (question) 2. The key (correct answer) 3. The distracters (plausible choices)	Factors to consider for the **stem**: • Match the question to the standard • Use clear wording • Ask a full question • Highlight critical words • Have a colleague review	Factors to consider for the responses (correct and distracters): • Be as brief as possible • Use *always, never, all of the above, none of the above* sparingly and purposefully • Make responses grammatically parallel

Examples (from TAKS release tests):
1. The U.S. Constitution's establishment of the executive, legislative, and judicial branches of government most clearly reflects which principle?
A Popular sovereignty
B Individual rights
C Separation of powers
D Federalism

1. What is the value of the expression $5 + 5(9 \div 3)^2$?
A 35 **C** 50
B 90 **D** 230

[19] Stiggins, R. (2006) *Classroom Assessment for Student Learning: Doing it Right—Using it Well*. ETS.

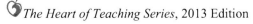

Performance Assessments

Performance assessment is assessment that is based on observation and judgment. Learners engage in an activity that requires them to apply a performance skill or create a product and we judge its quality.[20] When learners can perform the skill, we feel that learning has happened. We may also need to know whether they can perform the skills in a variety of conditions, at a later time, or under different circumstances.

A quality performance assessment has two parts:

1. **Performance Tasks** – the activities or exercises (reflecting a skill) in which learners engage that will be observed and judged for quality. Below is an example:

Task	Performance Criteria
Making a presentation in speech class	Body Language: • Strong, even stance with feet hip-width apart; no swaying, slumping, or pacing • Hands relaxed at side, except when making purposeful gesture; no flailing or playing with clothing or items; no hands in pockets • Eye contact with individuals in various places in the audience for 3-5 seconds, no scanning or staring Tone: • Tonal variety; not flat or monotone • Pacing variety; not too fast or slow • Pauses used for emphasis and thinking; no fillers Presentation Method • Strong opening with clear purpose statement • Transitions and connections between points • Strong closing with concluding statement or call to action

2. **Scoring guide showing the performance criteria** – the basis for judging the quality of the performance on the task, the standards.

Examples:
A scoring guide that awards points for certain parts of the performance or task
A rubric which describes levels of quality of the product or performance

Rubrics:

Rubrics are tools that formalize the process of evaluation. They can be summative and formative.
Simple steps in creating a rubric:
1. Make a list of the **desired characteristics** (or features) based on what you want to measure. There is no set number. These are based on what you want your students to be able to do. (Look at the criteria above for making a presentation.)
2. Decide on the **levels of quality**: Specifically describe what excellent, above average, average, and below average (or whatever terms you use) look like.
3. Assign a **weight** to each criterion.
4. Re-evaluate after each use to modify it.

---

[20] Rick Stiggins. (2006) *Classroom Assessment for Student Learning: Doing it Right—Using it Well*. Educational Testing Service.

Here is a simple example of a rubric for evaluating the speaker, using effective presentation skills:

		Body Language	**Vocal factors**	**Presentation Format**
Excellent	4	Strong stance, good eye contact with individuals in audience; hand gestures were purposeful; there were no distracting movements	Vibrant tone; pace was right; pauses were purposeful; there were no distracting fillers	Engaging opening Clear and concise statement of purpose Transitions & connections Purposeful closure
Above average	3	Mostly strong stance, good eye contact with audience; hand gestures were mostly purposeful; there were few distracting movements	Interesting tone; pace was slightly too fast or slow; pauses were somewhat short; there were few distracting fillers	Interesting opening Somewhat clear and concise statement of purpose Good transitions & connections Interesting closure
Average	2	Fairly weak stance, little eye contact with audience; hand gestures were not purposeful; there were some distracting movements	Little inflection in tone; pacing was at times good; pauses had some distracting fillers	Adequate opening Fairly clear statement of purpose Some transitions & connections Adequate closure
Below Average	1	Weak stance, little or no eye contact with audience; hand gestures were distracting; there were many distracting movements	Monotone; poor pacing; pauses had distracting fillers	Weak opening Weak or no statement of purpose Weak or no transitions & connections Weak or no closure

Practice:
Design a performance assessment (task, criteria, and scoring guide) for a lesson you teach.

Portfolios
A portfolio is a collection of artifacts to help students, teachers and others understand the depth, progress, and process of learning. It could represent an entire year of learning or a specific topic or unit. The best portfolios are created, presented, and assessed by the learner, not the teacher.

There are many types of portfolios for various purposes, including
- Growth portfolios – showing progress toward a standard or goal
- Project portfolios – showing the processes and product for a specific project

Portfolio contents (artifacts) vary depending on the type and purpose, but at the least would include
- Evidence samples – these are included based on the intended purpose and learning targets
- Goals or targets
- Journal or log – capturing growth or progress
- Self-reflection rubric

What might the portfolio of the above presenter contain?

What might the portfolio of the art student mentioned earlier contain?

Go back to your blueprint (p. 166) and add the assessment method to your plan.

Culminating Performance Sample

A **Culminating Performance** is an excellent example of a quality assessment and can be both formative and summative in design. It can be used at the end of a lesson or a unit.

A Culminating Performance provides **evidence** as it answers the big question, "What do I want my students to know, understand, and be able to do as a result of this unit of study?"

Lynne Erickson, in *Concept-based Curriculum and Instruction*, suggests using these three components as you design the assessment.

What – Begin with a higher-level cognitive verb "analyze, evaluate, investigate, etc." Tie it directly to the theme or conceptual topic.
Example: "Analyze the impact of Anglo migration into Texas from 1830 to 1900."

Why – Complete the *What?* statement by forcing the thinking beyond the topic to the significance or importance. Use a stem like, "…in order to…"
Example: "…in order to understand how cultures impact geography and how geography impacts cultures."

How – Begin a new sentence that frames how you want students to demonstrate their understanding of the *Why?* statement. If you want to measure deep understanding, the *How?* statement needs to demonstrate the *Why?*, not just the knowledge of facts in the *What?* statement. Use a stem like, "Students will demonstrate their understanding by…"
Example: "Students will demonstrate their understanding by selecting one side of the issue and prepare to debate which had the greater impact on the other: geography or culture. Students will present final findings by writing an essay that describes the reciprocal impact of geography and culture in Texas." (Notice the <u>process</u> and <u>product</u>.)

Teachers and students assess the Culminating Performance according to pre-defined criteria and a scaled set of performance indicators (a rubric).

Practice: Design a Culminating Performance for a lesson or unit you will teach.

What:

Why:

How:

Common Formative Assessments

"One of the most powerful, high-leverage strategies for improving student learning available to schools is the creation of frequent, common, high-quality formative assessments by teachers who are working collaboratively to help a group of students develop agreed upon knowledge and skills…and such assessments serve a distinctly different purpose than the state tests that have become the norm in North America..." (Rick DuFour, citing the experts: Fullen, Hargreaves & Fink, Reeves, Schmoker, and Stiggins, in *Learning by Doing*)

Common assessments
☑ Are created collaboratively by a team of teachers responsible for the same grade level or subject.
☑ Are given frequently enough to allow adjustments in teaching and student learning.
☑ Can be used to identify students who need more time and support.
☑ Can indicate which teaching strategies are and are not working.
☑ Can expose areas of concern with curriculum alignment and articulation.
☑ Generate improvement goals for individual teachers and for the team.

Benefits of Common assessments
☑ Ensuring that all students have access to the essential curriculum.
☑ Assessing student work according to the same standards.
☑ Reflecting whether the guaranteed curriculum is being taught and learned.
☑ Informing individual teachers of the effectiveness of their practice.
☑ Facilitating a systemic response to struggling students.

Using the Data – Data Teams
In *Common Formative Assessment*, Larry Ainsworth offers a five-step process for data team meetings based on his work and the work of others, including Doug Reeves and Mike Schmoker:
☑ Definition - A **Data Team** is defined as a grade-level or department team of educators comprised of teachers who all teach the same content standards to their students and who meet regularly for the express purpose of analyzing common assessment data. Teams meet at least twice in a grading/unit period.
☑ Function - Data teams apply the five-step process to their common formative *pre*-assessment results in order to improve student performance on their common formative *post*-assessments.
☑ **Five Steps** for the first **Data Team Meeting**:
1. **Chart the data:** Record the number and percentage of students who met or exceeded and those who did not meet the established proficiency score on the common pre-assessment.
2. **Analyze the results**: Identify strengths and areas of need.
3. **Set the Goal:** What is the specifically worded goal statement that represents achievable student improvements?
4. **Select Effective Teaching Strategies**: What are the most effective strategies to achieve the goal?
5. **Determine the results indicators**: How will the effectiveness of the instructional strategies be determined?
☑ These five steps culminate in the development of an action plan and lead to the second data team meeting to evaluate the post-assessment results to see if their goal has been met.

Data Team Action Plan

Questions to Address	Action Steps	✓
What needs to be done by each teacher to implement the selected instructional strategies?		
What resources, instructional materials, and additional collaboration time are needed?		
How will we further differentiate the delivery of our instructional strategies for non-proficient students?		
What informal classroom checks for progress need to be included, and when will they be done?		
Whom do we go to for help if we encounter problems implementing the identified strategies?		
What additional help or support do we need from our administration?		

Group Data Team Scoring Rubric Sample

Percentage Scale	4-point rubric score	Teacher 1 Number of students	Teacher 1 % of students	Teacher 2 Number of students	Teacher 2 % of students	Teacher 3 Number of students	Teacher 3 % of students	Team Totals
Above Proficient 90-100 %	4							
Proficient 80-89%	3							
Almost Proficient 70-79%	2							
Below 70%	1							

Process:
Plan your data team and meetings.

ASSESSMENT: PAST, PRESENT, and FUTURE

The Past

Benjamin Bloom's work included a strategy developed in the 1970s which he called ***Mastery Learning***. This strategy has teachers organize the important concepts and skills into learning units. After teachers taught these units using effective strategies, they administered a formative assessment that identified what students had learned and where they needed extra help. After corrective activities, students took another parallel assessment to see whether the correctives were successful in helping students learn. Research continues to verify the validity of Bloom's work.

The Present

Thomas Guskey and others have built upon Bloom's work in developing today's instructional models and interventions. These are the elements of Guskey's ***Mastery Learning***[21]:

1. **A diagnostic pre-assessment with pre-teaching**
   - Direct teaching of the concepts and skills (where deficit) to ensure success in lessons
2. **High quality, group-based initial instruction**
   - Instruction that is high-quality, developmentally appropriate, and differentiated
3. **Monitoring progress through regular formative assessment**
   - To monitor and give students prescriptive feedback
   - They measure the most important learning goals
4. **High quality corrective instruction**
   - Not just "reteaching," but different teaching—small group, individual, differentiated
5. **Second parallel formative assessment**
6. **Enrichment or extension activities**
   - Valuable, challenging, rewarding activities for learners who master material early

The Future

What do we want our children to KNOW, to BE ABLE TO DO, and to BECOME?
The question doesn't change…only the methods.

---

[21] Guskey, Thomas R. Lessons of Mastery Learning. ***Educational Leadership***. October 2010. 52-57.

Chapter Review...

Use specific content from this chapter to create the following analogies:

Effective instruction is like a hammer because...

Effective instruction is like a saw because...

Effective instruction is like pliers because...

Effective instruction is like a wrench because...

Effective instruction is like a level because...

Effective instruction is like a _____ because...

Discussion:
What are the most important concepts to remember from this chapter?

Research
A Comprehensive List of Strategies that Relate to Effective Teaching
(Robert Marzano)

I. CONTENT

A. Lessons Involving New Content
STRATEGY
1. Identifying critical information (e.g., the teacher provides cues as to which information is important) **A&S**
2. Organizing students to interact with new knowledge (e.g., the teacher organizes students into dyads or triads to discuss small chunks of content) **CITW**
3. Previewing new content (e.g., the teacher uses strategies such as: K-W-L, advance organizers, preview questions) **CITW**
4. Chunking content into "digestible bites" (e.g., the teacher presents content in small portions that are tailored to students' levels of understanding) **A&S**
5. Group processing of new information (e.g., after each chunk of information, the teacher asks students to summarize and clarify what they have experienced) **CITW**
6. Elaborating on new information (e.g., the teacher asks questions that require students to make and defend inferences) **CITW**
7. Recording and representing knowledge (e.g., the teacher asks students to summarize, take notes, or use nonlinguistic representations) **CITW**
8. Reflecting on learning (e.g., the teacher asks students to reflect on what they understand or what they are still confused about) **CAGTW**

B. Lessons Involving Practicing and Deepening Content That Has Been Previously Addressed
STRATEGY
9. Reviewing content (e.g., the teacher briefly reviews related content previously addressed) **CITW**
10. Organizing students to practice and deepen knowledge (e.g., the teacher organizes students into groups designed to review information or practice skills) **CITW**
11. Practicing skills, strategies, and processes (the teacher uses massed and distributed practice) **CITW**
12. Examining similarities and differences (e.g., the teacher engages students in comparing, classifying, creating analogies and metaphors) **CITW**
13. Examining errors in reasoning (e.g., the teacher asks students to examine informal fallacies, propaganda, bias) **A&S**
14. Using homework (e.g., the teacher uses homework for independent practice or to elaborate on information) **CITW**
15. Revising knowledge (e.g., the teacher asks students to revise entries in notebooks to clarify and add to previous information) **CITW**

C. Lessons Involving Cognitively Complex Tasks (Generating and Testing Hypotheses)
STRATEGY
16. Organizing students for cognitively complex tasks (e.g., the teacher organizes students into small groups to facilitate cognitively complex tasks) **CITW**
17. Engaging students in cognitively complex tasks (e.g., the teacher engages students in decision-making tasks, problem-solving tasks, experimental inquiry tasks, investigation tasks) **CITW**
18. Providing resources and guidance (e.g., the teacher makes resources available that are specific to cognitively complex tasks and helps students execute such tasks) **A&S**

II. ROUTINE ACTIVITIES

D. Communicating Learning Goals, Tracking Student Progress, and Celebrating Success
STRATEGY
19. Providing clear learning goals and scales to measure those goals (e.g., the teacher provides or reminds students about a specific learning goal) **CAGTW** 20. Tracking student progress (e.g., using formative assessment, the teacher helps students chart their individual and group progress on a learning goal) **CAGTW**
21. Celebrating student success (e.g., the teacher helps student acknowledge and celebrate current status on a learning goal as well as knowledge gain) **CAGTW, CITW**

E. Establishing and Maintaining Classroom Rules and Procedures
STRATEGY
22. Establishing classroom routines (e.g., the teacher reminds students of a rule or procedure or establishes a new rule or procedure) **CMTW**
23. Organizing the physical layout of the classroom for learning (e.g., the teacher organizes materials, traffic patterns, and displays to enhance learning) **CMTW**

III. BEHAVIORS THAT ARE ENACTED ON THE SPOT AS SITUATIONS OCCUR

F. Engaging Students
STRATEGY
24. Noticing and reacting when students are not engaged (e.g., the teacher scans the classroom to monitor students' level of engagement) **CMTW**
25. Using academic games (e.g., when students are not engaged, the teacher uses adaptations of popular games to reengage them and focus their attention on academic content) **A&S**
26. Managing response rates during questioning (e.g., the teacher uses strategies to ensure that multiple students respond to questions such as with response cards, response chaining, voting technologies) **A&S**
27. Using physical movement (e.g., the teacher uses strategies that require students to move physically such as "vote with your feet, " and physical reenactments of content) **CMTW**
28. Maintaining a lively pace (e.g., the teacher slows and quickens the pace of instruction in such a way as to enhance engagement) **CMTW**
29. Demonstrating intensity and enthusiasm (e.g., the teacher uses verbal and nonverbal signals that he or she is enthusiastic about the content) **CMTW**
30. Using friendly controversy (e.g., the teacher uses techniques that require students to take and defend a position about content) **A&S**
31. Providing opportunities for students to talk about themselves (e.g., the teacher uses techniques that allow students to relate content to their personal lives and interests) **CMTW**
32. Presenting unusual information (e.g., the teacher provides or encourages the identification of intriguing information about the content) **A&S**

G. Recognizing Adherence and Lack of Adherence to Classroom Rules and Procedures
STRATEGY
33. Demonstrating "withitness" (e.g., the teacher is aware of variations in student behavior that might indicate potential disruptions and attends to them immediately) **CMTW**
34. Applying consequences (e.g., the teacher applies consequences to lack of adherence to rules and procedures consistently and fairly) **CMTW**
35. Acknowledging adherence to rules and procedures (e.g., the teacher acknowledges adherence to rules and procedures consistently and fairly) **CMTW**

H. Maintaining Effective Relationships with Students
STRATEGY
36. Understanding students' interests and backgrounds (e.g., the teacher seeks out knowledge about students and uses that knowledge to engage in informal, friendly discussions with students) **CMTW**
37. Using behaviors that indicate affection for students (e.g., the teacher uses humor and friendly banter appropriately with students) **CMTW**
38. Displaying objectivity and control (e.g., the teacher behaves in ways that indicate he or she does not take infractions personally) **CMTW**

I. Communicating High Expectations
STRATEGY
39. Demonstrating value and respect for low-expectancy students (e.g., the teacher demonstrates the same positive affective tone with low-expectancy students as with high-expectancy students) **A&S**
40. Asking questions of low-expectancy students (e.g., the teacher asks questions of low-expectancy students with the same frequency and level of difficulty as with high-expectancy students) **A&S**
41. Probing incorrect answers with low-expectancy students (e.g., the teacher inquires into incorrect answers with low-expectancy students with the same depth and rigor as with high-expectancy students) **A&S**

© Robert J. Marzano (2009)
CITW: addressed in *Classroom Instruction That Works* (Marzano, Pickering, and Pol- lock 2001). **CMTW:** addressed in *Classroom Management That Works* (Marzano, Pickering, and Marzano 2003). **CAGTW:** addressed in *Classroom Assessment and Grading That Works* (Marzano 2006). **A&S:** addressed in *The Art and Science of Teaching* (Marzano 2007) but not addressed in CITW, CMTW, or CAGTW.

Chapter 7
Working With Parents and Families

I dreamed I stood in a studio and watched two sculptors there.
The clay they used was a young child's mind and they fashioned it with care.

One was the teacher—the tools he used were books, music, and art.
The other, a parent, worked with a guiding hand and a gentle, loving heart.

Day after day the teacher toiled with touch that was deft and sure.
While the parent labored by his side and polished and smoothed it o'er.

And when at last their task was done, they were proud of what they had wrought.
For the things they had molded into the child could neither be sold nor bought.

And each agreed they would have failed if each had worked alone.
For behind the teacher stood the school and behind the parent, the home.

--Author unknown

  Effective teachers pursue partnerships with parents and families in a professional manner for the benefit of students.

 Developing Positive Partnerships with Parents and Families
- What do I need to know about my students' families?
- How can I involve parents in a positive way?
- How can I keep the student's best interest in focus?
- How do I work with challenging parents?

Communicating with Parents and Families
- How will I develop an effective, proactive system of communicating with parents and families?
- How will I prepare for conferencing with parents and families in a positive, respectful, and confident manner?
- Do I know how to use effective communication skills in both pleasant and difficult conversations?

My Learning Goals:

Ideas I want to further explore:

Developing Positive Partnerships with Parents and Families

Preparing for Success
Here are some questions to get you started.
- ☑ What do I need to know about the families of my students?
- ☑ How can I involve parents in a positive way?
- ☑ What do I need to remember about dealing with parents?
- ☑ How will I first contact parents to inform them about my class?

It is important to know about the cultural, social, and economic makeup of the families in your school. You can assume that all families want the best for their children, even if they don't know how to show it. There are exceptions, but if we work from the premise that they care, we have a better chance of a win-win situation with parents. Because most parents love their children unconditionally, they usually cannot be objective about them. They will almost always be defensive about them. And if they think you might hurt them, they can become offensive. As a parent and grandparent, I am not always a normal, rational person about those I love; neither will the parents be of the children you teach. We must let parents know we have their child's best interest at heart at all times—all the children. One thing you cannot assume is that your students all live in families like yours or like those of other children.

Positive early communication with parents is essential.
- ☑ The earlier, the better! If the first contact with parents is positive and they understand who you are and what your expectations are, they are more likely to be supportive when you need to contact them with a problem.

- ☑ For elementary teachers, it is a wonderful idea to send a card or note to the parents and/or students before school starts, if possible. The week before my 5-year-old granddaughter started kindergarten, she received a postcard from her teacher. She taped it to her bedroom wall and displayed it to every visitor. It was her personal welcome to school from her teacher. Her parents were very impressed.

- ☑ For secondary teachers, it is usually impossible to send out a note before school starts. You can, however, have a letter prepared to go home with students on the first day to be signed and returned or an email if that is appropriate at your school. Be very careful about what is said and what the form of the letter or email is. Have your mentor or another teacher read it so that there are not any mistakes or misinformation. Nothing could be worse than a parent receiving a letter with misspelled words or grammatical errors. If you have a teacher webpage on your school's site, you could refer them there. Use great caution with electronic communication, whether with email, websites, or social media! This first communication to parents might have some of the following information:
  - o Welcoming information introducing yourself
  - o Goals for the student's learning
  - o Rules and procedures
  - o Instructional materials
  - o Invitation to visit or conference

Prepare for parents coming to school.

☑ Many schools offer opportunities for parents to visit their child's school and meet the staff. Elementary schools usually have a "Meet the Teacher" night the evening before the first day. Secondary schools often host a "Back to School" night a few weeks into the first semester. Whatever the case, be prepared. It is also important to notice which parents did not attend. There could be a variety of reasons; but it will help you to take notice of parent involvement early.

☑ Tips for "Meet the Teacher" night
  - Have an agenda, no "winging it."
  - Smile!
  - Dress like an adult; look and sound professional—overdo rather than underdo!
  - Explain your expectations, rules and procedures in light of your goals for your students, not as a drill sergeant.
  - Be confident and enthusiastic, not defensive and fearful.
  - Explain how they can help and how they may contact you.
  - Never apologize for being a new teacher.
  - Have a conference sign-up sheet available.

Respect

When dealing with parents, ALWAYS show professionalism and respect, even if the parent doesn't.

☑ General ideas for meeting parents:
  - Listen more than talk.
  - Be positive and hopeful.
  - Act confident, yet humble, not a know-it-all.
  - Avoid education jargon.
  - Involve parents in your excitement about your class.
  - Never promise anything you cannot do.
  - Never promise anything the school cannot do. It's always okay to say you need to check on something before you can answer.

What Parents Expect:

Author Lisa Feder-Feitel asked educators nation-wide to list what new teachers need to know to meet parents' expectations.

☑ She offers this top ten list. Parents need teachers to
  1. Know my child
  2. Set up clear expectations
  3. Know your curriculum
  4. Be available and keep me informed
  5. Let me know how I can help
  6. Provide a safe learning environment
  7. Promote success for my child
  8. Provide fair and consistent discipline
  9. Alert me if my child is struggling
  10. Ask my advice about my child

I would give you this advice: Treat each child as you would like a teacher to treat your own child, every day—good days and bad days. You can't go wrong following this Golden Rule.

Working With Different Kinds of Parents:

You will encounter a variety of types of parents and situations, both positive and negative. As with children, there is not one solution or formula for success. There are, however, some principles which will be helpful. Again…when dealing with parents, ALWAYS show **professionalism and respect**, even if the parent doesn't…especially if the parent doesn't.

Types of parents you may encounter:

☑ The <u>Over-involved</u> parent (sometimes called the "helicopter" parent—always hovering)
- Won't leave your classroom
- Wants to tell you how to teach
- Suggestions:
  - Give them specific tasks and times for them.
  - Meet them at the door.
  - Involve them in tasks away from the room.
  - Seek help from the office or your mentor.

☑ The Under-involved parent
- Never shows up for conferences
- Won't return calls or forms
- Suggestions
  - Document accurately and continue to try to contact.
  - Don't give up; keep trying.
  - Don't punish the child for his parent.

☑ The Over-familiar parent
- Wants to be your best friend, calls you by first name
- Calls you at home inappropriately
- Wants personal information
- Suggestions:
  - Be professional.
  - Call that person by Mr. / Mrs. in front of children and ask for the same.
  - Never give any information to a parent about anyone other than his child.
  - Avoid rumors and gossip.
  - Let them know when your conference period is for calls.

☑ The Over-impressed parent
- Thinks his child deserves special treatment or privileges
- Has an unrealistic view of his child
- Suggestions:
  - Listen, but be clear about standards for all children.
  - Send home enrichment work.
  - Give parent areas to assist child.

☑ The Over-to-you parent
- Blames any problem the child has on you
- Insists you are the only teacher the child has a problem with
- Wants you to solve all social and academic problems
- Suggestions:
  - Meet with parent with other teachers / team.
  - Document accurately.
  - Have colleagues observe student.

☑ The Overwhelmed parent or guardian
- May be single, unemployed, over employed, ill, etc.
- Suggestions:
  - Be compassionate!
  - Modify schedule to accommodate parent if possible.
  - Tell parent how to help.

Communicating with Parents and Families

☑ **General Conferencing tips**
- Sit in an arrangement where you are not behind your desk and the parent is not in a child's desk.
- Be friendly and make the parent feel welcome, not as if he or she is in trouble.
- Make the first statement about the student a positive one—even if you have to dig. Be sincere.
- Make clear the purpose of the conference.
- Be organized. Bring the documentation you need with you.
- Explain the situation in observable behavior terms, not opinions and generalizations. ("He has 4 zeros," not, "he's just lazy.") See list below for help.
- A conference suggests two-way communication, not a sermon.
- Don't ever compare the student to anyone else.
- Don't assume about the student's family situations.
- Don't let a parent berate you. Calmly end the meeting and suggest the parent come at another time when an administrator could be present.
- Be as positive as possible. Give parents a reason to hope.
- Don't dredge up the past. Deal with the situation at hand.
- Deal with the most important issues. Don't overwhelm parents with too many problems at once.
- Document everything that happened.
- Be clear, concise, honest.
- Treat a parent the way you would want to be treated if you were in his place.

☑ **Deciding when to contact parents**
- Use the "If it were your own child" test when unsure about whether or not to contact a parent.
- Make a phone call your first choice for reaching a parent. Emails can be misinterpreted.
- Prepare for a phone call as you would for a conference and document everything.
- Don't wait until the problem is huge—contact parents early enough that the problem can be resolved. The earlier the better.
- Be very, very careful when sending an email. Have someone else read it before you send it.

☑ **Choosing the right words** even when you have difficult things to say to parents is important. Give facts, not opinions; details, not a diagnosis. Avoid the negative list as much as possible; use the positive list.

Negative	Positive	Negative	Positive
Must	should	Stubborn	insists on his way
Lazy	has shown he can do more	Liar	said…
Trouble-maker	calls out in class	Wastes time	could make better use of his time
Uncooperative	does not work in a team	Sloppy	could do neater work
Cheats	copied a paper	Mean	difficulty in getting along with others
Stupid	can do better work with help	Poor work	achieving below his level
Never does	can do	Clumsy	not physically well coordinated
Truant	absent without permission	Profane	uses inappropriate language
Steal	took without permission	Selfish	does not share with others
Unclean	hygiene problems	Rude	inconsiderate of others
Help	cooperation	Bashful	reserved
Disinterested	not involved	Show-off	tries to gain attention
Insolent	outspoken	Will fail him	will pass if…

Contacting Parents by Phone

Student_____ Date of call_____

Parent_____ Phone number_____

1. **Begin with a statement of concern.**

2. **Describe the specific behavior that necessitated your call.**

3. **Describe the steps you have taken to solve the problem.**

4. **Get parent input.**

5. **Present your solutions to the problems:**
   - **what you will do**

   - **what you want the parent to do**

6. **Express confidence in the problem being solved.**

7. **Tell parents there will be follow-up contact from you.**

Parent Conference Summary

Student _____ Grade _____ Date _____

Conference requested by _____

Parents participating _____

Teachers participating _____

Others participating _____

Purpose of conference _____

_____

_____

Suggestions for school _____

_____

_____

_____

Suggestions for home _____

_____

_____

_____

_____

Comments _____

_____

_____

_____

Parent signature _____

Teacher Signature _____

Effective Communication Skills for Conferencing

Effective listening, according to Dr. Robert Bolton of the Ridge Associates, is ***understanding the thoughts and feeling being communicated from the speaker's frame of reference***. In order to do that, we need excellent communication skills—which must be learned and practiced. Most people know these things; it's just the <u>doing</u> it part that is challenging.

Let's start with the basics of effective communication—Active Listening. Then we will apply those skills as we learn various methods and protocols used in conferencing with parents…and with students.

Active listening skills can be divided into two major categories: Nonverbal & Verbal.

1. Nonverbal Skills

Body language of listening
- Maintain an open position without your arms crossed.
- Incline your body forward slightly.
- Responsive gestures show your interest.
- Maintain appropriate eye contact—not staring down or avoiding.
- Use head nods to show you are hearing, not that you necessarily agree.
- Your facial reactions should match what's being said.

Create an Environment conducive to communication
- Create privacy by moving away from others.
- Eliminate competing sights and sounds if possible
- Avoid furniture barriers; sit at the same level.
- Honor appropriate distance—don't be a close-talker!

Remember:
1. **What we <u>do</u>** will speak volumes before we ever open our mouth! **Eyes trump ears.**

2. <u>**How**</u> **we say what we say** is the key to authentic communication.
   - **Tone** – can communicate negative or sarcastic feelings
   - **Inflection** – can add an element of blame or doubt.
   - **Pace** – can be so fast without pauses that there is no time for thought or reaction

3. A skillful communicator can discern <u>**if something needs to be said**</u> and, if so, <u>**when is the best time?**</u> Consider these **context issues** that can affect communication.
   - **Health** – Illness and tiredness can make people react differently than when they feel healthy.
   - **Time of day** – Consider what the other is doing or is going to do after the conversation.
   - **Time of year** – Remember to consider the phases that new teachers experience.
   - **Personal issues** – Family, financial, or other problems can color one's perceptions.

4. New teachers often make three **mistakes** when conferencing with parents
   - They speak in their ***teacher voice*** ("you need to…"or ***parent voice*** ("you should…") instead of their ***adult voice*** ("Let's…).
   - They say too much or do all the talking.
   - They get defensive and try to "win" the conference instead of listening and finding a solution. You don't have to "win" to have a "win-win" situation.

2. Verbal Skills & Tools

Invitations encourage the other person to continue speaking.

Tell me more…
Fill me in…
Help me understand…
Uh-huh…
I see…

Restating or Paraphrasing –uses reflection to briefly summarizing what the speaker communicates to you. In your own words, restate what you think has been said. Examples: "So, Mrs. Jones, you are concerned about whether John is being treated fairly," or "It sounds like you were not aware of Sarah's absences." The entire point is to understand what is being said; not that you agree, but that you hear it and get it!

3 types of paraphrasing – depending on the conversation, a listener might employ one or all.
1. Paraphrasing that **acknowledges or clarifies**--
   ♦ "So, Mr. Vargas, you are upset that you didn't know about the failing grades earlier…"
2. Paraphrasing that **summarizes or organizes**--
   ♦ "So, Mrs. Thomas, there seem to be three separate concerns you have…___, ___, & ___."
3. Paraphrasing that **shifts the focus to a different level** --
   ▸ (Shifting up) "So, your goal is…" (Or, shifting down) "It sounds like our choice is…"

Inquiry – using open-ended **probing questions** (not derailing or diverting questions) to gather needed information for specificity.
Examples: "Mr. Davis, in what ways were you pleased with Jeremy's progress?" "Based on …, what do you think about…?" "How would you…"
Avoid using closed stems too often, like: "Did you…? Can you…? Will you…? Have you…?"
Listen for **entry points**—those comments that give you the opportunity to clarify underlying issues. Examples include:
   ▸ Generalizations or quantifiers– "everyone, all, none, no one, always, etc."
   ▸ Rules—"should, ought, must, can't…"
   ▸ Judgments—"bad, wrong, weak, lazy…"
   ▸ Comparisons—"better, worse, less…"
   ▸ Vagueness—"understand, prepare, know..."
   ▸ Victim language—"they, The School, teachers, parents…"
This statement from a parent offers several entry points, "No wonder Kimberly isn't learning anything; kids just don't care any more." Possible probing questions could be: "When you say 'not learning', what do you mean?" "By 'care', what do you mean?" "What are you seeing that causes you to think kids don't care?" Practice writing another probing question:

Input – After correctly identifying the issue or problem, the listener decides
• What level and type of input to offer.
• Which **format** or **protocol** to use depending on whether the goal is
☑ **Problem-solving** – Do we need to brainstorm solutions together?
☑ **Conflict-resolution** – Do we need to calm down emotions before issues can be resolved?
☑ **Assertion** – Do I need to stand by a position that is not negotiable?
☑ **Presenting information** – Do I simply need to inform?
☑ **Sharing resources** – Do I need to gather and share resources or bring in a resource person?
☑ **Other**

Reinforcing – The listener states the decision and schedules follow-up.
▪ "So we've decided to try the interventions for two weeks and check back after we see the results."

Conferencing Methods Using Effective Communication
Parent Concern Conferencing Method

This method can be followed when a parent comes to you with a problem or issue. You will use listening skills to solve the problem or find an answer for both of you. (For example: the parent questions your discipline policy.)

- Parent asks question or states concern or issue
- You listen, using effective skills (listen, invitations)
- You Restate/Paraphrase until the parent's problem/issue is correctly identified
- You ask what has been tried or other probing questions to gather needed information
- You invite yourself in to give advice or share information
- You give workable suggestions (in bite-size pieces)
- You check for reaction (Will that work?)
- Schedule follow-up.

Here's how it might sound with this cooperative parent example:
Parent (P) in 3rd week of middle school in response to Teacher (T) sending out progress report.
P: I can't believe that my daughter is failing your class! She has always been on the honor roll.
T: So, you weren't aware of Abby's grades until the progress report came.
P: No! We were shocked! This has never happened before. If we had known earlier, we could have done something to prevent this situation. She says it's because you are new and don't know how things work yet. We are worried this is going to ruin her class rank.
T: So you didn't receive the earlier messages I sent?
P: What messages? How? This is the first I've heard!
T: Mrs. Rhodes, I'm hearing several concerns. I think it will help if I address them. Will that work for you?
P: If you think you can.
T: Let's start with the communication issue. The report you have in your hand is a 3-week progress report. It lets parents know about students' progress in the middle of the grading period so that if there is a problem, there is time to correct it. I sent an earlier report home with Abby last week to let you know that she was not completing her assignments, and I sent an email to the address you provided at the Meet the Teacher Night. Here in her folder is a signature on that note that Abby returned to me. (Parent looks in disbelief at form.)
P: Well, I never got them. If you told Abby to give me a note, she would have. I don't know who signed that!
T: Let's look at the reason for Abby's failing grade. This is her folder with all of her assignments and graded work with a rubric showing expectations. Here on her assignment sheet you can see the work she turned in and those she hasn't completed. She has 7 zeroes. Even in lunch detention, she hasn't completed it. (Parent begins looking through folder.)
P: I can't believe this. This is not like her to do this kind of work. I didn't know she had detention.
T: Mrs. Rhodes, Abby is a very smart and talented girl. I really like having her in my class. My concern as a teacher is that she won't do work that she can do. I want her to be successful and I can tell you do too.
P: It is frustrating when you think you can trust them and find out they've lied to you. I think it's that new girl she's been hanging out with.
T: Let's talk about what we can do to get things back on track before the final grades come out.
P: Yes, please. The first thing my husband and I will do is have a "meeting" with her. May I have a copy of that assignment sheet and the thing with my forged signature? Can she still do any of this work?
T: Yes, most of it. That is a classroom norm. All learning work is acceptable until it is tested.
P: She will meet with you in the morning to find out which work that is.
T: Another concern you mentioned was about class rank. Let me reassure you on that issue. There isn't a class ranking in middle school, so her high school standing isn't impacted by these grades.
P: Oh, I didn't know that. We want her to go to college.
T: Of course. I do, too. So, what we've decided to do is meet with Abby and let her know we are on the same page. I'll let you know in a few days how it is going on this end and you can let me know if you have any further concerns. Is there anything else?
P: No…thank you so much!

Teacher Initiated Conferencing Method

This method is for when there is a need for you to tell someone you need them to do something or to assert your opinion or request: (For example: A student isn't cooperating with classroom rules) Having to confront someone over a problem is never fun and sometimes isn't the teacher's role. Check with a mentor before contacting parents for problems. Another perspective is helpful. This method can also be the vehicle for problem-solving when there are two or more opposing ideas…without conflict.

- ☑ Explain what your need / request is (Explain the concern)
- ☑ Listen using effective skills to understand other's viewpoint
- ☑ Restate until the other's opinion is correctly identified
- ☑ Restate your need and listen
- ☑ Restate the conflicting needs or opinions
- ☑ Invite to problem-solve, if appropriate
- ☑ Give workable suggestions
- ☑ Check for reaction (Will that work?)
- ☑ Schedule follow-up

See how it might sound with this cooperative parent example:

Teacher (T) in 4th week of school contacts Parent (P) of a 10th grader about discipline issue.

T: Thank you for coming in, Mr. Jackson. I appreciate your time. As I mentioned on the phone, I wanted to visit with you to see if we could put our heads together and come up with a plan to help Andy be more successful. He is a really good student; I enjoy having him in my class. But in the past two weeks, I've noticed a big change in him. His work is not of the same quality, and he seems to want to sleep in class. I have met with him a couple of times about it. Yesterday when I asked him to wake up and participate, he threw all his books off the desk and made some pretty rough comments. I wondered if you were seeing any changes in his behavior or if there is anything going on I need to know about?

P: Well, we have had a big change at home…we brought our twin babies home last week…that's why my wife couldn't come…it's been pretty crazy…really, we are all tired and overwhelmed. I haven't noticed any big changes in Andy at home…just what we thought was normal teenage sulking. We've all had less sleep than normal.

T: Congratulations on the twins. I didn't know…Andy said he was an only child…

P: Yeah…I think he's kind of embarrassed about the age difference…his world has been turned upside down. And now that I think about it, I haven't been able to spend much time with him lately…I just can't believe he would act like that.

T: Sounds like big changes for all of you. The usual consequence for Andy's behavior is for him to serve afterschool detentions all week.

P: I know he needs to be punished, but are there any other options? He has an after-school job that is helping him learn responsibility and money management. I really don't want him to lose that job, but I also don't want him acting that way.

T: Under the circumstances we can come up with some options. Could he serve either early morning or lunch detentions?

P: With the twins right now, I think lunch would be better…and might make a bigger impression to miss that time with his buddies.

T: How about if Andy meets with you and me tomorrow to talk about things and set some expectations?

P: Yes, and I'll be meeting with him at home as well.

T: Sounds good. We'll work on this together.

⊙ **Practice:** Using a scenario from your experience with a new teacher, role-play with a partner using one of the methods above to practice effective listening skills.

Case studies:

🍎 Read the case study and decide how you would conduct the parent conference. Which method will you use? What other information do you need to find out? If you are working in a team or with a partner, role-play the conference between the teacher and parent or guardian.

Michael

Michael has lived with his aunt, who has several children of her own, since the beginning of this school year. His mother passed away two years ago. The year before he came to live with his aunt, he was in three different schools and had lived with four different relatives. He is older than the other students in your class and can't seem to find a group where he fits in. In the beginning he was cooperative. Lately he has been bullying other kids and is openly defiant to you. You think he is very smart but is very far behind where he should be. You would like for him to get some tutoring help in order to catch up. His aunt has refused your request for him to join an afterschool tutorial club. She is coming in for a conference after school.

Jessica

Jessica is a very outspoken and outgoing student. Without working very hard, she has always made straight A's on everything until your class this year. You've checked with your mentor and others to be sure that your assignments are valid. Other students are doing well. Jessica has complained since the first of school about how hard this class is and questions every grade. She received a zero yesterday for copying someone's assignment. She blew up in class and informed you that her father, the school board president, would be hearing about this. During a phone call to the mother, you learn that Jessica has been complaining to her all year about how ridiculous the class is, that you are new and don't know what you're doing. She is coming in after school for a conference.

Gracie

Gracie is a likeable student, but has become a constant disruption. She calls out in class during whole group instruction. During small group work, she dawdles and gets the group off task. You have talked with Gracie, moved her to different groups, and assigned consequences. Nothing has worked. You sent a note home informing the parents and asking for a conference. Today Gracie tells you that her mother is mad. She is taking off work and coming to school to see the principal because you are always picking on her and won't help her with her work. The principal schedules the meeting for you to meet with the mother.

Working with Parents and Families
Reflect on your learning in each of the three categories.

....

Professional – How will this impact your work?

....

Personal – How will this impact your life?

....

Peculiar-What was unique or interesting?

....

Chapter 8
Being a Professional Educator

You may bring to your office and put in a frame a motto as fine as its paint,
But if you're a crook when you're playing the game,
That motto won't make you a saint.
You can stick up the placards all over the wall,
But here is a word I announce:
It is not the motto that hangs on the wall, but the motto you live that counts.
If the motto says, "Smile," and you wear a frown;
"Do it now," and you linger and wait,
If the motto says, "Help," and you trample men down;
If the motto says "Love," and you hate -
You won't get away with the mottoes you stall,
For truth will come forth with a bounce.
It is not the motto that hangs on the wall, but the motto you live that counts.
"Mottoes," Kalends, in *The New Speaker's Treasury of Wit and Wisdom.*

 Effective teachers exhibit professionalism and high standards at all times in and out of the classroom.

 ## The Professional Teacher
- How will I demonstrate that I understand what educator professionalism means as it applies to actions, attitudes, dress, speech, and habits?
- What are the legal issues affecting teachers and how will I gain an understanding of those issues?

My Professional Development
- Why is it important that I am an open and active learner through my personal and professional development?
- How will the models of professional development aid me as I design a professional learning plan?
- How will the criteria describing a highly qualified beginning teacher help me assess my professional progress?

My Learning Goals:

Ideas I want to further explore:

The Professional Teacher

"You don't get a second chance at a first impression"

What does it mean to you to be a professional educator? That seems to be difficult to define in this day and age. If we want to be respected as the professionals we are, then we must conduct ourselves in a professional manner. In the first year when you are making an impression on the administration, parents, colleagues, and students, you especially want to leave no doubt in anyone's mind about your professionalism. It is true and it is sad that there are those in our profession who give the rest a bad name. Every year there are those whose names appear in the news for crimes against their students or their schools. There are also many whose crimes aren't worthy of the news, but are still just as damaging to the profession. I look back in regret at many of my actions that were less than what they should have been as a teacher. What seemed right at the time proved not to be the best thing or the right thing. How nice it would be in life to be able to press the delete or backspace button to correct mistakes or redo something like we do on a computer. You will make mistakes. Don't be defeated by them, but do learn from them. Knowing what it means to be professional and knowing what the law says leaves the choice to each of us as individuals to decide to do the right thing…no matter what.

This will be a brief overview of issues for your awareness. I encourage you to seek out more information for yourself from others. Remember, just because other teachers do one thing doesn't make it right. Always check it out. Your best resource is the principal. Sometimes other teachers haven't had training in legal issues, or they are not aware that the laws have changed. When in doubt? Ask! You've heard some teachers say that it's easier to ask forgiveness than to ask permission? That may be true for a veteran, but <u>NEVER</u> true for a first-year teacher. <u>ALWAYS ASK</u>. Ask more than one person. Go as high as you need to in order to get the right answer. And when you do make a mistake, tell your supervisor as soon as possible, so he has a chance to help you fix it. I promise, even if it's bad—really bad—he would rather hear it from you than from the superintendent or the newspaper!

Professional Issues -

- ☑ Appearance – dress appropriately for your grade level, community, assignment
  - o Remember you are an adult, not a student.
  - o Research says that dress has a direct impact on respect that students have for teachers and discipline.
  - o I recently watched a group of high school students put on a little performance for the entire community, imitating their teachers. Most was funny, but some was not. They acted out how improperly, and even sleazy, several teachers-men and women-dressed, walked and acted.

- ☑ Speech—be careful what you say
  - o Pretend that there are always two invisible people—your principal and a parent—with you in your classroom, the workroom, and the lounge. How would you talk in that case? That's the way to talk all the time. With today's technology what you say in third period can be on YouTube by lunchtime.
  - o There is a generational issue here. Each generation seems to have slang that is not considered inappropriate to them, but sends the previous generation into fits! Please be careful to use

professional business language with your students. Casual is okay, but be careful about slang. I recently heard a teacher tell her high school students (with me in the room), "I know, it s---s, but there's no need to be p---ed off about it." She didn't think it was inappropriate at all. My advice: how you speak on your own time is truly your business, but on school time, honor a higher standard.

- o Most teachers don't know that it is against the law to speak in an unprofessional way about their administration, colleagues, students, and parents. Check out your state's teachers' code of ethics. Wow!
- o What about freedom of speech? You certainly have freedom of speech as it pertains to issues that are concerns for the general citizenry, like a tax increase. But you do not have the freedom to share information that is confidential, and you do not have the right to speak publicly against your employers as it pertains to your assignment or a school policy.

☑ Duties— TCB--Take care of business
  - o Be on time to work, faculty meetings, hall duty, bus duty, staff development, and other events.
  - o Complete requirements, such as paper work, forms, and documentation.
  - o Professional development—be a learner, not a back-row complainer.

☑ Chain-of-command
  - o Find out what the proper chain-of-command is in your district and follow it.
  - o Don't go around your principal to the central office. The only exception would be if you feel you are being asked to do something illegal or immoral. In that case, inform your supervisor and seek other advice.
  - o Don't ever contact a school board member without being told to do so.

☑ Legal Issues—Ask your mentor or principal about the topics on this list.
  - o Touching students—what is the policy?
  - o Religion in the classroom – teachers' rights and students' rights
  - o Politics—what are my rights concerning elections, political opinions, etc.?
  - o Transporting students—under what conditions can I provide transportation?
  - o Documentation—how much, when, and who gets to see it?
  - o Special Education issues—modifications, IEPs, etc.
  - o Homework and grading—can students trade and grade?
  - o Harassment—what constitutes it?
  - o Speech—how much do I have to endure, what can I say?
  - o Discipline issues—corporal or not, what can I do, where do I send kids?
  - o Reporting abuse—when, to whom, what happens?
  - o Technology – what is the local policy about using phones and other technology and social media?
  - o Resources for legal issues in most states can be found through links on the State Education Agency's website. In Texas that is the Texas Education Agency-www.tea.state.tx.us.

☑ Professional Development— The professional teacher is a life-long learner.

*Effective professional development is driven by what teachers' needs are in order to be successful in achieving the vision of **high levels of learning for all**.*

Models of Professional Development

Effective professional development is driven by what teachers' <u>needs</u> are in order to be successful in achieving the vision of ***high levels of learning for all***. Effective districts and campuses have <u>clear goals and objectives</u> for the continuous growth and development of all educators. Effective professional development requires a commitment from the district of time and money. The payoff for the investment can be tremendous if the professional development is effective. Remember, professional development doesn't just mean workshops! Tom Gusky (*Evaluating Professional Development*. 2000. Thousand Oaks, CA:Corwin.) suggests the following seven models of professional development:

- **Training**—This is the most common form of professional development and can be very effective. We must be careful not to overwhelm teachers with training. Everyone needs time to process what is being learned in order to implement it. There should be a thoughtful plan for the teacher's professional development, considering amount, time of year, and expected outcomes. Training without follow-up and feedback is rarely implemented in the classroom and usually a waste of time and money.

- **Observation and Feedback**—Schedule time for the teacher to observe other teachers and time for the teacher to be observed and be given specific feedback from other teachers. This method is beneficial to the observer and the one being observed. This requires a commitment of time and requires training in observation skills and coaching.

- **Improvement/planning processes**—Teachers can benefit greatly from being on a team of teachers planning curriculum and instructional strategies. What makes this model most effective is when these teams of teachers base instruction on student achievement data derived from regular formative common assessments as part of a learning community.

- **Study groups**—Whole faculty study groups have proven to be greatly successful as a way to learn together, investigate research, and solve common problems. Teachers can grow professionally by being a part of a focused, organized, research-based group.

- **Inquiry / Action Research**—This method allows educators to identify a problem, collect data related to the problem, study the research, create a plan, and take action. This method of professional development is a good match for teams of teachers working as true professional learning communities.

- **Individually guided activities**—This allows educators to determine their own needs for professional development and select activities to meet those needs. For new teachers, this model is not as effective as others since many of them don't know what their needs are or what is available to meet those needs. We can use this in conjunction with mentoring, however, to help them determine their needs and help them design professional development activities to meet those. E-learning opportunities are now abundant in schools, universities, and through web-based companies.

- **Mentoring**—This tried and proven strategy is the most powerful tool we have to help new teachers or struggling teachers succeed. Effective mentoring requires that the helping teacher have a certain set of knowledge and skills, which requires training.

☙ **Think about it:** Create a graph or (use the one on the next page) of the seven models and list the professional development you have had in a column next to the model. Make columns to answer the following questions:
- What professional development has been most effective for you? (You learned and are implementing the knowledge and skills successfully.)
- Which of the models has most of your professional learning followed?
- How could you diversify your learning opportunities in all seven models?

Analyzing Professional Development

Model of Professional Development	List of professional development activities	Level of implementation and effectiveness	Needed to increase effectiveness	My Plan
Training				
Observation and Feedback				
Improvement and Planning Process				
Study Groups				
Inquiry / Action Research				
Individually Guided Activities				
Mentoring				

The Highly Qualified Beginning Teacher
Source: National Commission on Teaching and America's Future

We looked at this list in Chapter 2. Look at it again here with professional learning in mind. These criteria are based on the teaching profession's consensus about what a highly qualified teacher, including beginning teachers, should know and be able to do to help students learn.

Highly qualified beginning teachers should be able to meet state licensing standards that require candidates to

☑ Possess a deep understanding of the subjects they teach

☑ Evidence a firm understanding of how students learn

☑ Demonstrate the teaching skills necessary to help all students achieve high standards

☑ Create a positive learning environment

☑ Use a variety of assessment strategies to diagnose and respond to individual learning needs

☑ Demonstrate and integrate modern technology into the school curriculum to support student learning

☑ Collaborate with colleagues, parents and community members, and other educators to improve student learning

☑ Reflect on their practice to improve future teaching and student achievement

☑ Pursue professional growth in both content and pedagogy

☑ Instill a passion for learning in their students

Think and Plan:
With these 10 criteria as the vision of an effective highly qualified teacher, create a professional learning plan for yourself that will serve as a guide for your professional growth. Use the charts on the following pages as a tool. Remember to consider the 7 models of professional development as you plan.

Standards for a Highly Qualified Teacher Action Plan

Standard (Where I need to be)	Current Status (Where I am now)	I Need	My Plan
Possess a deep understanding of the subjects I teach			
Evidence a firm understanding of how students learn			
Demonstrate the teaching skills necessary to help all students achieve high standards			
Create a positive learning environment			
Use a variety of assessment strategies to diagnose and respond to individual learning needs			
Demonstrate and integrate modern technology into the school curriculum to support student learning			
Collaborate with colleagues, parents and community members, and other educators to improve student learning			
Reflect on their practice to improve future teaching and student achievement			
Pursue professional growth in both content and pedagogy			
Instill a passion for learning in their students			

Standards for a Highly Qualified Teacher Rubric

Think about it: Brainstorm the variations of growth toward the IDEAL for each of your first three years. Describe what success would look like.

The IDEAL The Standard	Successful Third Year Development	Successful Second Year Development	Successful First Year Development
Possess a deep understanding of the subjects I teach			
Evidence a firm understanding of how students learn			
Demonstrate the teaching skills necessary to help all students achieve high standards			
Create a positive learning environment			
Use a variety of assessment strategies to diagnose and respond to individual learning needs			
Demonstrate and integrate modern technology into the school curriculum to support student learning			
Collaborate with colleagues, parents and community members, and other educators to improve student learning			
Reflect on their practice to improve future teaching and student achievement			
Pursue professional growth in both content and pedagogy			
Instill a passion for learning in their students Other			

Chapter 9
Working in Learning Community And With Mentors

Take good counsel and accept correction—that's the way to live wisely and well.
Arrogant know-it-alls stir up discord, but wise men and women listen to each other's counsel.
Become wise by walking with the wise; hang out with fools and watch your life fall to pieces.
Book of Proverbs

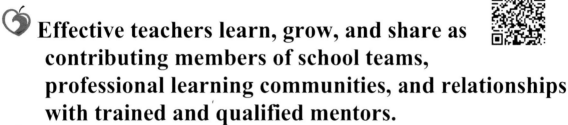 **Effective teachers learn, grow, and share as contributing members of school teams, professional learning communities, and relationships with trained and qualified mentors.**

Working with a Mentor
- What do I need to know in order to understand the mentor-new teacher relationship?
- How will I grow and share professionally through mentoring and coaching?

 Professional Learning Communities
- What is a professional learning community?
- What is my role as a team member?
- What are the characteristics of effective team members?

My Learning Goals:

Ideas I want to further explore:

Working with a Mentor

"Refuse to take good advice and watch your plans fail;
Take good counsel and watch them succeed."
Proverbs

☑ The law and intent –
   o Some states require that every teacher with zero years experience be assigned a mentor to provide support. It is the intent of any mentoring relationship that the first year teacher receive knowledge, skills, and support from such a relationship. The ultimate goal of mentoring and induction programs is the <u>retention</u> and <u>growth</u> of new teachers so that all students succeed.

☑ Mentor's role and types of help
   The mentor's role is to provide support in several areas depending on your needs.
   As a new teacher you can expect mentoring assistance in seven specific areas:
   o Instruction—planning, preparing, and teaching the curriculum
   o Systems—understanding the processes and culture of a school - "how we do things here"
   o Resources—Where to get and how to use materials and supplies
   o Emotional—personal support
   o Managerial—organizing and managing time, space, and materials
   o Parental—how to conference, keep parents informed, etc.
   o Disciplinary—guidance and ideas, interventions

☑ The new teacher's role –
   o Seek help when you need it; don't wait.
   o Don't be afraid to ask; everyone has been where you are!
   o Be willing and able to grow and to share—your mentor (and other veterans) will learn a great deal from you and will have a lot to share.

Information about my mentor

Name:

Assignment:

Room Location:

Phone #:

Our plan for meeting -

Categories of Support Worksheet

Use this form to prepare questions for your meeting with your mentor.

Category of Support	My Questions	My Needs	Mentor's Ideas	Whom to Ask/ Where to go for help
Instructional: Planning, Teaching, Assessing				
Systems: Campus procedures, culture, customs, etc.				
Resources: Where to get things, supplies, teaching materials, etc.				
Emotional: Stress Management, Parents, etc.				
Managerial: Time, space, materials, student procedures				
Parental: Communication, problems, involvement, etc.				
Disciplinary: Disruptive, uncooperative students, etc.				

Professional Learning Communities

The most promising strategy for sustained, substantive school improvement is developing the ability of school personnel to function as professional learning communities.
–Rick DuFour, author *of Professional Learning Communities at Work.*

What is a professional learning community?
Those three words capture the essence of what PLCs are.
- **Professional** – a person who is (and continues to be) trained, knowledgeable, and skilled in a particular field
- **Learning** – ongoing study and practice in pursuit of continuous improvement
- **Community** – a group linked by common interest

A professional learning community is <u>not</u> something we DO; it is who we ARE.

Definition
Richard DuFour and others define a Professional Learning Community as
- Educators committed to working <u>collaboratively</u> in ongoing processes of collective inquiry and action research in order to achieve better <u>results</u> for the students they serve. PLCs operate under the assumption that the key to improved learning for students is continuous, job-embedded learning for all educators. (DuFour, DuFour, Eaker, 2006)

Why PLCs?
- The National Commission of Teaching and America's Future recommended that if schools are going to be effective, they must be restructured to become genuine learning communities for both students and teachers.
- The National Staff Development Council's first standard states that staff development that improves the learning for all students organizes adults into learning communities whose goals are aligned with those of the school and district. (NSDC, 2001)
- With the focus on learning for all, schools can no longer function as they have in the past, with teachers in isolation working as independent contractors. It's too hard. There is too much at stake.

Education systems of the future will have understood that the most significant factors determining whether students learn well are the competence, caring, and commitment of teachers and administrators....Educators in these schools will have become true professionals through their work as a professional learning community—working just as the three words connote: professionals coming together in community to continuously learn, to increase their effectiveness so that students become increasingly successful learners. Shirley M. Hord, *Journal of Staff Development*, Summer 2007

Six Characteristics of a Learning Community

You cannot have students as continuous learners and collaborators without teachers having the same characteristics.
–Michael Fullen

Shared mission, vision, values, goals
- Mission explains why we exist; it must be understood by all.
- Vision is the picture of what we are trying to become.
- Values are how we behave, the guiding principles that govern our behavior as we accomplish our work.
- Goals are the measurable specific steps taken to achieve the desired results.

Collaborative teams focused on learning
- Professionals working interdependently toward a common goal for which they are mutually accountable.

Collective inquiry into best practice and current reality
- Professionals relentlessly questioning the status quo, seeking new methods of teaching and learning, testing the methods, and learning from the results.

Action orientation/experimentation
- Professionals turning their learning into action and testing new ideas.

Commitment to continuous improvement
- Professionals never satisfied with the status quo, seeking ways to achieve better results.

Results orientation
- Professionals recognizing that the only valid judgment of improvement is observable and measurable results.

The Four Big Ideas of PLCs
- Ensuring that Students Learn – ensuring, not just providing the opportunity
- A Culture of Collaboration – learning and working interdependently toward a common goal is the norm
- A Focus on Results – shifting the focus from intentions to results
- Hard Work and Commitment – success is entirely dependent on the professionals who are the heart and soul of an effective school

Working in Community

Effective people and groups have certain qualities and do certain things in order to be high functioning. Ineffective people and groups also have certain characteristics and exhibit behaviors that cause them to be dysfunctional.
Patrick Lencioni in *The 5 Dysfunctions of a Team*

Dr. Shirley M. Hord, author and scholar emerita with the Southwest Educational Development Laboratory in Austin, Texas, is the researcher who first proposed the idea of professional learning communities for educators. She stated in a recent article that in order for collective learning to become the hallmark of effective schools, those schools must create the structural and relational conditions that support a community of learners. One structural challenge in making learning in community possible is arranging the time and schedules so that staff can come together to work on the work. A major relational consideration is assuring that all professionals have the knowledge and skills to work and learn together, along with the tools for efficient teamwork.

What are the attributes of effective teams?
According to Lencioni, functional groups share these 5 qualities:
- High levels of trust among all members
  - As evidenced by vulnerability and a confidence among members that other teammates' intentions are good and that there is no need to be protective, defensive, or careful around the group. That leads to
- Unfiltered conflict around ideas
  - As evidenced by team members' ability to passionately discuss concepts, issues, and ideas without being mean-spirited or fearful of hurting feelings. That leads to
- Commitment to decisions and action plans
  - As evidenced by knowing what other team members do and how everyone contributes to the collective good. As evidenced by the team's ability to make clear, concise decisions with complete buy-in from every team member once the decision is made, even those who were not in favor of it. That leads to
- Holding one another accountable
  - As evidenced by the willingness of team members to challenge one another's performance or behaviors that might hurt the team. That leads to
- Focus on the achievement of collective results
  - As evidenced by the team making desired results clear and rewarding only those behaviors and actions that contribute to those results, such as sharing resources and ideas.

❂ Think about it:
Think about a team of which you have been or are now a member. How would you describe its effectiveness based on the above criteria? Did you notice that these five are hierarchical, meaning that each is dependent on the previous one? For example, teams cannot have unfiltered conflict around ideas without a high level of trust. What area would your team need to work on first in order to improve?

What is my role as a team member?
What are the characteristics of effective team members?

As a new teacher you will find yourself on a number of teams. Some of those teams might be grade-level, subject-area, vertical content, improvement planning, campus-wide, or district-wide, just to name a few. Whether the team is large or small, effective or not, here are some tips that will help you become a productive, positive member.

Tips for being a good team member:
- Come prepared with questions and ideas
- Listen thoughtfully and constructively
- Speak your mind freely
- Know your strengths and use them
- Relate discussion to the action
- Value others' opinions and ideas
- Make your point while it's relevant
- Be mentally present and focused
- Do what you say you will do
- Assume the best intentions of others
- Think win-win

Some Don'ts of teamwork:
- Don't fight over the ownership of an idea
- Don't monopolize the discussion
- Don't overturn the team's decision
- Don't keep quiet
- Don't play politics
- Don't attack people
- Don't avoid issues
- Don't withhold information
- Don't argue
- Don't judge
- Don't have side conversations
- Don't work on other work

Think about it: Which of these tips would also be appropriate for your students as they work in teams? Make a list in language that would fit the age of your students. How will you incorporate these tips into your procedures for student learning?

Chapter 10
Managing Stress

To keep a lamp burning we have to keep putting oil in it.
--Mother Teresa

Effective teachers have a plan to be healthy and happy as professionals by being able to identify and manage stress.

Understanding Stress
- How will I demonstrate that I understand the physical, emotional, social, and mental impact of stress?
- How have I identified personal and professional stressors?

Identifying & Managing Stress
- What must I know in order to develop a plan for managing and eliminating stress?

My Learning Goals:

Ideas I want to further explore:

Understanding Stress

Being a teacher is stressful. There is more to do than time to do it. There are zillions of decisions to be made every day. There is constant change. There is the pressure to meet standards. You are by the very nature of your position as a new teacher highly stressed. Many of you have experienced enough stressful events in the last few months to put you in the hospital: new degree, new job, new town, new life mate, new baby, new colleagues, new home, etc. And those are all good things! All of these good things, coupled with the negative stress, can work together to create burnout. We want you to learn to take good care of yourself and create a life-long pattern of being in control of this stress-filled life called being a teacher.

So, what is stress?

- Stress is our body's response to any change, threat, or pressure put upon it—from outside forces or from within.
- We can also look at stress as a state of imbalance between demands from the inside or outside and our perceived ability to meet those demands.
- Stress is our body's attempt to regain its normal state and protect itself from potential harm.
- Stress is inevitable and its purpose is to keep us alive! To be without it is to be DEAD!
- Stress can be
  - pleasant=eustress (excitement before a game, joy of marriage)
  - unpleasant=distress (fear of heights, your mother-in-law)
- But whether pleasant or not, too much stress can be harmful.

☑ Stress is inevitable, but it must be <u>eliminated, reduced, or managed</u> if we are to be healthy.

Symptoms of Stress

Cognitive
Confusion in thinking
Difficulty making decisions
Lowered concentration
Memory dysfunction
Lowering of all higher level thinking

Physical
Dizzy spell
Increased heart rate
Elevated blood pressure
Rapid breathing
Fatigue
Gastrointestinal disturbance
Sleep / appetite disturbance
Sexual dysfunction
Nausea
Muscle tremors
Headache

Emotional
Anxiety / fear / anger
Grief
Depression
Feeling overwhelmed
Irritability
Intrusive thoughts
Numbness
Denial of feelings

Behavioral
Changes in ordinary patterns
Changes in eating habits
Decreased personal hygiene
Withdrawal from others
Prolonged silences
Hypersensitivity
Outbursts of anger
Substance abuse

Identifying & Managing Stress

1. List every possible stressor you can think of in the columns below.

Personal	Environmental	Professional
Example: large debt	Example: house is dirty	Example: new job assignment

2. Designate each of the above items as either positive or negative (+ / -).

3. After completing the stress management scale and life satisfaction scale on the following pages, begin to work on your stress management plan. For each item on the above chart decide:

☑ Which ones will I <u>eliminate</u>? Designate with an X.

☑ Which ones will I <u>change my perception about</u>? Designate with a star.

☑ Which ones will I <u>develop better coping skills for</u>? Highlight those.

4. What specific actions will you take?

Stress Cycle

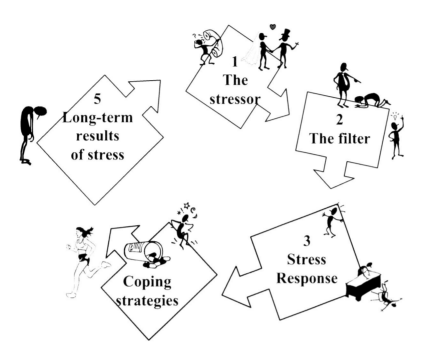

Stress has a cycle and it takes its toll if not managed.

☑ **1. The stressor**—There are three categories of stressors:
- ○ Job stressors, personal stressors, and environmental stressors
- ○ Stressors can be
  - ▪ Internal—our biology, our personality, lifestyle choices
  - ▪ External—change, relationships, personality, events, job, schedule
- ○ For something to be labeled a stressor, it must be <u>perceived</u> as one.
  - ▪ For example, for some people, height is a stressor; for some, it is not.

☑ **2. The filter**—what causes something to be perceived as a stressor
- ○ Our personalities, early messages, past, values, expectations from others and of ourselves cause something to be perceived as a stressor. When it is, <u>it causes</u> a stress response.

☑ **3. Stress Response**—the physiological response to stress: outpouring of adrenaline and release of other stress hormones into the bloodstream causing increased heart rate, faster breathing, tensing of muscles, etc. (fight or flight)
- ○ There are physical, emotional, cognitive, and behavioral reactions
- ○ Our body exhausts itself trying to counter stress

☑ **4. Coping strategies**—attempts to deal with stress
- ○ healthy-exercise, diet, organization, and deep breathing
- ○ unhealthy-drugs, alcohol, abuse, running away

☑ **5. Long-term results of stress**—stress-disease link, burnout, relationships, memory loss

Quick Review...

Label the phases of the Stress Cycle and give examples from your perspective.

Life Events Stress Test

Check the events that have taken place in your life in the past 12 months.

Life Event	Value ✓	
Death of a spouse	100	_____
Death of a child	100	_____
Divorce	85	_____
Separation from mate	80	_____
Arrest or incarceration	85	_____
Major illness or incapacitating injury	80	_____
Marriage	75	_____
Conviction of a felony	75	_____
Firing or layoff from job	70	_____
Birth or adoption of new family member	68	_____
Death of close family member	63	_____
Purchase and move to new home	60	_____
Foreclosure on mortgage of home	60	_____
Change in job / career	58	_____
Giving up job to return to school	58	_____
Change of residence (no purchase)	52	_____
Major change in health of family member	47	_____
Major change in lifestyle	45	_____
Retirement	45	_____
Building or remodeling a home	42	_____
Pregnancy	40	_____
Death of a close friend	38	_____
Major change in work environment New boss, promotion, etc.	35	_____
Major change in financial condition Inheritance, spouse loses job, etc.	35	_____
Starting a new romantic relationship	33	_____
Trouble with in-laws	29	_____
Major change in health of in-law	28	_____
Addition or loss of household member Son or daughter leaves, parent moves in, etc.	27	_____
Acquiring a substantial loan	26	_____
Beginning or ending school	25	_____

Winning a significant award		
College degree, publishing a book, etc.	25	_____
Trouble with boss	23	_____
Changing schools	23	_____
Minor change in physical health:		
Headaches, minor surgery	21	_____
Minor change in emotional health:		
Insomnia, minor depression	19	_____
Change in church activities	19	_____
Major change in eating habits	19	_____
Change in social habits		
Going out more/less, change friends	16	_____
Conviction of a misdemeanor		
or minor law violation	15	_____
Planning and taking a vacation	15	_____
Change in number of family gatherings	15	_____
Celebrating a major holiday	10	_____
Acquiring a new hobby / skill	10	_____
Other (assign value) _____		_____
_____		_____
_____		_____
_____		_____

Total Score _____

Add the value of all checked items.

If an event occurred more than once, give your self 1.5 times the value of the item.

___below 150___ = low susceptibility to stress-related illness

___150 – 300___ = medium susceptibility to stress-related illness

___over 300___ = high susceptibility to stress-related illness

❧ Life Satisfaction Scale

Circle the number that best describes your response. Don't leave any blank! If it is not applicable or neutral, check the middle column.

	Definitely true	Somewhat True	Neutral or Unsure	Mostly untrue	Definitely Untrue
The work I do is challenging	4	3	2	1	0
I have adequate responsibilities	4	3	2	1	0
The work I do suits my ability and skills	4	3	2	1	0
The people I work with are supportive	4	3	2	1	0
I have reasonable authority to make decisions	4	3	2	1	0
My job/career meets my financial needs	4	3	2	1	0
My lifestyle is comfortable	4	3	2	1	0
I am able to save a reasonable amount of money	4	3	2	1	0
My spouse/partner is comfortable with our income level	4	3	2	1	0
I am preparing adequately for retirement	4	3	2	1	0
I am comfortable with my current level of spending	4	3	2	1	0
I am comfortable with my body (size, shape, color)	4	3	2	1	0
I enjoy spending a quiet evening at home	4	3	2	1	0
My home is a place where I can relax and be myself	4	3	2	1	0
I have a hobby I enjoy	4	3	2	1	0
My home is a place of serenity and beauty; it nurtures me	4	3	2	1	0
I take pride in my home	4	3	2	1	0
I laugh frequently	4	3	2	1	0
I attend movies, plays, etc. fairly often	4	3	2	1	0
I can and do laugh at myself	4	3	2	1	0
Sometimes my sense of humor helps me get through difficult times	4	3	2	1	0
I believe I am making a valuable contribution to the world in some way	4	3	2	1	0
I feel needed and appreciated by those who matter to me	4	3	2	1	0
I have a plan for my life and I am following it	4	3	2	1	0

I have a belief in the meaning of my life	4	3	2	1	0
There is someone in my life with whom I can confide almost anything	4	3	2	1	0
I enjoy my social life	4	3	2	1	0
I enjoy my spiritual life	4	3	2	1	0
I have friends outside my immediate family with whom I socialize	4	3	2	1	0
My friends and I sometimes share our problems with one another	4	3	2	1	0
I have a relationship of mutual respect with my friends	4	3	2	1	0
I feel comfortable with members of the opposite sex as friends	4	3	2	1	0
I enjoy a physical relationship with my spouse	4	3	2	1	0
I am satisfied with my marital status	4	3	2	1	0
My partner frequently lets me know he/she cares	4	3	2	1	0
I feel safe disagreeing with my partner	4	3	2	1	0
My partner and I are able to talk through our differences and resolve most of them	4	3	2	1	0
My partner and I share interests and have fun together	4	3	2	1	0
I am usually able to focus on the positives in life, rather than the negatives	4	3	2	1	0
I've lived my life so that if I died tomorrow, I'd feel fulfilled	4	3	2	1	0

Column total ___ ___ ___ ___ ___

Total of all columns _____

Add the value of all checked items.

Over 120 = high level of satisfaction

60 - 120 = medium level of satisfaction

Below 60 = low level of satisfaction

Graphing Your Stress and Satisfaction Levels

From the tests, find your stress and satisfaction levels and mark them on the graph.

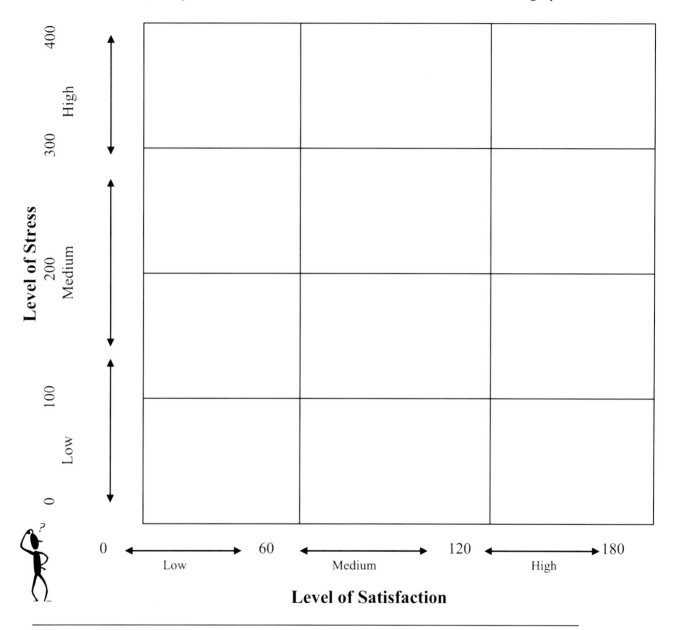

Discussion:

What do you need to do to lower your stress level?

What can you do to increase your satisfaction level?

Lowering Stress and Improving Life

There are 3 ways to lower stress and improve our life—3 places to intervene in the stress cycle

#1 Eliminate or reduce stressors
--may involve major life changes

#2 Change our perception of the stressor
--learning to respond differently

#3 Add and increase healthy coping strategies
--easiest to do

❂ Look back at your lists on page 208 and work on your stress reduction and management plan.

Stressors to Eliminate	Perceptions to Change	Coping Strategies

A joyful heart is good medicine, but a broken spirit dries up the bones.

Stress Reducing Tips

Change the stressor

Time and money management

Learn to say no

Use problem-solving techniques

Possibly leave a job or relationship

Seek professional help if you cannot get out of the cycle or it leads to depression

Change your thinking

Look at things more positively

See problems as opportunities

Refute negative thoughts

Keep a sense of humor

Look at things from the big picture or in the long run

Change your lifestyle

Exercise regularly

Decrease caffeine

Eat a well-balanced diet

Eat slowly

Get adequate sleep –7-8 hours

Have leisure time—do something for yourself every day

Use relaxation techniques—stretching, breathing

Take small joy-breaks often

Find a trusted friend to talk it out with

Meditate or pray

Research

Chronic Stress Can Prematurely Age Your Brain

"There's always going to be stress in the environment," says Howard Fillit, MD, clinical professor of geriatrics and medicine at New York's Mount Sinai School of Medicine and executive director of the Alzheimer's Drug Discovery Foundation. "But what's damaging is the distress we feel internally in response to it."

Fillit's distinction points to the bodywide reaction our bodies experience when we routinely respond to stress by going into fight-or-flight mode. In our brains, the stress response can cause memory and other aspects of cognition to become impaired, which is a risk factor for Alzheimer's disease and accelerated memory loss with aging. One thing that can happen is you can start feeling a lot older, mentally, than you are.

"Patients come in complaining of faulty memory and wonder if they're beginning to get Alzheimer's," says Roberta Lee, MD, vice-chair of the Department of Integrative Medicine at Beth Israel Medical Center and author of *The Superstress Solution* (Random House, 2010). "Their workups and MRI scans look normal. In the interview, I ask them about their lifestyle and almost invariably they have compounded stress."

The Research

Studies at the University of California–San Francisco have shown that repeated instances of the stress response (and their accompanying floods of cortisol) can cause shrinkage of the hippocampus — a key part of the brain's limbic system vital to both stress regulation and long-term memory. Call it the downside of neuroplasticity.

Why It Matters to You

Aside from the obvious — no one wants his or her brain to age faster than it's already going to — this research matters because it suggests that you have some influence over the rate of your own cognitive change.

To protect the brain from cortisol-related premature aging, Lee suggests building stress disruptors into your regular routine: "A five-minute period in the middle of every day during which you do absolutely nothing — nothing! — can help a lot, especially if you are consistent about it," she says.

Her other recommendations include eating breakfast every day — complex carbohydrates (whole grains, veggies) and some protein. "Breakfast helps your metabolism feel like it won't be stressed — caught up in a starvation-gluttony pattern," she explains.

And when anxiety does strike, a good way to initiate the relaxation response is her "four-five breath" routine: breathing in through the nose to a count of four, then out through the mouth to a count of five. "Repeat it four times and you'll feel the relaxation," she says. "Best of all, do the four breaths twice daily, at the beginning and end of the day."

Read more: http://www.care2.com/greenliving/6-surprising-things-that-affect-your-brain.html#ixzz2IFnXDsY4

❺ Chapter Reviews & Reflection

What are the key points you want to remember from the chapters?

Using the graphic organizer, list the concepts and content in the left column and depict your ideas in the right column with drawings, symbols, etc.

Section	Key Ideas	Symbols / Drawings
1		
2		
3		
4		
5		
6		
7		
8		
9		
10		

Overall main ideas to remember…

Suggested Resources

Beginning Teachers

Emmer, E. T., Evertson, Carolyn, etal. (2003). *Classroom Management for Secondary Teachers, 6th Edition.* Boston: Allyn and Bacon.

Evertson, Carolyn, Emmer, E.T., & Worsham, M.E. (2003). *Classroom Management for Elementary Teachers,* 6th Edition. Boston: Allyn and Bacon.

Koening, Larry. (2000). *Smart Discipline for the Classroom; Respect and Cooperation Restored.* Thousands Oaks: Corwin Press.

Kohn, Alfie. *Punished by Rewards.* (1993). New York: Houghton Mifflin Company.

Lindberg, Jill, et al. (2008). *Common-Sense Classroom Management Techniques for Working With Students with Significant Disabilities.* Thousands Oaks: Corwin Press.

Marzano, Robert J and others. (2003). **Classroom Management That Works: Research-based strategies for Every Teacher.** Thousands Oaks: Corwin Press.

Orange, Carolyn. (2000). *25 Biggest Mistakes Teachers Make and How to Avoid Them.* Thousands Oaks: Corwin Press.

Shelton, C. and Pollingue, A. (2000). *The Exceptional Teacher's Handbook.* Thousands Oaks: Corwin Press.

Strohmer, J. and Carhart, C. (1997). *Time-Saving Tips for Teachers.* Thousands Oaks: Corwin Press.

Sousa, David. (2009). *How The Brain Influences Behavior.* Thousands Oaks: Corwin Press

Wong, Harry and Rosemary. (1998). *How To Be An Effective Teacher The First Days Of School.* Mountain View, California: Harry Wong Publications, Inc.

Induction, Mentoring, and Coaching

Boreen, J., Johnson, M., et al. (2000). *Mentoring Beginning Teachers: Guiding, Reflecting, Coaching.* Stenhouse.

Bolton, Robert and Dorothy G. (1996). *People Styles at Work: Making Bad Relationships Good and Good Relationships Better.* New York: AMACOM.

Bolton, Robert. (1986). *People Skills.* New York: Simon and Schuster.

Breaux, A. L. & Wong, H. K. (2003). *New Teacher Induction: How to train, support, and retain new teachers.* Mountain View, CA: Harry K. Wong Publications.

Covey, Stephen R. *The 7 Habits of Highly Effective People* (Nov 9, 2004)

Educational Leadership. May 2005. Entire issue dedicated to Induction Issues.

Johnson, S. M., & Kardos, S. M. (2002**). "Keeping new teachers in mind."** *Educational Leadership, 59*(6), 13–16.

Killion, J & Harrison, C. (2006). *Taking The Lead: New roles for teachers and school-based coaches.* National Staff Development Council.

Kosmoski, G. and Pollack, D. (2001). *Managing Conversations With Hostile Adults.* Thousand Oaks: Corwin Press.

Lipton, L., Wellman, B. and Humbard, C. (2001). *Mentoring Matters: A Practical Guide to Learning-Focused Relationships.* Sherman, CT: Mira Via, LLC.

Podsen, I. and Denmark, V. (2001). *Coaching & Mentoring First-Year & Student Teachers.* Larchmont, New York: Eye On Education.

Smith, T. M. & Ingersoll, R. M. (2004). "**What are the effects of induction and mentoring on beginning teacher turnover?**" *American Educational Research Journal, 41(3), 681-714.*

Professional Development, Professional Learning Communities & Leadership

Barth, DuFour, Fullan, et al. (2005). *On Common Ground: The Power of Professional Learning Communities.* Blooomington, IN: Solution Tree.

Collins, J. (2001). *Good To Great!* New York: Harper.

Dickmann, M. & Stanford-Blair, N. (2002). *Connecting Leadership to the Brain.* Thousands Oaks: Corwin Press.

Dickmann, M., Stanford-Blair, N., & Rosati-Bojar. (2004). *Leading With the Brain in Mind: 101 Brain-compatible Practices for Leaders.* Thousands Oaks: Corwin Press.

DuFour, R., DuFour, R., Eaker, R., & Karhanek, G. (2004). *Whatever It Takes: How Professional Learning Communities Respond When Kids Don't Learn.* National Education Service.

DuFour, R., DuFour, R., Eaker, R., et al. (2006). *Learning By Doing: A Handbook for PLCs at Work.* Blooomington, IN: Solution Tree.

DuFour, R., & R., Eaker, R (1998). *Professional Learning At Work.* Alexandria, VA: ASCD.

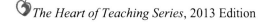

Fullan, Michael. (2003). *Change forces with a vengeance.* New York: Routledge.

Garmston, R.J. & Wellman, B. (1992). *How To Make Presentations That Teach and Transform.* Alexandria, VA: ASCD.

Gladwell, M. (2002). *Tipping Point: How little things can make a big difference*. Boston: Little Brown.

Glickman, Carl D. (2002.) *Leadership for Learning: How to Help Teachers Succeed.* Alexandria, VA: ASCD.

Guskey, T., (2003) "**What Makes Professional Development Effective?**" *Phi Delta Kappan*, 84(10), 748-750.

Hord, S. (1997) *Professional Learning Communities: Communities of continuous inquiry and improvement*. Austin: SEDL

Knowles, M.S., Holton, E.E., &Swanson, R. S. (2005). *The Adult Learner.* Amsterdam: Elsevier.

Lezotte, L. (2004) *Revolutionary and Evolutionary: The Effective Schools Movement.* www.effetiveschools.com/freestuff.

---. (2010)*What Effective Schools Do: Re-Envisioning the Correlates.*

National Staff Development Council. (2001). *Standards For Staff Development, revised*. Oxford, OH: NSDC.

National Staff Development Council. (2003). *Moving NSDC's Staff Development Standards For Into Practice: Innovation Configurations.* Oxford, OH: NSDC.

Marchese, T. (1998). *The Adult Learner.* Seattle, WA: New Horizons.

Reeves, D. (2004). *Accountability for Learning: How Teachers and School Leaders Can Take Charge.* Alexandria, VA: ASCD.

Reeves, D. (2006). *The Learning Leader: How to Focus School Improvement for Better Results.* Alexandria, VA: ASCD.

---. (2008). *Reframing Teacher Leadership: To Improve Your School.* Alexandria, VA: ASCD.

---. (2004). *Accountability for Learning: How Teachers and School Leaders Can Take Charge.* Alexandria, VA: ASCD.

Sousa, D. (2003). **The Leadership Brain: How to lead today's schools more effectively**. Alexandria, VA: ASCD.

Curriculum, Instruction, Assessment

Armstrong, Thomas. (1998). *Awakening Genius in the Classroom*. Alexandria, VA: ASCD.

---. (2006). *The Best Schools*. Alexandria, VA: ASCD.

Cook, John E. (2006) *The RTI(Response To Intervention) Guide: Developing and Implementing a Model in Your Schools.* LRP Productions.

Danielson, Charlotte. (1996). *Enhancing Professional Practice A Framework for Teaching*. Alexandria, VA: ASCD.

---. (2002). *Enhancing Student Achievement: A Framework for School Improvement*. Alexandria, VA: Alexandria, VA: ASCD.

Diamond, Marian and Hopson, Janet. (1998). *Magic Trees of the Mind: How to Nurture Your Child's Intelligence, Creativity, and Healthy Emotions form Birth Through Adolescence.* New York: Dutton.

De Bono, Edward. (1992) *Six Thinking Hats for Schools*. Perfection Learning Corporation. www.debonogroup.com

English, Fenwick. *Deciding What to Teach and Test, Millennium Edition*. Corwin Press.

Erickson, Lynn. (2002). *Concept-based Curriculum and Instruction: Teaching Beyond the Facts.* Thousand Oaks: Corwin Press.

---. (2006). *Concept-based Curriculum and Instruction for the Thinking Classroom.* Thousand Oaks: Corwin Press.

---. (2007). *Stirring the Head, Heart, and Soul.* 3rd Edition. Thousand Oaks: Corwin Press.

---. (2008). *Facilitator's Guide to Stirring the Head, Heart, and Soul.* 3rd Edition. Thousand Oaks: Corwin Press.

Gardner, H. (1994) "Reflections on Multiple Intelligences: Myths and Messages." *Phi Delta Kappan.* Vol. 78 No. 5. pgs. 200-207.

---. (1983). *Frames of mind: The theory of multiple intelligences*. New York: Basic Books. Tenth Anniversary Edition with new introduction, New York: Basic Books, 1993. Twentieth Anniversary Edition with new introduction. New York: Basic Books, 2004.

---. (1993). *Multiple intelligences: The theory in practice.* New York: Basic Books.

---. (1999). *Intelligence reframed: Multiple intelligences for the 21st century*. New York: Basic Books.

---. (2005). *The development and education of the mind: The collected works of Howard Gardner.* London: Taylor and Francis.

Garner, Betty K. (2007). *Getting To Got It!: Helping Struggling Students Learn How to Learn*. Alexandria, VA: ASCD.

Given, B.K. (2002). *Teaching to the Brain's Natural Learning Systems.* ASCD.

Gregory, Gayle H. & Chapman, C. (2002) Differentiated Instructional Strategies. Thousand Oaks: Corwin Press.

Guskey, T. (2002). *How's My Kid Doing? A parent's guide to grades, marks, and report cards*. San Francisco: Jossey-Bass.

Hunter, M. (1982). *Mastery Teaching.* El Segundo, CA: TIP Publications.

Jacobs, Heidi Hayes, editor. (2004). *Getting Results With Curriculum Mapping*. Alexandria, VA: ASCD.

Jensen, Eric. (2005).*Teaching With the Brain in Mind.* 2nd Edition. Alexandria, VA: ASCD.

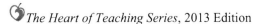

Kagan, Dr. Spencer & Miguel Kagan. (2008).*Cooperative Learning, revised*. San Clemente, CA: Kagan Cooperative Learning.

Marzano, R. (2007). *The Art &Science of Teaching*. Alexandria, VA: ASCD.

---. (2004). *Building Background Knowledge for Academic Achievement*. Alexandria, VA: ASCD.

---. (2006). *Classroom Assessment & Grading that Work*. Alexandria, VA: ASCD.

Marzano, R., Pickering, D., and Pollock, J. (2001). *Classroom Instruction that Works*. Alexandria, VA: ASCD.

Marzano, R., Waters, T., & McNulty, B. (2005). *School Leadership that Works*. Alexandria, VA: ASCD.

Marzano, R. & Kendall, J.S. (2006). *The New Taxonomy of Educational Objectives, 2nd Edition*. Thousand Oaks: Corwin Press.

McCarthy, Bernice. (2000). *About Teaching: 4MAT in the Classroom*. Wauconda, Illinois: About Learning ,Inc.

Pollock, Jane S. (2007). *Improving Student Learning One Teacher at a Time*. Alexandria, VA: ASCD.

Popham, W.J. (2008). *Transformative Assessment.* Alexandria, VA: ASCD.

Rogers, Spence. (1997). *Motivation and Learning: A Teacher's Guide to Building Excitement for Learning and Igniting the Drive for Quality.* Evergreen, Colorado: Peak Learning Systems, Inc.

Schmoker, Mike. (2006). *Results Now.* Alexandria, VA: ASCD.

Sousa, David. (2005). *How The Brain Learns.* 3rd Edition. Thousand Oaks: Corwin Press.

---. (2006). *How The Special Needs Brain Learns.* 2nd Edition. Thousand Oaks: Corwin Press.

---. (2005). *Facilitator's Guide to How the Brain Learns, 3rd Edition*. Thousand Oaks: Corwin Press.

Sprenger, Marilee. (1999). *Learning and Memory: The Brain in Action.* Alexandria, VA: ASCD.

---. (2002). *Becoming a "Wiz" at Brain-Based Teaching.* Thousand Oaks: Corwin Press.

---. (2003). *Differentiation Through Learning Styles and Memory.* Thousand Oaks: Corwin Press.

Stiggins, R. (2006) *Classroom Assessment for Student Learning: Doing it Right—Using it Well.* ETS.

Sullo, B. (2007). *Activating the Desire to Learn.* Alexandria, VA: ASCD.

Sylwester, R. (2005). *How To Explain a Brain: An Educators' Handbook of Brain Terms and Cognitive Processes.* Thousand Oaks: Corwin Press.

Sylwester, R. (1997). "**The Neurobiology of Self-Esteem and Aggression**". *Educational Leadership.* Vol.54, No.5. 75-79.

---. (1995). *A Celebration of Neurons: An Educator's Guide to the Human Brain*. Alexandria, VA: ASCD.

The Brain, the Mind, and the Classroom. Alexandria, VA: ASCD.

Tomlinson, Carol. (1999).*The Differentiated Classroom: Responding to the Needs of All Learners.* Alexandria, VA: ASCD.

Tomlinson, Carol & McTighe, J. (2006). *Integrating Differentiated Instruction and Understanding By Design.* Alexandria, VA: ASCD.

Wiggins, G. and McTighe, J. (2005). *Understanding by Design, Expanded 2nd Edition*. Alexandria, VA: ASCD.

Willis, Judy, MD. (2007). *Brain-Friendly Strategies for the Inclusion Classroom: Insights from a neurologist and classroom teacher*. Alexandria, VA: ASCD.

Wolfe, Patricia. (2001). *Brain Matters: Translating Research into Classroom Practice*. Alexandria, VA: ASCD.

Other

Goleman, D. (1995). *Emotional Intelligence: Why It Can Matter More Than I.Q.* New York: Basic Books.

Gelb, Michael J. (1988). *Present Yourself.* Torrance, California: Jalmar Press.

Gregorc, Anthony F. (1982). *An Adult's Guide to Style.* Columbia, Conn,: Gregorc Associates.

Keirsey, David, and Marilyn Bates. (1978). *Please Understand Me: Character and Temperament Styles.* Del Mar, Calif.: Prometheus, Nemesis.

Kushner, Malcolm. (1996). *Successful Presentations for Dummies.* Foster City, California.

Lambert, Linda. (1998). *Building Leadership Capacity in Schools.* ASCD.

Lencioni, Patrick. (2002). *The Five Dysfunctions of a Team.* Jossey Bass.

Payne, Ruby K. (2005). *A Framework for Understanding Poverty, 4th Edtion.* Highlands, Texas: RFT Publishing.

Tucker, Ginger LaGrone. (2002). *The Heart of a Teacher: Sailing The High Cs (The Affective Characteristics of Effective Educators.* Amarillo, Texas: GKT Publishing.

---. (2009). *Teacher Handbook: Tools for Effective Classrooms.* Amarillo, Texas: GKT Publishing.

---. (2009). *Teacher Handbook: Foundations for Effective Classrooms.* Amarillo, Texas: GKT Publishing.

---. (2013). *Mentoring New Teachers: Induction Program Notebook.* Amarillo, Texas: GKT Publishing..

---. (2011). *Leading Adult Learners.* GKT Publishing, Amarillo, Texas.

Websites, On-line Articles, and Other Resources:

www.disciplinehelp.com - tons of behavior management ideas

www.kaganonline.com - Kagan Cooperative Learning

www.true-colors.org - personalities and styles

www.dinah.com - Dinah Zike's Foldables site

www.teachers.net - resource site

www.dana.org - for brain research and other resources

http://www.nctaf.org - National Commission on Teaching and Americans Future

http://www.**newteacher**center.org - New Teacher Center, UCSC

http://www.theteachersguide.com/ClassManagement.htm -management and discipline resources

http://drwilliampmartin.tripod.com/reallybest.htm - has 55 sites on classroom management

Alliance for Excellent Education. (2004). *Tapping the potential: Retaining and developing high-quality new teachers.* Washington, DC: Author. Retrieved July 25, 2005, from http://www.all4ed.org/publications/TappingThePotential/TappingThePotential.pdf.

Center for Strengthening the Teaching Profession. (2005, May). *Effective support for new teachers in Washington state: Standards for beginning teacher induction.* Silverdale, WA: Author. Retrieved July 25, 2005, from http://www.cstp-wa.org/Navigational/Policies_practices/Teacher_induction/Complete_Guideline.pdf

Education Week. (2005, January 6). Quality counts 2005: No small change [Special issue]. *Education Week, 24(17).* Retrieved July 25, 2005, from http://www.edweek.org/ew/toc/2005/01/06/index.html.

National Commission on Teaching and America's Future. (2003). *No dream denied: A pledge to America's children.* Washington, DC: Author. Retrieved July 25, 2005, from http://www.nctaf.org/article/?c=4&sc=16.

National Commission on Teaching and America's Future. (2003, September). *Summary of NCTAF national summit: The first three years of teaching.* Washington, DC: Author. Retrieved July 27, 2005, from http://www.nctaf.org/documents/nctaf/Summit1summary.doc.

New Teacher Center. (2002). *Teacher induction: e-Mentoring for student success.* Santa Cruz, CA: Author. Retrieved July 25, 2005, from http://newteachercenter.org/eMSS/overview.php.

Texas Center for Educational Research. (2000). *The cost of teacher turnover.* Austin, TX: Texas State Board for Educator Certification. Retrieved July 25, 2005, from http://www.sbec.state.tx.us/SBECOnline/txbess/turnoverrpt.pdf.

Add your sites:

*

Ginger Tucker's

First Year Teacher Academy

Participant Worksheets

"I touch the future—I teach." --Christa McAuliffe

Ginger Tucker

GKT Consulting, Inc. 806-353-7291 ginger@gingertucker.com
www.gingertucker.com

FYTA Pre Test

Keep this and refer to it at the beginning and the end of each session. Change your responses as you learn.

Yes	Maybe	Not Yet	
☐	☐	☐	1. I can name at least 3 things that define an effective teacher.
☐	☐	☐	2. I know the main 3 things that must be ready on the first day.
☐	☐	☐	3. I know several things a student needs to know on the first days.
☐	☐	☐	4. I know 4 major things that must be managed in the classroom.
☐	☐	☐	5. I have a list of procedures to teach the first days and know how to teach them.
☐	☐	☐	6. I know the difference between rules and procedures and can give examples.
☐	☐	☐	7. I know the guidelines for writing rules.
☐	☐	☐	8. I can explain the difference in classroom management and classroom discipline.
☐	☐	☐	9. I know the standard operating procedure for managing behavior.
☐	☐	☐	10. I understand brain-based learning principles and can apply them.
☐	☐	☐	11. I can explain and give examples of the 3 parts of the Nested Concept.
☐	☐	☐	12. I can use a higher level of thinking taxonomy in planning lessons
☐	☐	☐	13. I know the 4 personality styles and how to work with all.
☐	☐	☐	14. I know how to design a lesson using a planning format.
☐	☐	☐	15. I know how to involve all my students in the learning process.
☐	☐	☐	16. I know the modalities and how to teach to all.
☐	☐	☐	17. I know all the words to several sitcoms' theme songs. (Why do I know this and not something important?)
☐	☐	☐	18. I have a plan for working with parents.
☐	☐	☐	19. I understand what a mentor's role is.
☐	☐	☐	20. I understand how to manage stress.

First Year Teacher Questionnaire

Teaching Level	Special Education	Special Assignment	Alternative Certification	School Size
P E M H	Y or N	_____	Y or N	S M L

Part 1:
Please **circle** the number that best indicates your **level of mastery**.

1=Little/None	2=Some	3=Moderate	4=High	5=Very High

1. Maintaining student discipline   1 2 3 4 5

2. Organizing and managing my classroom   1 2 3 4 5

3. Managing my time and work   1 2 3 4 5

4. Completing paperwork   1 2 3 4 5

5. Communicating with the principal and other administrators   1 2 3 4 5

6. Communicating with other teachers and staff   1 2 3 4 5

7. Obtaining instructional resources and materials   1 2 3 4 5

8. Evaluating student progress   1 2 3 4 5

9. Motivating students   1 2 3 4 5

10. Assisting students with special needs   1 2 3 4 5

11. Dealing with individual differences among students   1 2 3 4 5

12. Understanding the curriculum   1 2 3 4 5

13. Communicating with parents   1 2 3 4 5

14. Understanding my legal rights and responsibilities as a teacher   1 2 3 4 5

15. Dealing with stress   1 2 3 4 5

Part 2: List (in order) your top 5 concerns or areas in which you would like assistance or for which you need information in the space below.

*

Today's FYTA Agenda
Date_____

☐ Opening

☐

☐

☐

☐

☐ Closure and Evaluation

Personal Learning Goals Today:

Summary of learning:

Today's FYTA Agenda
Date_____

☐ Opening

☐

☐

☐

☐

☐ Closure and Evaluation

Personal Learning Goals Today:

Summary of learning

Today's FYTA Agenda
Date_____

☐ Opening

☐

☐

☐

☐

☐ Closure and Evaluation

Personal Learning Goals Today:

Summary of learning

Today's FYTA Agenda
Date_____

☐ Opening

☐

☐

☐

☐

☐ Closure and Evaluation

Personal Learning Goals Today:

Summary of learning

Today's FYTA Agenda
Date_____

☐ Opening

☐

☐

☐

☐

☐ Closure and Evaluation

Personal Learning Goals Today:

Summary of learning

FYTA Expectations

Participate Actively

Ask Questions

Take Care of Yourself

Be a Learner

Respect Confidentiality

Value Others

Manage Electronics, please…

Have Fun!

Teammates

Name	School	Subject/grade taught
1.		
2.		
3.		
4.		

Make-a-Date

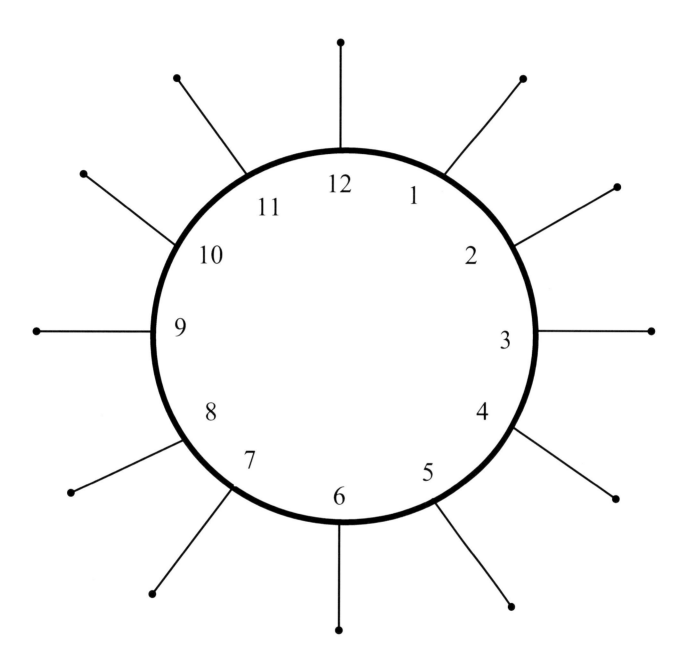

Stand and greet someone. Write his/her name on your "Make-a-Date" clock at a certain hour and have him/her write your name on the same hour of his or her clock. Find a new partner and select a time when you both have the same hour available. Exchange names. Continue to match times with partners until your entire clock is complete.

The presenter will ask you to find a partner for a given time. You will stand and find the person whose name you have that matches the given hour.

Find Someone Who

Meet someone and ask one of the questions. Write the answer in the space. Get the person's signature on the line. You ask; you write, he signs. Go to another person and repeat. You cannot ask your teammates until you have asked everyone else. You can't ask one person more than one question. When you are finished, go back to your seat.

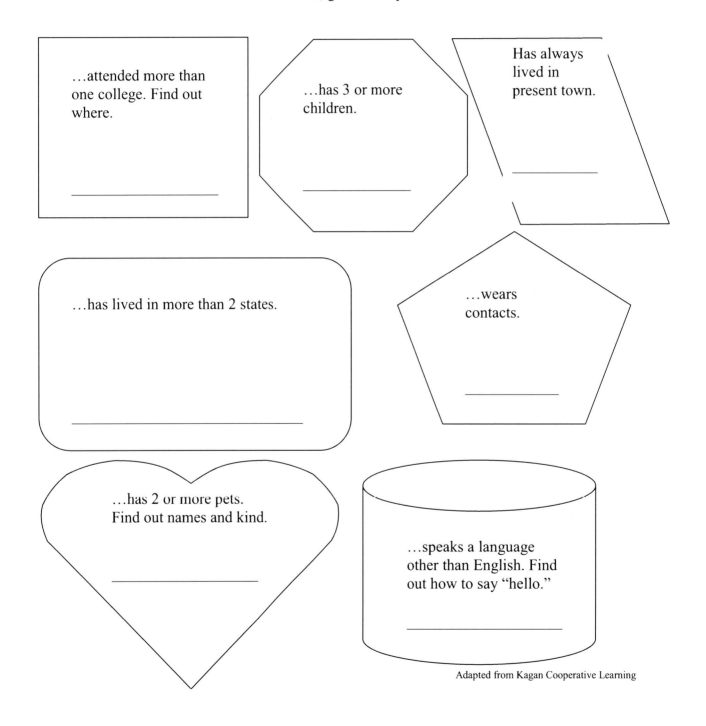

Adapted from Kagan Cooperative Learning

True Colors™ Word Cluster Sheet

4 = most like you; 3=next most; 2 next most; 1 = least like you

Active Opportunistic Spontaneous	Parental Traditional Responsible	Authentic Harmonious Compassionate	Versatile Inventive Competent
☐	☐	☐	☐
Competitive Impetuous Impactful	Practical Sensible Dependable	Unique Empathic Communicative	Curious Conceptual Knowledgeable
☐	☐	☐	☐
Realistic Open minded Adventuresome	Loyal Conservative Organized	Devoted Warm Poetic	Theoretical Seeking Ingenious
☐	☐	☐	☐
Daring Impulsive Fun	Concerned Procedural Cooperative	Tender Inspirational Dramatic	Determined Complex Composed
☐	☐	☐	☐
Exciting Courageous Skillful	Orderly Conventional Caring	Vivacious Affectionate Sympathetic	Philosophical Principled Rational
☐	☐	☐	☐
Total	Total	Total	Total
☐	☐	☐	☐

Think of the things you:

☐ Value

☐ Dislike

☐ Dream of

☐ Respect

☐ Consider your strengths

☐ Are stressed by

After completing the style inventory on the previous page, graph your score. Label the columns on the previous page in the same order as this page.

	Orange	Gold	Blue	Green
25				
20				
15				
10				
5				

Dealing Positively with Parents:
Effective Communication Practice

Practice # 1.
Communicating Effectively with Parents –

Listen to the scenario and write your response in the space provided.
Time: 1 minute each.

1.

2.

3.

4.

5.

Dealing Positively with Parents:
Effective Communication Practice

Practice # 2.
Communicating Effectively with Parents –

Listen to the scenario and write your response in the space provided.
Time: 1 minute each.

1.

2.

3.

4.

5.

First Year Teacher Questionnaire

Teaching Level	Special Education	Special Assignment	Alternative Certification	School Size
P E M H	Y or N	_____	Y or N	# students_____

Part 1:

Please **circle** the number that best indicates your **level of mastery**.

1=Little/None	2=Some	3=Moderate	4=High	5=Very High

1. Maintaining student discipline   1 2 3 4 5

2. Organizing and managing my classroom   1 2 3 4 5

3. Managing my time and work   1 2 3 4 5

4. Completing paperwork   1 2 3 4 5

5. Communicating with the principal and other administrators   1 2 3 4 5

6. Communicating with other teachers and staff   1 2 3 4 5

7. Obtaining instructional resources and materials   1 2 3 4 5

8. Evaluating student progress   1 2 3 4 5

9. Motivating students   1 2 3 4 5

10. Assisting students with special needs   1 2 3 4 5

11. Dealing with individual differences among students   1 2 3 4 5

12. Understanding the curriculum   1 2 3 4 5

13. Communicating with parents   1 2 3 4 5

14. Understanding my legal rights and responsibilities as a teacher   1 2 3 4 5

15. Dealing with stress   1 2 3 4 5

Part 2: Describe your philosophy about teaching, learning, and impacting students.

*

Ginger Tucker's
First Year Teacher Academy
Participant Reflections

I'm glad I **learned**…	As a result of today's session, I **will**…
The part I **liked** most was…	If I forget everything else, I want to always remember…
I **need** more information about…	**Additional comments**…

My overall summary of the training:

FYTA Date _____   FYTA Location_____

Trainer_____

*

Ginger Tucker

Ginger Tucker's experience as an educator includes her years as a high school classroom teacher and department chair. Following her classroom experience, she worked as a curriculum specialist and Title I Coordinator at a regional education service center, and then as Executive Director of Curriculum and Professional Development for a school district. Since 1996 she has owned her own consulting company and trains school, business, and church personnel. Ginger has served on the board of the Texas Staff Development Council and presents at local, state, and national conferences. Ginger's education includes a bachelor's degree in history and English education from Hardin Simmons University, a master's degree in history and geography from West Texas A&M University, and a mid–management certification from WTAMU. Her published works include *The Heart of a Teacher: Sailing the High Cs; Helping New Teachers Succeed: Mentor Manual; Teacher Handbook: Tools for Effective Classrooms; Leading Adult Learners; Dancing on Daddy's Feet and Other Stories of God's Love,* and other works.

Ginger's professional mission is to provide quality resources and services in a way that enhances educators' morale and performance so that they can make a difference in the lives of children.

Ginger Tucker's *Heart of Teaching Series* Materials Order Form 2013

Name_____

Address: _____

Phone #_____ email_____

City_____ State_____ Zip_____

Ginger Tucker's Resources: See catalog for description or visit www.gingertucker.com

Resource	Cost each	Quantity	Total
First Year Teacher Notebook, Revised Edition (Yellow Spiral Book), 2013	$ 25.00		
FYTA Certified Trainer Manual with notes, 2013	$ 150.00		
FYTA Certified Trainer Resource CD, 2013	call		
Mentoring and Coaching: Helping New Teachers Succeed, *Revised Edition* (Blue Spiral Book), 2013	$ 25.00		
Mentor Training Manual, 2013	$ 150.00		
Mentor Trainer's Resource CD, 2013	call		
Leading Adult Learners (Orange Spiral Book)	$ 25.00		
Teacher's Handbook: <u>*Foundations*</u> *for Effective Classrooms* [Same content as FYTN, but for veteran teachers (Purple Spiral Book)	$ 25.00		
Teacher's Handbook: <u>*Tools*</u> *For Effective Classrooms* for 2nd and 3rd Year Teachers and others (Green Spiral Book)	$ 25.00		
Teacher's Handbook: Tools For Effective Classrooms Trainer Manual	$ 150.00		
The Heart of a Teacher: Sailing the High Cs	$ 15.00		
Dancing on Daddy's Feet and Other Stories of God's Love	$ 15.00		
Add 10% shipping and handling			
Total			

Method of Payment
- ☐ **Bill my school   (PO enclosed)**   ☐ **Check enclosed**
- ☐ **You may order by credit card online.**

Mail or fax your order to:
GKT Consulting, Inc.
7505 Pennsylvania Drive
Amarillo, Texas 79119

Contact us at:
Phone: 806-353-7291
Fax: 806-353-7526
Email: ginger@gingertucker.com
www.gingertucker.com